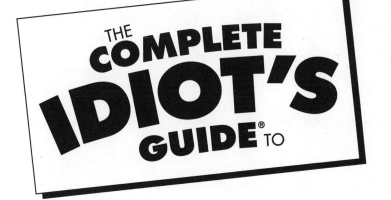

THE **COMPLETE IDIOT'S GUIDE**® TO

Success as a Personal Financial Planner

by John P. Napolitano, CFP®, CPA, PFS, MST

ALPHA

A member of Penguin Group (USA) Inc.

ALPHA BOOKS

Published by the Penguin Group

Penguin Group (USA) Inc., 375 Hudson Street, New York, New York 10014, USA

Penguin Group (Canada), 90 Eglinton Avenue East, Suite 700, Toronto, Ontario M4P 2Y3, Canada (a division of Pearson Penguin Canada Inc.)

Penguin Books Ltd., 80 Strand, London WC2R 0RL, England

Penguin Ireland, 25 St. Stephen's Green, Dublin 2, Ireland (a division of Penguin Books Ltd.)

Penguin Group (Australia), 250 Camberwell Road, Camberwell, Victoria 3124, Australia (a division of Pearson Australia Group Pty. Ltd.)

Penguin Books India Pvt. Ltd., 11 Community Centre, Panchsheel Park, New Delhi—110 017, India

Penguin Group (NZ), 67 Apollo Drive, Rosedale, North Shore, Auckland 1311, New Zealand (a division of Pearson New Zealand Ltd.)

Penguin Books (South Africa), (Pty.) Ltd., 24 Sturdee Avenue, Rosebank, Johannesburg 2196, South Africa

Penguin Books Ltd., Registered Offices: 80 Strand, London WC2R 0RL, England

Copyright © 2007 by John P. Napolitano

International Standard Book Number: 978-1-59257-686-9
Library of Congress Catalog Card Number: 2007930857

09   08   07   8   7   6   5   4   3   2   1

Interpretation of the printing code: The rightmost number of the first series of numbers is the year of the book's printing; the rightmost number of the second series of numbers is the number of the book's printing. For example, a printing code of 07-1 shows that the first printing occurred in 2007.

Printed in the United States of America

Note: This publication contains the opinions and ideas of its author. It is intended to provide helpful and informative material on the subject matter covered. It is sold with the understanding that the author and publisher are not engaged in rendering professional services in the book. If the reader requires personal assistance or advice, a competent professional should be consulted.

Publisher: *Marie Butler-Knight*
Editorial Director: *Mike Sanders*
Managing Editor: *Billy Fields*
Senior Acquisitions Editor: *Paul Dinas*
Development Editor: *Lynn Northrup*
Senior Production Editor: *Janette Lynn*
Copy Editor: *Lisanne V. Jensen*

Cartoonist: *Steve Barr*
Cover Designer: *Bill Thomas*
Book Designer: *Trina Wurst*
Indexer: *Tonya Heard*
Layout: *Ayanna Lacey*
Proofreader: *John Etchison*

Contents at a Glance

Contents

Appendixes

Introduction

Timing is everything! With more people entering their retirement and pre-retirement years than ever before, I can't think of a career with better potential than financial planning. Financial planning continues to be one of the top growth industries. It's no wonder—in these days of confusion in the financial markets, tax laws, pension plans, and job security—that people need guidance across a broad range of interrelated financial issues.

The majority of people who tend to hire a financial planner are over age 50 with concerns about their investments, retirement, insurance, homes, Social Security, lifestyle, and families. These people hire a planner for guidance and direction with the expectation that they will be better off with a planner than without one.

From none to hundreds of thousands of professionals now calling themselves financial planners is major progress, especially in fewer than 50 years. But when compared to the older financial professions like banking, accounting, law, or insurance, financial planning may still be in its fledgling stage. What it will take, beyond just time, to get to the level of success equal to other financial disciplines is the trust of the general public and more professional planners who can earn that trust.

That trust is coming, thanks to the efforts of the many ethical, hardworking planners in the business today—but it still has a long way to go. The industry needs more ethical, caring professionals who have a desire to serve that is greater than their desire for monetary success. Don't worry, though. With a strong, ethical desire to serve, it would be difficult not to have financial success.

All too often, the popular press likes to create headlines because of a rogue broker, insurance agent, or advisor who takes advantage of an unknowing client and bilks them out of their life savings. These headlines prevent many from hiring a financial planner and stop potential planners in their tracks from joining the ranks in favor of less-controversial pursuits. Don't let it stop you. The thousands of ethical, caring professionals who do help their clients live their dreams day in and day out may go unnoticed in the press, but they are rich with the gratitude of their paying clients and a financially rewarding career.

Why You Need This Book to Succeed

For many years, the failure rate for new financial advisors was very high. That was, in large part, due to the unknown. Unsuspecting, aspiring financial planners were seduced into a sales environment—only to find out a few months later that their success would be determined by how many insurance policies they sold or how much in commissions they would generate.

I fell prey to this trap in my first financial planning job. I was on the job for two months until I realized that I wasn't there to do planning for the firm's clients; rather, my duty was to generate clients and sell them life and disability insurance. The boss didn't really care whether I ever mentioned the words "financial planning" as long as I sold enough policies to justify my taking up cubicle space. I don't want this situation to happen to you. I did leave this firm after six months and returned to my roots in a small CPA firm, where I became the architect of my dream to be a financial planner. As the first CPA to register as a financial planner while still engaged in the practice of public accounting, I built a financial planning division and became a partner in the firm by the time I was 27 in 1983. Now, 25 years later, my passion for the financial planning business is greater than it was then.

Not that selling life insurance, annuities, or investment products is a bad thing. Somebody has to do it. But doing it with your eyes open in an environment that gives you every chance of success is the best situation. It's even better if your prospective employer is honest with you and lets you know how you will be judged and what you need to do in order to succeed.

By reading this book, you will enter the profession with your eyes wide open. You will know what questions to ask. You will gain insight into what to expect and guidance on what knowledge and natural talents you need to become a success. You will learn what training to get, where to get it, and how to zero in on a specialty that fits with your unique abilities. You will pass the fledgling stage and become successful. If you want, you'll even get a good dose of reality regarding what it takes to open your own financial planning business. Then, you can take that business to even greater heights with world-class systems, processes, and associates who can become your most valuable financial asset.

You will also learn how to deal with—and maybe even anticipate—the constant change that this industry brings and soar into the upper echelon of financial planners in the United States. While you will need to be hardworking, innovative, a good leader, and fair to your staff and clients, you do not need to have the business mind of a Warren Buffet. The trail is well marked from the many planners who have "been there, done that." I have captured much of that tried-and-true experience on the road to success in this book to help you get there with greater ease and more success than the early pioneers.

Don't be intimidated by the enormity of the subject areas that a financial planner will touch. No one expects you to know everything; you just need to know where to go to get the answers. What you need to know most is your client. You need to know their goals, objectives, vision, values, and passions. The chapter on life planning and the wisdom of Susan Galvan from the Kinder Institute will guide you through this mandatory skill.

In this business, you should earn a great living, meet wonderful people, and have a ton of fun. How many people do you know who can say that about their jobs?

What You'll Learn in This Book

Part 1, "Your Future Is in Front of You!", explains why the future for financial planners looks so bright. Regardless of what you've done in a prior career or in school, the financial planning community needs bright, energetic, and caring people to meet the demand for services.

Part 2, "Earning a Living," tells you how to get a job and gives you a clear understanding of the types of employers looking for new financial planners. Learn about compensation structures, advancement, and success in your new career.

Part 3, "Be Your Own Boss," describes how you can become the owner of a financial planning business. Do the right things and avoid the common mistakes of the many people before you who learned the hard way.

Part 4, "Growing Your Success," discusses how you can be more than a self-employed financial planner. It shows you how to build a business that will grow and expand with talented associates. After reading this section, your business will be on a track that will someday have great value.

Extras

You'll also find four types of sidebars sprinkled throughout the chapters to help enhance your understanding of financial planning:

def•i•ni•tion

These boxes define key words and phrases that are crucial in understanding the career of personal financial planning.

In the Know

Check these boxes for inside advice on how to enhance your business or better serve your clients.

Walking the Walk

These boxes share words of wisdom from successful financial planners and other financial professionals.

Pitfalls

Heed these cautions about time-wasters, tricks by financial vendors, or regulations that could adversely affect your business.

Acknowledgments

Writing this book has been on my mind for years. It would not have happened without the aid of some very important people in my life.

Thanks to my family for their support and encouragement and for sticking with me during nights and weekends spent at the keyboard instead of with you. Joan, Laura, Julia, Rob, and Tom … I love you and owe you some undivided attention!

I am grateful for everyone in my office, whose professional attitude and abilities allowed me to be noticeably vacant for an extended period. Especially to George Clarke, Dennis McCarron, Peter Donohoe, Barbara Purslow, and Helen Griffin for doing things that I should have done!

I am deeply appreciative for the contributions of two renowned professionals for their contributions in specific chapters. To Susan Galvan, cofounder of the Kinder Institute for Life Planning, my thanks for contributing the firsthand material for Chapter 10. To Darren Oglesby, owner of Oglesby Financial Group in Monroe, Louisiana, and one of the finest financial planners that I know, your work on Chapter 16 adds great value for all readers.

I want to thank my fellow directors of the Financial Planning Association of Massachusetts for their leadership and wisdom as we collectively try to make this profession better for all planners. And a special thanks to Dee Lee for steering me to Alpha Books and the opportunity to serve future successful planners through this book.

And last, to the hardworking people at Alpha Books for making this book a reality … thank you.

Trademarks

All terms mentioned in this book that are known to be or are suspected of being trademarks or service marks have been appropriately capitalized. Alpha Books and Penguin Group (USA) Inc. cannot attest to the accuracy of this information. Use of a term in this book should not be regarded as affecting the validity of any trademark or service mark.

The following trademarked and registered terms are mentioned in this book:

> Certified Financial Planner (CFP®)
> CERTIFIED FINANCIAL PLANNER™
> Chartered Financial Analyst (CFA®)

Chartered Financial Consultant (ChFC®)

CEBS®

CFA®

CLF®

CLU®

Junior Achievement™

Morningstar®

REBC®

RHU®

The Entrepreneurial Time System®

The Strategic Coach®

Part 1

Your Future Is in Front of You!

Forget about the past—your future as a personal financial planner is so bright that you'll need to keep the sunglasses handy! There are millions of people who need a good financial planner and almost as many ways for you to get into this business. The style of practice you want to build will determine what licenses you will need to chart the course that's best suited for you.

Personal Financial Planning: A Profession Whose Time Has Come

In This Chapter

- ◆ The emergence of the financial planning industry
- ◆ Six steps of personal financial planning
- ◆ Personal financial planning goes boom!
- ◆ The changing roles of brokers and agents
- ◆ What's ahead for the financial planning profession

If you ask your grandfather what a personal financial planner is, there's a good chance that he won't know. In fact, the older he is, the less likely he can answer.

Personal financial planning is a profession that both started and gained prominence in the late twentieth century. In the twenty-first century and beyond, the future is very bright for the profession. There are demographic reasons, complexity issues, and lifestyle dreams that all benefit from the guidance of a skilled financial planner.

A big issue for the industry is that a high percentage of current practitioners are over age 50. What the industry needs is an influx of non-gray-haired professionals who will continue to work as financial planners for as long as their clients will live! This huge challenge for the industry brings an even larger opportunity for those who are ready for the career of their lives. Neverending opportunity, the chance to be your own boss, and more clients than you could possibly serve—what could be better?

The Early Days

Prior to what we now call the financial planning movement, stockbrokers sold stocks and bonds, mutual fund salesmen sold mutual funds, insurance salesmen sold insurance products, and banks sold depository accounts and loans. That was it. Never did one sell the others' products, and rarely would the related professionals work together or even discuss clients' overall needs.

In September 2005, Texas Tech University in Lubbock, Texas, announced that it would house the first historical archive of the financial planning profession in the United States. Memorabilia and other documents describing professionals acting as personal financial planners date back to the 1950s. While this may seem like some time ago, compared to the legal, accounting, architecture, or engineering professions, the financial planning industry is still in its infancy.

def•i•ni•tion

Holistic financial guidance is a type of advice that considers the entirety of a client's life situation, dreams, and financial condition. It refers to giving advice on one matter while considering all of the related issues that may be impacted by that one matter.

Families with extreme wealth may say that their predecessors received proactive and holistic advice from their trust officers, attorneys, or accountants for generations. This statement may be so, but there are still families today with wealth passed down through generations that obviously got very little, or pretty bad, *holistic financial guidance*. Most of those professionals merely gave advice on their particular area of expertise but rarely on matters beyond their core knowledge. (That only happened as an accommodation or incidentally to their primary business.)

Trust officers gave advice beyond trusts and investments to keep the clients from looking for other advisors in an attempt to lock them in for generations. Attorneys gave advice beyond estate planning and business law to keep the family engaged with the firm for all of their legal needs. Accountants gave advice beyond the preparation of tax returns and financial statements only when they were asked. But very few had ever held themselves to be the one source for proactive and holistic financial advice. For those who did get it—lucky you—you were in the minority.

The Birth of Financial Planning

According to the Financial Planning Association, financial planning as a distinct profession was born in 1969. It emerged through the perseverance of 13 visionaries meeting in Chicago on December 12, 1969. These visionaries comprised a diverse group of insurance agents, investment brokers, investment advisors, attorneys, and accountants. Out of this meeting, the College for Financial Planning and The International Association for Financial Planners were created.

Like most new ideas, the financial planning movement took immense dedication and great courage for the pioneers. These visionaries were determined to "build a better mousetrap" for the financial services industry. They had hoped to build a system that worked better for both the industry and its clients.

These new ideas came with an action plan. The first part was to create a professional certification. As a result, the Certified Financial Planner (CFP) designation was born. The mission for the CFP was twofold:

1. To serve the client well and put the client's best interests ahead of their own

2. To guide clients on the path toward reaching their specific financial objectives and to be there as an advisor for the ongoing financial issues that arose in clients' lives

The Evolution from Sales to Service

In the early days—and still to some extent today—not all planners were so idyllic. Some are aggressive salespeople hiding behind the veil of financial planners. It was also common in the early days for new planners to start with only one tool: the telephone book. Companies only hired people who weren't afraid to make hundreds of cold calls per day. If you had prior success at doing that—or if someone thought that you had that skill in you—you were hired. Today, that is a little different. Industry regulations have very strict rules about cold calling, and most consumers are sick and tired of those dinner-interrupting phone calls—making this tactic far less effective.

These aggressive sales types don't want to deliver holistic financial planning solutions for their clients and often advocate that their one solution or product is the right answer for everyone. Of course, it is not possible to have a one-size-fits-all solution in the context of personal financial planning. The good news is that the public is becoming educated on what to expect from a planner—and more advisors are joining the ranks of financial planning professionals and following the intent of the financial planning pioneers.

What Is Personal Financial Planning?

The next part of creating the profession was to define the *financial planning* process. It involves taking stock of all your existing resources, developing a plan to utilize them, and systematically implementing the plan in order to achieve your short- and long-term goals. The plan must be monitored and reviewed periodically so that adjustments can be made, if necessary, to assure that it continues to move you toward your financial goals.

This process is further broken down for CFP practitioners and is known as the six-step financial planning process.

def•i•ni•tion

Today, **financial planning** is defined as the process of establishing personal and financial goals and creating a way to reach them.

1. Establish the Planner-Client Relationship

In this step, you (as the planner) should explain the appropriate issues and concepts related to the overall financial planning process. You will also explain your services and how you will document your advice. You will also talk to the client about his or her responsibilities, such as the need to be truthful about finances and to provide you with complete and accurate information. You will also discuss with the client your responsibilities as the planner and how you will be compensated.

2. Gather All Relevant Data to Determine the Client's Goals and Expectations

In this step, you will gather as much information as you need to determine what your client owns, what those assets are worth, how the assets are owned, what your client owes, what he or she makes, and what he or she spends. You will gather this data through interviews and questionnaires and gathering backup documentation. You'll want documentation such as tax returns, wills and trusts, insurance policies, investment statements, retirement plans, mortgage and other loan statements, bank statements, and anything else to support the client's financial condition. During this step, you will help the client define his or her personal and financial goals, needs, and priorities. At this step in the planning process, you'll need to learn about the client's values, preferences, financial outlook, and desired results as they relate to his or her goals, needs, and priorities.

Clients will often need help with identifying goals and values. Basic goals, such as retiring comfortably or educating children, are easy to elicit—but values-based goals, such as devoting more time to charity or spending more time with family, will frequently need prodding by the planner.

 Pitfalls _____

Sometimes a new client will withhold important information about his or her life or financial condition. Make it clear, and in writing, that your advice is only valid if the client reveals everything about his or her financial situation.

3. Clarify the Client's Financial Status

In this step, you will assess the client's cash flow, net worth, and tax status and identify any problem areas or opportunities. Topics often discussed include capital needs, risk management, investments, tax planning, retirement planning, estate planning, and special needs such as elderly parents or special-needs children.

4. Present a Financial Plan to the Client

In this step, you will tailor a plan to the client's needs, goals, values, and risk tolerance. You should make recommendations in writing, and be certain that they're easy to understand. You may also discuss with your client alternative strategies or other strategies considered in this step.

5. Implement the Recommendations

The best-laid plans are of no value unless they have a chance to come to fruition. In this step, you may have to coordinate the services of other professionals, such as attorneys, Certified Public Accountants (CPAs), investment advisors, or insurance professionals. The key here is to see that the plan is implemented. Not implementing the planning recommendations may later cause a problem or prevent a client from achieving a life goal.

6. Monitor the Process

Depending on the plan or client complexity, the final step—monitoring—should be done at least annually. It is a good idea before you conclude the planning engagement to decide exactly how often the follow-up will occur. During a review or monitoring engagement, you will review what has changed since the original engagement, track progress of the original plan, and discuss with the client if their goals and life dreams are the same and if the qualitative factors that have gone into the planning recommendations are still on target and agreeable.

In the Know

Make it clear to your clients that steps five and six are especially critical for their success. It may take extra encouragement on your part to have them implement planning recommendations and to help them understand that today's recommendations may be inappropriate as time goes on, due to changing circumstances or economic realities.

While every financial planner on earth may have a particular process or methodology, this six-step process—as outlined by the "fathers" of modern-day financial planning—is still appropriate and being used today by financial planning practitioners. Don't be intimidated by this process. Once you get good at financial planning, you will commit the process to memory and even be able to delegate much of the clerical tasks to others in your firm.

A Few Words of Caution

There are still plenty of advisors who call themselves financial planners but give very short attention to the entire comprehensive process. Many professionals say that they don't like comprehensive planning engagements because they take too long or that their clients don't want them. Whether you end up charging separately for the financial planning service or it is wrapped up with another fee or commission that you may receive, it could be dangerous to not give holistic advice based on your client's entire set of circumstances and desires. Either limit your work to clients who want the comprehensive planning process, or document that you are not performing a comprehensive financial plan. Like anything else, the first few plans that anyone creates are inefficient and take longer than expected.

Also, in this litigious society, keep in mind that documenting the scope of an engagement and obtaining the client's written acquiescence could help you in the event of a lawsuit. Lawsuits are often originated by heirs or the beneficiaries of deceased or disabled clients. Having the client's written understanding of the scope of your services could prevent a suit from going anywhere.

Why the Sudden Wave of Popularity?

Considering that the first time anyone really heard the term personal financial planning was fewer than 50 years ago, the whole movement can be looked at as a sudden wave. But starting in the 1990s, the term—and the profession—has really been catching on in a big way.

Several factors are causing the planning explosion. In short, they are: demographics, complexity, disappointment, information, promotion, and convenience. I'll discuss each of these aspects in the following sections.

Boomers: Their Time Has Come

Hardly a day goes by when you don't hear some wild statistic about the largest generation of Americans, known as baby boomers—people born between 1946 and 1964. This is such a huge bulge of people that the boomers are single-handedly responsible for putting many companies and industries on the map. For example, the boomer generation can directly be traced to the early success of Johnson & Johnson, Band-Aid, Coke and Pepsi, automobiles, and housing. Why would the financial services business be any different? It isn't. There are many millions of people who will need advice on what to do with their finances in order to fulfill their life dreams and financial goals.

Boomers are now in the process of contemplating retirement. Historically, this age group—more than any other—has sought out financial advice. Many issues are converging on them at once. When should I stop working? Will I have enough money to retire comfortably? Should my investments be monitored or changed to meet my needs? Does my estate need a plan? Can I help my children afford their first house? How do I care for my aging parents? There are many other questions that need to be answered, and many boomers will want the help of a professional.

Beyond the traditional questions of aging and retirement, boomers also appear to be reinventing retirement. They are living longer, healthier, much more active, working full or part time for an extended period, and are used to getting what they want. An

Associated Press survey found that most boomers expect to retire around age 63—but 66 percent of them expect to work for pay after retiring. 43 percent will do so because they want to stay busy; 27 percent say they'll keep working to make ends meet; and another 19 percent will work so that they can afford "extras."

More Choices Means Greater Complexity

We live in an extremely complex world, and it's not getting any simpler. Every component of financial planning now has more to it than the entire world of personal finance had 50 years ago. Taxes, investments, exchange traded funds, mutual funds, estate laws, insurance products, annuities, mortgages, reverse mortgages … the list goes on and on. New products and concepts are introduced nearly every day. It's hard enough for the financial professional to keep up with these new trends—so imagine how an untrained client feels. He or she will be overwhelmed, to say the least.

In the Know

In a 2004 survey by Del Webb Corp., a builder of homes for retirees, only 36 percent of boomers think that they'll have enough money to live comfortably in retirement. Conversely, that 64 percent who don't feel that they have enough will be scrambling to find help.

Take the tax code, for example. In 1913, that simple one-page return could be completed by nearly everyone without the help of a professional. Now, the tens of thousands of pages of code, regulations, and cases are not understandable by many CPAs.

Now, you can earn specialty Master's degrees in taxation—with subspecialties within the tax area because of its intense complexity. Most personal financial planners never really become tax professionals, but they sure do need a general understanding of the individual, business, trust, and estate tax laws. Conversely, most tax professionals do not usually make really good personal financial planners. Their minds are so geared toward minute details that they have a hard time conveying broader concepts that are draped in uncertainty and soft issues, such as the client's feelings and related financial issues.

The trust and estate tax laws are even worse. They are so convoluted and confusing that you'd better have an estate planning specialist to help you implement that part of the financial plan. They are further complicated by state laws, which vary from state to state. The core of most estate planning issues is rooted in the financial planning decision-making side of the engagement. Estate planning issues such as giving gifts to children, to other family members, or to charity tie right into the client's personal desires and do not depend on the tax code. In this area, individuals often make very poor choices—mostly because they are misguided by generalist lawyers who are not estate planning experts. There is also the constant threat of changing tax laws. Many clients do nothing because of rumors that a change to the estate tax code is coming.

How about mortgages? In the good old days, there was only one option: a fixed loan with all of the interest deductible. Today, you get a loan with fixed rates, variable rates, interest only, reverse mortgages, lines of credit, negative amortization … and you can choose your payback terms. This situation is further complicated by changes to the tax code that disallow certain home mortgage interest higher than a certain amount and that disallow refinance or home equity lines of credit beyond a certain amount. It's no wonder that your client, who is buying a second home in Florida, needs more than a mortgage broker to help decide which loan—if any—is right for him or her, given the entire financial picture.

Likewise, the investment world is more complicated than ever before. Today, there are more mutual funds available than stocks on the New York Stock Exchange. Compound this with emotion, and you have one very dizzy client who really doesn't know what he or she has and why. One year, it's stocks; the next year, it's bonds; the next year, it's gold and precious metals; and the next year, it's real estate. Emotion makes even the smartest do-it-yourself investor an accident waiting to happen. They often chase past performance, headlines, and media gurus and are often so late to the game that they are doing the opposite of basic Investing 101 philosophy: buy low and sell high. How many investors do you know who were lined up to buy stocks or stock-based mutual funds in the early 2000s? Unfortunately, not many! They were all on the sidelines, crying in their milk and reaping the lowest money market yields in decades.

The same is true for real estate. Sure, many a vast fortune was built through property ownership. But many a Chapter 7 filing was fueled by excessive debt and falling real estate prices. The real estate boom that followed the stock market crash had many investors dumping all of their money into residential real estate. Florida snowbirds who had rented for years not only bought a condo for their personal use, but they also bought two or three more on speculation that they would be able to sell them for substantially more 12 months later. Recent price declines have made this impossible, and many will not be able to hold the property long enough and may be forced to sell their properties at a loss.

What could be worse than selling a losing portfolio of stock-based mutual funds to load up on real estate at its peak? Investors need an unemotional, rational professional to guide them through the good times and the bad times. Unfortunately, many investors don't understand or believe that.

Walking the Walk _____

I frequently see clients whose investments are a mess. They have a little of this, a little of that and really didn't know what they should be holding, buying, or selling. It is gratifying to help them create a portfolio that is more likely to accomplish their objectives and reduce the time that they spend worrying about their investment choices.

—Timothy McCarthy, CPA, ChFC, Avon, Connecticut

Insurance is another great example of this complicated world in which we live. For your grandparents, it was simple: they insured their home, health, car, and their lives—and the world was not lawsuit crazy. Today, you not only need homeowner's coverage—you also need umbrella liability coverage, replacement cost coverage, earthquake insurance, and flood coverage added to your base policy.

It's not good enough to have life insurance to pay the mortgage and provide for the survivors. You need coverage for estate planning, college education, business continuity, and to replace the cost of long-term care that was not covered by your health insurance or Medicare.

Long-term care insurance didn't even exist when the financial planning profession was started. Today there are many different policy types and lots of options within the coverage available, but very few clients want to own it. They wait until they are 65 or older to look into it and by then the premiums are quite costly. This insurance is far less costly over a 20-year period than the cost for just one year of long-term care, but nevertheless costly. In the next 50 years long-term care insurance will be as common as health insurance is today.

I could devote an entire book to the complexities in today's financial world. Fortunately, you have 300-plus great pages of sage advice where you'll get plenty of examples of our changing financial world and why you should do very well as a personal financial planner.

Realistic Expectations

Some people are simply too optimistic, and because of that they feel disappointed or let down in financial matters. They are disappointed in their 401(k); they are disappointed when the insurance company tells them that their claim will not be fully paid; and they're disappointed when they read about the potential problems with our Social Security system.

A big part of the planning process is to shed light on the reality of financial life and to help properly set expectations. There's a lot of water cooler talk about money and financial issues where someone is given false hope. Getting someone to understand the consequences of his or her actions (or inactions) early on can be a lifesaver when he or she gets to a destination or wants to do something different, like retire or relocate.

Rarely do clients point the finger of disappointment at themselves. It's always an investment or mutual fund that didn't do its job, or that insurance salesman who didn't sell the right long-term care insurance, or the mortgage broker who inappropriately recommended an adjustable rate mortgage. Accountability is a two-way street. You, as a financial planner, are accountable to your clients—and you must show them that they will be accountable for implementing planning recommendations and attending review sessions with you.

Too Much Information

For your computer, there may be no traffic jams on the information superhighway. But the average financial consumer is on information overload. The availability and flow of information on just about any topic is readily available. Combine that with the technical nature of financial information and all of the opposing viewpoints—and people sometimes just can't make decisions. The move that they make today might be shot down by someone else tomorrow—and what they shoot down tomorrow might be the hot topic on your favorite talk show as the best thing ever.

Newspapers, magazines, the Internet, television, radio, and every living person from your Uncle Louie to co-workers at the water cooler are trying to give you financial advice. In many cases, the advice may be good for some but not necessarily for you. Taken out of context, any advice may sound good on any given day. That's why clients need and want your guidance more than ever to sift through the information and make their way toward the right decisions for them.

Personal financial planners once thought that all of this free and low-cost information would weaken their franchise or reduce their opportunities. At first, it may have. But the reverse situation is actually happening now. The more that is written, discussed, and viewed, the more it makes a savvy consumer seek expert guidance and advice. This trend will only continue to accelerate over the years and cause the wave of popularity of financial planning to continue to grow.

Now Hear This

Financial services companies and planners alike are getting better at promoting their products and services. Their advertisements use catchy rock-and-roll tunes; they sponsor the most visible athletic events in the world; and they know how to tug at your emotions.

You are surrounded daily by blimps, parades, sports arenas, and infomercials promoting a financial services company. Do you have a mug, a T–shirt, or a hat given to you by a financial services company?

Whether disseminated directly or subliminally, all of this noise keeps the public's eye focused on financial issues. It, like everything else we've talked about so far, also increases client confusion about what an advisor does, where to get good advice, or whether you can handle finances yourself. These constant reminders only help create awareness in potential clients' minds of the services that a good planner can provide.

One-Stop Shopping

During these days of fast and accessible information and superstores for one-stop shopping, people are conditioned for simplicity and want more of it. We all want things to be convenient and easy. At the core of our capitalistic society is letting the free market rule, and the free market has spoken. We want to make it easy and convenient to do just about anything.

Pitfalls

When it comes to financial issues, sometimes "too easy" is not a good thing. Just think of all the trouble that people get themselves into by clicking a button to borrow from their retirement plans or clicking a button to borrow $100,000 against their house to make a very aggressive purchase in their investment account.

The one-stop-shopping concept so well perfected by the big-box stores is now taking a foothold on the financial services world. Consumers want convenience and ease of doing business. In the process of running their financial lives this way, there is often a lack of guidance and expertise. Financial planners do not need to be threatened by the financial supermarkets or financial services websites. This actually creates an opportunity. With the advent of technology, great resources are also available to personal financial planners—allowing even the smallest shop to access great technology and work with experts from a variety of disciplines.

What Happened to Brokers and Agents?

Brokers and agents once dominated the financial planning industry. While the ranks of pure brokers and agents are dwindling, brokers and agents haven't become extinct. Some of them are personal financial planners; some of them are not. Brokers and agents are typically paid commissions for assisting in the planning process or performing a transaction.

Recently, however, the concept of being a *fiduciary* has taken center stage. There is a long-standing requirement that a financial planer must act in the best interests of his or her clients and therefore as a fiduciary. The question arises as to whether or not a broker or agent can be a fiduciary. One side says no, that the conflict of interest is way too prominent. The other side says yes, as long as he or she discloses compensation and offers alternative ways for the clients to obtain the same result.

def•i•ni•tion

A **fiduciary** is someone who is hired to act or advise on behalf of another. The duties of a fiduciary are to always keep the best interests of the clients first and foremost in decision-making and advising.

The hot debate about brokers, agents, planners, and fiduciary responsibilities has raged for years. Other countries, such as Great Britain and Australia, have settled the score for their advisory communities by having strict disclosure requirements for financial planners regarding compensation. Expect some movement in this direction within the United States in the near future.

Regardless, many financial professionals will enter this profession as brokers and agents and do fine jobs assisting their clients with achieving their lifetime dreams and goals. Some will pursue a financial planning slant, and others may choose to be specialists in an area that is best served by a broker or agent. As long as you always do the right thing by your clients, you'll be fine.

Where Do We Go from Here?

Hopefully, you go right on to the next chapter and see what it takes to make the grade as a personal financial planner. Then, get ready to launch the best career you've ever had. But the industry will continue to change and grow, with or without you. The leaders of the profession today are passionate, educated, and motivated to see that the world is a better place because of the financial planning profession.

The profession is working hard to attract smart, energetic talent to the ranks. There are financial literacy projects and campaigns underway as you read this book to wipe out financial illiteracy among our citizens. There have been, and will continue to be, billions of investment dollars funneled into this industry.

Most employment surveys and career counselors rank a career in financial services as one of the top two or three fields for the next millennium. Financial planning is considered one of the top growth segments of the financial services industry. Like anything else that the boomers have moved through, the financial planning industry can do nothing but explode. The only thing missing is you.

The Least You Need to Know

- ◆ The financial planning profession is still emerging and will continue to evolve.

- ◆ Financial planning is a process for reaching personal and financial goals. The process requires discipline and time and is best overseen by a financial planning professional.

- ◆ Our complicated financial world needs trained advisors. Too many people make financial decisions based upon hearsay or news headlines.

- ◆ The millions of aging baby boomers will fuel the growth of financial planning for decades.

- ◆ Financial planning is a fast-growing career that needs dedicated young talent to reach its full potential to serve the millions in need of advice.

Making the Grade

In This Chapter

◆ Beginning the self-assessment process

◆ The outlook for new grads

◆ Completing a successful career change

◆ Understanding the skill sets you'll need

◆ The importance of passion

In this chapter, you will find out whether you have what it takes to be successful as a personal financial planner. Certain characteristics are non-negotiable; you must possess them in order to succeed. Others, however—depending on how you enter the profession—are not deal killers.

The failure rate for starters in the financial planning profession used to be very high. Your success largely depended on your ability to sell. Today, there are still some entry points to the business that depend on you selling commission-based financial products—but there are finally some established career tracks that resemble other professions (such as accounting, management, or finance). And yes, if you can communicate well and are a good salesperson, you will earn more than the analytics who have a tough time with persuasion.

The combination of smarts, personality, passion, and empathy will get you to the top of the heap in personal financial planning. Excelling at any one or two of these areas can also make you a valuable asset to many firms—especially one that is building a collaborative organization based upon the unique skill sets of several talented employees.

Who Is Best Suited?

Your career in financial planning will be filled with unlimited opportunities and challenges that you may have never encountered. The opportunities will range from the unlimited earnings potential inherent in the planning industry to enjoying some really cool people that you love to spend time with as clients. The challenges will come in the form of dealing with difficult people or difficult economic conditions all the way through mastering the art and science of financial planning. A good planner will stay current with the financial markets and keep an eye open for new opportunities for his or her business and clients as they arise. That same good planner must always accept a future of guaranteed challenges in the form of ever-changing tax laws, new investment opportunities, or the guaranteed changes in direction of this great emerging profession.

At the end of the day, it is your clients who will decide whether you are a great financial planner. After all, it is they who will pay your fees and/or buy financial products from you. And thankfully, the old saying about different strokes for different folks also applies to careers in financial planning. Some planners are as analytical as engineers, and others are as smooth as car salespeople. Both types can earn a great living as personal financial planners.

The question "Who is best suited?" can be further broken down. Who is best suited in the first few months or years? Who is best suited from a socioeconomic standpoint? Who is best suited from a geographic point of view? Who is best suited from a lifestyle point of view?

And while these are all good questions or angles to consider, the answer to all of them is, "It depends."

It depends on where you first start to work as a financial planner, what type of education you have, where else you have worked, your current financial condition, and a host of other factors that you'll have a good handle on by the time you're finished reading this book.

Walking the Walk

A successful career has a lot more to do with what you love doing rather than what you know how to do. Very few people start in any career already knowing how to do the job well, but many who start doing what they love become world-class professionals driven by their passion for what they are doing.

—Greg Rutan, division director, Robert Half International

Certain skill sets are commonly looked at as the cornerstone of making a successful financial planner:

- Good people skills, including strong communication abilities and listening skills
- Analytical abilities
- Problem-solving skills
- The ability to work independently with a strong work ethic
- Curiosity
- Mathematical abilities
- Leadership skills
- Decision-making ability
- Integrity
- Organizational skills
- Learning ability
- Computer skills
- Creativity
- Empathy and compassion

While there may be few, if any, financial planners who excel at all of these skill sets, the best ones figure out how to be good and improve—or surround themselves with talent that can complete their skill set. (I'll discuss the importance of many of these skills in detail later in this chapter.)

Hiring New Grads

In the early days of the financial planning industry, new college graduates were typically hired to sell financial products. There were actually very few true financial planning firms. Most firms with names such as Cross Street Financial Group were just titles to disguise the fact that the group was really in business to sell insurance for some large insurance company. Owners of these firms were often *general agents (GAs)* for a large insurance company. They would hire as many new college grads as they could get their hands on with the full knowledge that within three years, 90 percent of their recruits would fail. Three years was a common length of time because, by then, your guaranteed base salary—as small as it was—would cease. If you were one of the few who made it to your third year, you knew that from year four onward, you were on a 100 percent commission basis.

def•i•ni•tion

A **general agent (GA)** is a person who is hired by an insurance company to manage an office that is often owned by and paid for by the insurance company. The GA's job is to recruit, manage, and train a sales force of agents and an administrative support staff for that sales force.

The same was pretty much true for some of the most prestigious names on Wall Street. You were given a desk and a phone and were told to "Go get 'em." Who you were getting and for what reason was secondary; you simply knew that you had to sell them something.

If you had what it took to be a good salesperson, you probably would have made it. In fact, if you had great sales skills and great contacts, you probably made it big.

Today, the large insurance companies are hiring far fewer new grads than they did 20 years ago. This method of throwing spaghetti against the wall to see who would stick was far too expensive. The failure rate was also embarrassingly high. There are still some insurance and investment firms that hire new college grads. The same desires and sales skills need to be present, but the training and focus on financial planning is far more prevalent. Many employers of rookie planners have implemented mentor programs where junior advisors are teamed with successful veterans to help with some of the low-end tasks and marketing while they learn.

Financial planners generally fall into two broad categories: generalist comprehensive planners and specialist planners (whose knowledge is concentrated in one or a few areas). Commonly, new planners are asked to focus on a single area (or two) of expertise, such as annuities, mutual funds, or long-term care insurance. With some specialized knowledge, the failure rate is lower and the new planner can make a good living while he or she learns.

In addition to the large insurance and Wall Street firms, there are ample opportunities today for gaining specialized knowledge related to financial planning in many industries. Commonly, this type of experience can be gained in banks, trust companies, discount brokerage firms, mutual fund companies, asset management companies, retirement plan firms, annuity companies, and *broker dealers*.

def•i•ni•tion

A **broker dealer** is a company that is registered with the Securities and Exchange Commission (SEC) to sell stocks, bonds, mutual funds, and other securities products for a commission.

In the past 10 years, there has been an emergence of companies that practice only financial planning. These firms have opened a new career track that didn't exist 20 years ago for recent college grads. These firms will hire new grads on a salary basis with good training and experience that has nothing to do with their ability to sell. These firms or their principals do a fine job of attracting new clients; they just need good, young talent to do the analysis, research, and planning work.

Trends today for new college grads are favorable as the financial services industry continues to grow. New grads need not worry about having a business degree. Firms are looking for young talent who can read and write and relate to people while they are trained in the specifics of the financial industry. If you do have a business degree or even a degree in financial planning—and possess all of the language and interpersonal skills that firms are seeking—you may be at the top of the candidate interview list.

Career Changers

Much to the surprise of many, career changers are the most common newcomers to the financial planning industry. Some career changers were downsized one too many times and wanted to enter a profession in demand where they could control their own destinies. Some simply hated what they did and always wanted to pursue a career related to an area that they found more appealing. Then there are other career changers who were touched so deeply by an advisor who helped change someone's life for the better that they couldn't resist the opportunity to do the same.

def•i•ni•tion

A **natural market** refers to a group of prospects, often referred to as a market, with which you have a close and personal relationship. This relationship can develop from training, experience, or exposure to that group over an extended period in a highly visible way.

Career changers are also among the most successful financial planners. Kind of like that person you met in college who went back to school in midlife, they are often so serious and focused on why they are there that success is virtually inevitable.

Career changers can have unique experience in two ways. First is through professional contacts with a qualified *natural market* of prospects. Second is through a related discipline, such as accounting, tax, or corporate finance, which offers great financial credibility and technical training in one or more of the subject areas of financial planning.

The Natural

Let's talk about the person who has great personal integrity as well as other desirable characteristics and a natural market of prospects. You don't even need to be a financial person for this scenario to work. A good example could be someone who started his or her career as a teacher.

One former teacher who made a successful career change is Tim, who taught in a difficult yet respected public school system. Tim has been on the job in one of the East Coast's most challenging inner-city public school systems for more than 10 years. With a heart of gold and a deep curiosity for learning and love of helping others, Tim has gotten to know many of the teachers in his city's schools. He participated in many of the parent-teacher associations, was involved in several student extracurricular activities, and also represented his school on both the county and state advisory boards. Over the course of his 10-year teaching career, Tim became good friends with many of the area's most successful teachers, administrators, and superintendents from towns all over the state.

Tim has superior dedication and understands the needs of his students and the school district. During daily social interactions in the teachers' lounge, the discussions frequently wander way beyond talk of troubled students, union haggles, or creative new ideas to engage students. Subjects as personal as family relationships, relations with other teachers, or weekend social activities are common. Because Tim has such a great ability to connect, is sincere, and communicates openly and confidentially, he quickly became a source of sage advice and mentoring. Tim was often asked to speak in front of large groups of teachers at annual meetings and to lead discussion groups during teacher training. Tim not only spoke of his successes but frequently exposed his vulnerability and spoke of his failures and the corrective actions that he took to make a situation better.

Tim knew a lot about his colleagues' lives outside school. Conversely, other teachers around the state got to know a lot about Tim. They knew that he was a former college football player and armed forces veteran, that he loved watching the Discovery Channel, and that he had a passion for money and business issues. He was frequently called upon to guide his colleagues through the selection of mutual funds for their 403(b) plans and the selection of insurance benefits from the menu provided by the various school systems. The union even asked Tim to consult on the benefit plans offered and opine on the types of benefits that were important to the retention of high-quality teachers.

As in many government areas, budget cuts and the bureaucracy of politics were wearing thin on Tim, and after two years of steady deterioration, Tim realized that he was not having fun anymore. It was time for him to move on. A careful saver and investor, Tim had the luxury of time and the freedom to plan a career change. After careful research, he thought that a career in the financial services industry would suit him well. Tim found a job with a large CPA firm. At the same time, out of curiosity and with a passion for the subject, Tim pursued advanced education in the area of personal finance while studying for his CPA exam. Within five years, Tim had earned both his CPA designation and the Chartered Financial Consultant (ChFC) designation. (We'll talk more about financial services designations in Chapter 7.)

Tim then left the large firm and started his own accounting practice with a focus on taxes and personal financial planning. Naturally, many of his clients were teachers and their spouses. Tim knew that most teachers came from a two-income household, where the second breadwinner was often a business owner or someone with a successful professional career. Therefore, they would need both a CPA and a financial planner. Five years after Tim left the teacher's lounge, his former colleagues learned about his new business and immediately wanted to benefit from his new knowledge and services. His natural market came through for him, and today his business is a nice mix of small business and individual clients for whom he does tax, accounting, and financial planning work.

Not all career changers are as motivated and successful as Tim, however. Tim had the vision and perseverance to pursue his dream and in five short years was again happy with his career. He made three times as much money as he ever made in the classroom. If you are ready for the work required and have a respected natural market, your transition can be just as successful as Tim's.

Those with Relevant Experience

Now, let's talk about those candidates whose prior careers are a great start for building credibility or whose knowledge is particularly applicable in financial planning. Personal financial planning is a broad subject area. Most financial professionals will admit that they have never met any person who is truly an expert in each specific area of financial planning (although there are some who claim to be). But some, by virtue of their previous training and experience, may truly be experts in one or more of the related disciplines.

The person who has relevant experience has a head start over other career changers when starting in the field of personal financial planning. It can help on a number of fronts to go deep into a few of the knowledge areas needed to serve a client well. All clients' needs are different. Some have problems with tax issues, some with insurance issues, and some with retirement planning issues. Your previous relevant experience can help build a client following whose needs center on the area of your prior experience—making you both qualified and a good fit for their initial needs.

In the Know

Generally speaking, any person with a natural market and desirable personal characteristics can succeed in personal financial planning and will be viewed favorably by many prospective employers.

Pitfalls

If your past career was very successful, be prepared to take a salary cut. Make sure that you can adapt your lifestyle or supplement your earnings with savings for the first year.

Your relevant experience can help with respect to marketing your practice around the core competencies gained from a prior career. Clients who have specific needs want to feel comfortable that they are getting the best advice available, and your prior experience gives that. Other professionals are often the first to recognize when a client needs advice from another professional, and your prior experience may make you the best choice. In fact, professionals and referral sources from that prior career are excellent financial planning prospects themselves.

Many professions and specialties lead nicely to a career in personal financial planning. There are a few, however, that stand out as giving a notable head start—at least in the areas of technical know-how—because of that prior training and experience.

Certified Public Accountants (CPAs)

Many CPAs can only look into the rearview mirror, and you know what would happen if you drove down the highway with both eyes focused there! These CPAs are very good at telling you what happened last year and reporting it as required by accounting regulations and the taxing authorities. Yet, very few ever take their eyes off the rearview mirror and help their clients plan for the future—except when asked. Even then, the planning offered is most commonly limited to tax or business planning, with comprehensive and holistic financial planning done only incidentally and at a very general level.

The good news about CPAs is that most have a thorough understanding of tax and basic business issues. Some are even experienced or trained with knowledge in estate planning, retirement plans, business succession, business valuations, and risk management. These CPAs have a genuine head start to success as personal financial planners.

Passing the CPA exam is no small feat. This rigorous exam demonstrates your ability to grasp tough concepts and consider the entire situation while tackling a specific issue. Most CPAs possess the intellectual curiosity required of a personal financial planner and the problem-solving abilities to create knowledge-based solutions.

If you are a CPA who is tired of only looking into the rearview mirror and is trained or experienced with any deeper understanding beyond accounting and taxes, you are ready to look at the road ahead. When you take at least one eye off the rearview mirror to plan for your clients, you have the most unique advantage of all career changers. You already have clients who trust you, like you, and want to interact with you.

Attorneys

Like them or not, lawyers are very well trained for a career in financial planning. A lawyer's ability to pass the bar exam—like the CPA exam—indicates a core level of intelligence. Attorneys are good readers, are able to understand complex fact patterns, and often have good training and experience with asking provocative questions.

Similar to financial planning, the law is complex and is made up of many specialty areas. Divorce lawyers often know nothing about not-for-profit entities, and business lawyers often do not practice in the area of land use. Those who have the best relevant experience, however, are those whose prior careers have taught them about taxation, estates and probate, trusts, business, or family issues. These are not the only areas where prior experience as an attorney is helpful, however. Every area of financial planning—no matter how specialized it may be—has a legal connection and can be helpful for a career in financial planning.

An example of a legal specialty that is helpful to a new career as a personal financial planner would be an attorney who has practiced with special-needs children. From care and education options to financing that care, the spectrum of expertise required to be a good lawyer for young special-needs children can make you uniquely qualified to do financial planning for those families.

Financial Analysts

Financial analysts come in many varieties. Some are corporate financial analysts comparing the financial consequences of one action over another. And some may be analysts for an investment company looking into the historical financial statements and projected financials of a company to determine whether it would be a good investment.

Much of the technical side of financial planning has to do with financial analysis. Some clients will gain comfort from knowing that a respectable company has trained you and that you helped them make important financial decisions. There is also a lot of similarity in the process of analyzing financial data and simulations in a corporate environment to personal financial planning situations. While the actual data and the purpose may be different, your experience with using a process to discover, analyze, and make recommendations will be very helpful.

While personal financial planning is a broad and pervasive profession, clients and prospects often consider the investment part of planning as the most important. Clients love to talk about investments and will often decide on a financial planner based on their perception of how good he or she is with investing. Maybe that is because so many large investment companies are the ones marketing financial planning services—or because the heritage of the financial planning profession has such strong roots in the investment community. Whatever the reason, a background in financial analysis brings you close to what is near and dear to the hearts of many financial planning clients.

College Finance and Business Professors

A person who has taken business courses in college has a soft spot for the professor who so skillfully taught a subject in which he or she had no prior knowledge. The perceptions alone of the wise, experienced, professorial type make them very credible in the eyes of clients and other professionals.

On the nuts-and-bolts side, these professionals have taught many of the concepts that form the foundation of personal financial planning. Whether that professor taught economics, accounting, finance, or taxation, these topics are at the very core of personal financial planning. The expertise required to teach the subject is certainly more than adequate to gain proficiency as a financial planning practitioner.

Also, college teachers know how to learn. The academic environment is very keen on research and lifelong learning for their professors, and they become very good at it. The financial planning world and all of its technical subcomponents is always changing. You and your clients will benefit from a commitment to stay current and know how to research areas beyond specialized areas of expertise.

> **In the Know**
>
> While professors may possess in-depth knowledge in many of the required areas of financial planning, it doesn't guarantee that they will find success. Professors face the same challenges as any other new person with regard to business development and finding clients.

Intellectual Abilities

You already know that you can't be devoid of any intellectual ability to be a good personal financial planner—but you don't need to be a Rhodes Scholar, either. You have to be able to pass both licensing exams and then certification exams. None of these are simple, but if you have good learning skills, decent study habits, and commit the time to preparation, you should do fine.

The primary areas of intellectual ability involve analytical, mathematical, and computer skills. Don't let any of these scare you.

Good analytical skills require looking at a situation, evaluating the alternatives, and making a decision about which way to go based on your analysis. To do this, you will have access to research tools, specialists, intuition, and experience. In the real world, there are a couple additional safety nets to prevent you from making fatal mistakes. A good client will challenge your analysis if it doesn't feel right—often requiring you to rethink your decision. Professional colleagues or others outside your office are always willing to act as sounding boards. The client's other professional advisors are also good resources for aiding in decisions. These other professionals are there for guidance so that the client's team of advisors can collaboratively give the best advice possible. And when you do make a wrong decision or give advice where another alternative may have been better, don't hide it. Even the best-laid plans are subject to revision.

When I speak of good mathematical skills, I'm not talking about geometry or calculus. I'm referring to basic addition, subtraction, multiplication, division, and a little bit of algebra. The stuff you learned by eighth or ninth grade is often good enough. For the mundane tasks of basic math, you'll have the aid of calculators, the Internet, and software programs that are fairly intuitive. What you will need regarding mathematical skills is the ability to understand how numbers relate to other facts and goals. You'll need the ability to see that if a client is spending too much money on recreation today, he or she won't be able to retire early or buy a second home in 10 years. You'll need to understand the significance of investing your entire nest egg in a 5 percent certificate of deposit when the inflation rate is 4 percent and your client is in a 30 percent tax bracket. Although the calculator or software program will give you the answer, you need to understand the process and come up with alternative solutions.

Pitfalls

Many career changers avoid personal financial planning because they fear a lack of knowledge. This is a career where you can start at an entry level and get your training and advanced education while on the job. Don't assume that you can't do it.

Most people today have some basic computer skills. If you don't, though, just ask your local librarian— or your seven-year-old niece—to point you in the right direction. A basic understanding of how to use the Internet, a word processor, spreadsheets, and presentation software (such as PowerPoint) are the main ingredients and can be learned in a few days. Learning how to use the entire Microsoft Office suite is ideal, and you can master it in a few months. Once you have that down, you'll learn how to use some specific financial planning application software. Some are a bit challenging, but all offer training courses and tutorials built right into the program to assist you.

Interpersonal Skills

Take a look back at your high school or college classes and see who the most successful people are 20 years later. While it may be the valedictorian, it is just as likely that the class clown or the person who had a B average has enjoyed equal career success. Your ability to interact with people is probably the number-one characteristic that will define your success.

A good planner will be empathetic—always focused on the client's feelings and desires. You need genuine compassion and care about your clients, realizing that their goals are important to them. Their plan is about them, not you.

Good communication skills are imperative. Both the speaking and listening sides are equally important. You need to hear clearly what is important to your client and address those issues first. Even if you do a great job with what you see as the major holes in a client's financial plan, you run the risk of client dissatisfaction if you do not thoroughly address what he or she feels is the most pressing need.

After you've demonstrated your care by listening well, you'll also need to speak effectively. You can master this skill for addressing large groups, but in small client settings your speaking ability has to come somewhat naturally from genuine care and concern for helping your client. You must also be persuasive. Some of the decisions are difficult for a client to make, but you know that they must be made. An example is the client who has a tough time dealing with his or her own mortality and has not drawn up a will. If that client has a spouse and minor-age children, the consequences of not preparing a will could be devastating. In this case, you must be persuasive and stress the significance of neglecting this imperative planning tool and figure out a way to get it done. You may need to be creative and outline scenarios that you know your client would like to avoid as possible consequences of this inaction.

In the Know

As a financial planner, you need to do more listening than speaking to gain the confidence of your clients and to find career success. There is an old adage that says, "You have two ears and one mouth for a good reason. Listen twice as often as you speak."

You need to be able to work well in groups. All clients will need specialists who can do work that they cannot. Whether they need an attorney to draft wills and trusts or a third-party administrative company to design and maintain the client's profit-sharing plan, you cannot complete these tasks alone.

The person who has great interpersonal skills can often succeed in personal financial planning where the great technicians cannot. He or she should be highly personable and often a good leader and a good judge of abilities and character. This person intuitively knows his or her strengths and weaknesses and will frequently surround himself or herself with others who can deliver what he or she cannot.

Burning Desire

There is no substitute for burning desire. While it is easy to get into the financial planning business without it, you will never find great success. You need a burning desire for success, to learn and to be competent for your clients, to be ethical, and to always keep your client's best interests in mind.

People are attracted to others who possess passion and a burning desire to succeed. This person is often the one who exceeds expectations, goes above and beyond the call of duty to make something right, and always does the right thing. While we should not take integrity for granted, it is impossible to lack integrity and possess a burning desire for success as a financial planner. Success in your own mind is one thing, but success in the eyes of your clients and colleagues only comes when they feel that you have treated them fairly. Only those who have the intent to deceive can possess a burning desire for success and lack integrity at the same time. These deceitful people usually get into regulatory trouble or end up in lawsuits.

Burning desire is a two-way street. Your clients must also possess a burning desire for reaching their financial planning goals. If they don't, the relationship will be marginal at best. But when they do possess that same passion for their personal finances that you have, you will have a lifelong relationship as long as you live up to your half of the bargain.

The Least You Need to Know

- The characteristics of a successful financial planner include a blend of interpersonal, technical, and work ethic skills along with a genuine curiosity and thirst for knowledge.

- Opportunities for new grads are prevalent in insurance companies, investment firms, banks, and financial planning firms.

- Career changers have a natural advantage because of their real-life skills and contacts from their previous career.

- Effective listening and genuine concern for your client's life dreams and financial goals will deepen the client relationship and build the trust needed for an effective planner-client working relationship.

- A burning desire to succeed is critical in this entrepreneurial profession and will help deliver early success as you get started.

Chapter 3

Getting in the Game

In This Chapter

- Understanding financial planning lingo
- How financial planners get paid
- What you should know before you embark on a career in financial planning
- The necessary education
- The licensing requirements
- Things that could keep you out of the game

Like any new game, playing without knowing any of the language or basic rules is nearly impossible. How would you feel if you were dropped into the middle of a bridge game with Warren Buffet and Bill Gates—if you never played bridge? It's pretty much the same story for a career changer or for a college senior who is interviewing with a financial services company recruiter who is looking for new associates. The only difference there is that they don't expect you to really know anything about the industry specifics. But if you do, it's fair to say that you will leave a very favorable impression on the interviewer.

In this chapter, you'll become familiar enough with the industry to carry on intelligent conversations with financial planners and prospective employers. The financial services industry has its own jargon and rules that are complex and not intuitive. The regulatory side has rules enacted by different regulatory authorities, and each state may add its own requirements.

Some of the bare minimum requirements to be in the financial planning business include a myriad of licenses and a clean record that is free from criminal activity. Depending on the type of business you work for, you may need all of the licenses or some—but you will need something.

Learning the Language

The language of the financial planning business is extensive. This section is not meant to define every term that you'll run across—there's a glossary for that (see Appendix A)—but I'll hit the high points. Let's start with the basic term *financial planner*. Some call themselves financial planners while other firms use names such as financial advisors, wealth managers, financial consultants, wealth consultants, wealth advisors, and probably a few more titles that are being coined as we speak.

 Pitfalls

Holding yourself out as a financial planner if you have no intention of doing complete financial planning for a client could be a short-term gain at best. While you may get clients today you're likely to lose them for the services you are not delivering to them in the future.

The real issue isn't what you call yourself. Rather, it's what you do for your clients and what style of practice you have. If you are going to call yourself a financial planner, then deliver planning services as the founders of the financial planning movement intended. Have it be comprehensive, proactive, holistic, and in the client's best interests.

In the world of certified public accountants (CPAs), planning engagements have been further broken down. We have devoted much of our attention to comprehensive, holistic financial planning. But the CPA profession has coined a term: a *segmented engagement*, where you are merely giving advice on a segment of the client's overall financial plan. While most clients will benefit from an overall comprehensive engagement, it isn't always what they want. Commonly, clients will see an advisor and just want input on their portfolios or on a revised estate plan. While the planner would still need to consider factors from other parts of the client's financial life to properly advise on the specific segment, this type of engagement would be considered a segmented engagement. There is nothing wrong with segmented engagements; just make sure that you have properly documented the nature of the engagement and obtained the client's signature as acceptance of this limitation. If you are committed to comprehensive, holistic planning only, this is an engagement that you should not take. Refer to another advisor who is willing to offer segmented advice.

Compensation Methods

There are several different revenue models in the financial planning business. In general, revenues may be generated from fees, commissions, or both. The issue of which compensation method is best for the client is hotly contested. Your preference, employer, or industry focus will help shape the decision as to which is best suited for you and your client.

At the end of the day, it really shouldn't matter which compensation method you choose to use as long as you subscribe to one of the many financial planning codes of ethics promulgated by various industry groups. All of the trade associations and industry designation-granting authorities have strict codes of ethics that mandate serving the client's best interest first. As you may expect, however, there are numerous stories about advisors whose advice is geared toward maximizing commissions from the sale of financial products. If they are not holding themselves out as financial planners—and their industry does not have commission disclosure requirements—it ends up as a buyer-beware situation. The industry needs to fix this baggage in order to gain wider acceptance among the public. A simple solution would be to require full disclosure of all compensation for anyone who is holding himself or herself out as a financial planner. As simple as that sounds, there is strong industry opposition from the securities and insurance industries, who fear that full disclosure may weaken their sales and give consumers a reason to look for less costly alternatives.

Fee Only

Fee-only practitioners are the most outspoken about their method of compensation. Fee-only practitioners derive compensation solely from the client. They do not receive commissions and are often not even licensed to accept them. Fee-only planners have created an industry association called The National Association of Personal Financial Advisors (NAPFA). Planners join NAPFA to enhance skills, market services, and be part of a collective, influential voice on matters that affect them and their clients. NAPFA fee-only members subscribe to a set of core values that are similar to other financial planning organizations—except that NAPFA members subscribe to a fee-only method of compensation because they believe that it facilitates objective advice.

In theory, fee-only planning makes sense. In practice, however, a new planner may not be able to afford to earn a living from fees only. Also, if you decide that life insurance is going to be your specialty, there are not enough commission-free products on the market to satisfy all of your clients. Another practical problem is working with other professionals. For a practitioner to be completely objective, he or she must refer to other professionals the part of plan implementation that involves the sale of commissionable products. Many fee-only advisors only refer to a small network of professionals with whom they have had a previous relationship that includes cross-referrals. There are also plenty of fee-only practitioners who will refer that commission-based business to family members. Is that facilitating objective advice or steering clients toward someone whom you want to succeed? If you intend to practice as a fee-only planner, you should join NAPFA to learn and adopt their strict code of ethics.

Commission Only

Commission-only financial planners—once the majority—are now a fast-shrinking population. Commission-only planners derive their compensation strictly from commissions on the sale of financial products. Now, recall the distinction between the services provided to the clients. There are still plenty of industry specialists such as life insurance professionals who don't ever intend to be comprehensive financial planners. But there are still some financial planners who are performing comprehensive planning engagements for their clients and get paid strictly from commissions.

In the Know

Your method of compensation may start out one way early in your career and change to another later. Compensation methods do not reflect on your abilities in any way.

Fee and Commission

Fee and commission planners get paid a combination of fees, commissions, or both. But just as with the commission-only planner, the method of compensation is not necessarily the main issue. What matters is which service you hold yourself out as performing and that you do competently deliver all of the services that your client expects of you.

What You Need to Know

Before embarking on a career in the financial planning industry, you need to know certain things. Be aware that you will not be a planning sensation overnight. It takes time to build your knowledge and client base. In addition, just like any other professional services career, your ability to generate new business is critical for making it all the way to the partner or self-employed level. In rare circumstances, you may rise to the partner level as the service partner actually doing the work of a partner who is better at sales and obtaining new clients—but that is not likely. And if you do rise to that partner level, it's unlikely that you will be an equal owner or equal in compensation.

You need to come to grips with the fact that you'll never be an expert in everything—and you'll need to build a team of professionals upon whom you can rely to support your planning business. Although you are competent, this is such a relationship-based business that you will do best when working with clients whose style is compatible with yours. Technical know-how alone does not make you the right planner for everyone.

In the Know

When interviewing new clients, the intangible factors and your ability to get along with and like your clients are important. You will never accurately judge your ability to get along with a new client 100 percent of the time, but trust your instincts and don't work with clients you don't like or feel you won't get along with, regardless of the financial opportunity.

The regulatory side of the financial planning industry is fast-moving. New regulations come out frequently, and you may need to hire people or adjust how you do things just to comply with new regulations. Regulations vary among states, and you must comply with the regulations of each state in which your clients reside. So, for example, if your practice is in Manhattan, it's likely that you'll need to be registered and keep up with the regulations in New York, New Jersey, and Connecticut that govern financial planners. As clients move south or get transferred to other states, you'll then have to comply with those regulations. Compliance with all federal and state laws can be a full-time job in a medium-sized practice. In a small practice, it can consume 10 or more hours per week.

The good news: you don't need to know everything! Outsourcing has arrived in the financial planning industry, and planners can now outsource some of the compliance and billing functions—and just about any area of technical expertise where you don't want

Pitfalls

Don't get hung up as a perfectionist and feel that you have to know everything there is to know about financial planning. You will never know everything.

to be the expert. You will, however, be responsible for supervising others' work and seeing that it is appropriate for your client and consistent with your planning recommendations. While you may outsource some of the specific duties, it does not relieve you from the responsibility of ensuring that the overall system is appropriate for your practice, in place, and compliant with all appropriate regulations.

Where to Get the Education

Until recently, few options existed for obtaining a financial planning education. A few industry associations offered courses as well as the few major designations or courses of study in related areas at colleges and universities.

When you think of education for financial planning, most people go right to the nuts and bolts of the financial planning world. But there is a lot more than that. You will need education in sales and business development, practice management, leadership, dealing with people and their most private issues, computer software, the planning process, and maybe even management training.

Thorough technical knowledge is important and the only way to develop a solid foundation for success. But often, mastering the other nontechnical skills separates good financial planners from the most successful ones. These are the finely tuned issues that are necessary to continue growing in your chosen style of practice. It isn't possible to do everything all at once, however; you must take baby steps. The order of those steps, however, may not be clear to you until you figure out your entry point into the profession. Each style of practice and employer will stress a different educational track, given their experience and business model.

On the Job

On-the-job training used to be the main way in which people developed their skill sets as financial planners. You learned by doing with a little supplement: in-office training sessions. A new planner often accompanies the sales manager on calls to lend credibility and to show you how to make a presentation in a live client situation.

Today, many firms have developed extensive training modules and perfected systems that have been tried and tested. While there is no substitute for formal technical training, there is also no substitute for good on-the-job experience.

From your on-the-job experience, you can expect a heavy dose of process training—training on the systems and processes that your company uses to do just about everything.

You'll need to learn their system for communicating with clients and documenting those communications. You'll need to learn about the services that the firm offers. Some do not offer comprehensive financial plans, and some do—and still others may have variations. There will be learning time devoted to using the various software programs deployed by your firm.

Many firms have formal mentoring programs. The office manager will actually assign you to a seasoned veteran as your role model and sounding board. Some of these mentoring programs are required; others are optional. A good mentor will help you decide on critical areas such as business development, specialization, and the direction of your career path.

Another common method for firms today is assigning you to a team—often made up of three to five professionals who have varying degrees of experience and knowledge. All members of the team will usually get involved in nearly every case that the team develops. The team method is good because it lets you see the timeline of other professionals along your career path. It helps for you to see what you may (or want to) be doing in a few years' time.

In the Know

On-the-job experience will give you good, practical information. Pay attention to what *not* to do also, and learn from the mistakes of others to shorten your learning curve.

There should also be a formal component to your on-the-job training—whether the firm actually sends you to a home office-type training event or it's held right at your local office. What's important is that there is some formal element to the program that you can evaluate up front as part of your decision to join that particular firm. In addition to an up-front type of cram session—which can last up to three weeks or longer—there should be some sort of regular weekly or at least monthly training offered to all new professionals.

A College Degree in Financial Planning

If you looked for a university degree in financial planning 20 years ago, you may have found a few. Today, there are literally hundreds. In fact, you can enroll in a certificate program or obtain a Bachelor of Science (B.S.), Bachelor of Business Administration (B.B.A.), Master of Science (M.S.), Master of Business Administration (M.B.A.), Master of Arts (M.A.), or a Doctorate (Ph.D.) degree in financial planning. Some are specifically degrees in personal financial planning while others are degrees in finance or accounting with either a concentration or a minor in personal financial planning. All this in the past 20 years gives solid evidence of the profession's coming of age and bright future.

If you do not have one of these degrees or are halfway through an undergraduate degree in marketing, please do not think that you blew it. The industry still wants you with another degree and will ask you to obtain industry-specific training at the Master's, certificate, or designation level. On the other hand, if you are halfway through another degree and have a burning desire to start your financial planning education today, look seriously into transferring. Most colleges today have distance-learning programs that enable you to attend classes from anywhere—as long as you have an Internet connection. You can get information about formal educational programs from the CFP Board of Standards website at www.cfp.net/become/programs. asp. For other educational programs, contact your local college or university, local library, or high school guidance office.

For the certificate programs, you may need an undergraduate degree in just about any discipline. Each school sets its own curriculum, but typically schools will try to conform to what the CFP Board of Standards deems necessary to qualify for taking the CFP exam. There are between five and six courses, each lasting about 30 hours spread over 6 to 10 weeks. There are many, however, that offer executive-style education where you will go for three or four full-time days in a row and complete a part in much less time. Distance learning is very popular and available through many institutions.

Financial planning undergraduate degrees are going to be pretty much the same as any other business-based undergraduate degree. You'll have to take a smattering of basic liberal arts courses such as English, literature, history, psychology, and some basic science courses. The major portion of your studies will be economics, accounting, taxation, insurance, investing, retirement plans, and financial planning. Emphasis in most of the programs is on understanding financial products, base theories of the subject areas, and the decision-making process. Full-time attendance will take four years to complete.

A Master's degree in financial planning is far more focused than any undergraduate program. Master's degree courses cover much of the same financial planning content as the undergraduate courses—without all of the liberal arts or science requirements. The presumption and prerequisite here is that you already have an undergraduate degree. In addition to the core financial planning courses, you usually may choose from four or five electives that are much deeper and more challenging than those offered in undergraduate programs.

Walking the Walk _____

At Bentley College, we decided to offer a Master's of Science in financial planning because of demand for the education and the lack of a graduate program in the Boston area. Our students are ready for a career in planning when they complete the program and have very little trouble finding gainful employment.

—Jack Lynch, MSFP director, Bentley College, Waltham, Massachusetts

The Ph.D. program in financial planning is currently only offered by one university. Texas Tech University in Lubbock, Texas, is the first to launch such a program. This program is very advanced with a major emphasis on research. Candidates for this degree are typically not doing it to further their career as financial planners; rather, they are planning for a career in academia.

When to Get the Credentials

We'll discuss professional credentials more in Chapter 7, but for now, let's discuss them in the context of getting in the game. Too many people, especially career changers, become focused on credentials way too soon. There are more important issues early on in your planning career. It is, of course, a good idea to have credentials—and sooner is good. But wouldn't you like to know whether or not you'll enjoy a career as a financial planner before you invest so much time and money? If you have the luxury of good savings and are not in any rush to start your career in financial planning, go ahead and get started on a course of study that will lead to a designation. The worst case is that you will develop personal knowledge that will guide your own financial affairs.

But, speaking from a practical point of view, it is better to get in the game, make sure that you like it, get your licensing squared away, and then focus on a credential. Many employers will provide financial assistance or full reimbursement for any training and credentialing examinations that will arise. Those same employers will usually agree to pay your credential licensing fees and foot the bill for any continuing education required during the term of your employment.

What About Licensing?

Early critics of the financial planning profession cried that there were no criteria or licensing requirements. Of course, all that has changed—and now, licensing has become a major expense and time-consuming for all planners. The style of practice you choose will determine which licenses(s) you will need. So if you choose to be a fee-only financial planner, you wouldn't need to get an insurance or securities license—only those that are applicable to financial planning. Conversely, if you only want to sell insurance, you don't need to be securities licensed or licensed as a financial planner. It is a bit confusing, and conflicting advice is common among practitioners and employers alike. Here, you'll get the straight scoop.

When you think about licensing as a financial planner, there are many different fronts you need to consider: licensing as a securities representative, licensing as a financial planner, and licensing as an insurance broker or agent.

The first area I'll review is for the sale of securities. Securities are investment products such as stocks, bonds, mutual funds, variable annuities and life insurance, unit trusts, and direct participation programs. Suffice it to say that any investment sold for a commission is probably classified as a security. The securities industry is overseen and regulated by the U.S. Securities and Exchange Commission (SEC). The mission of the SEC is to protect investors, to maintain fair, orderly, and efficient markets, and to facilitate capital formation. As it relates to dealing with financial planners, the SEC is concerned primarily with promoting the disclosure of important market-related information, maintaining fair deals, and protecting against fraud.

The securities industry is also overseen by the National Association of Securities Dealers (NASD). The NASD is a private-sector provider of financial regulatory services and oversees the activities of more than 5,100 brokerage firms and 659,000 registered securities representatives. The NASD licenses individuals and admits firms to the industry, writes rules to govern their behavior, examines them for regulatory compliance, and disciplines those who fail to comply.

The North American Securities Administrators Association (NASAA) is yet another group involved in the regulation and oversight of the securities and financial planning industries. NASAA is a voluntary association whose membership consists of 67 state, provincial, and territorial securities administrators in the 50 states, the District of Columbia, Puerto Rico, the U.S. Virgin Islands, Canada, and Mexico.

In the United States, NASAA is the voice of state securities agencies that are responsible for efficient capital formation and grassroots investor protection. Their fundamental mission is protecting consumers who purchase securities or investment advice, and their jurisdiction extends to a wide variety of issuers and intermediaries who offer and sell securities to the public.

Last on the list of potential licenses would be insurance. Most financial planning practitioners who sell insurance limit it to life insurance, annuities, disability insurance, long-term care insurance, and health insurance. Homeowners, automobile, and other property and casualty insurance is not commonly sold by financial planners; however, some property and casualty agents are either starting to offer financial planning services or hiring a person to create that division within their agencies.

Series 6

The NASD administers this exam. Upon successful completion of the Series 6, an individual will have the qualifications needed to sell mutual funds, variable life insurance, and variable annuities. To take this exam, you must be sponsored by an NASD-member firm. And that's only likely to happen if you are interviewing for a position or have already accepted one.

The exam is 100 questions and multiple-choice, and you have 2 hours and 15 minutes to complete it. A passing score is 70 percent. Study guides, review courses, and online tutorials are readily available. This is the easiest of all of the securities exams.

Series 7

The NASD administers this exam. An individual who passes will earn the qualifications necessary in order to make different types of trades with all types of corporate securities—except commodities and futures. Passing this exam overrides the need to take a Series 6 exam. To take this test, you must be sponsored by an NASD-member firm.

The exam has 260 multiple-choice questions that are broken down into two parts. There are 125 questions on each part, plus 10 pretest questions that do not count toward your grade. You will be given 3 hours for each part of the exam. A passing grade for this exam is 70 percent. This test is considerably more difficult than a Series 6 exam. Study guides, review courses, and online tutorials are readily available. Unless you have significant industry experience or are good at independent study, the review course is strongly recommended.

In the Know

Many insurance- and mutual fund-based sponsor firms will be reluctant to sponsor you for the Series 7 exam as you get started. It is more costly and harder to pass—possibly delaying your ability to sell their products. Ask for the Series 7 sponsorship. If you don't get it, you can always take it later in your career when you need it.

The review course for the Series 7 exam lasts 40 hours. Your study time for the exam will easily exceed 50 hours in addition to the review course. The failure rate for those not taking a review course is very high. A Series 7 license is also a prerequisite for obtaining a supervisor's license. While you won't need that as you start in the financial planning business, you may if you ever go out on your own or want to open a branch office. Ask your sponsor firm to sponsor you for the Series 7 if you have a vision of doing either in the future.

Series 63

The Series 63 exam is also administered by the NASD and is considered the uniform securities agent state law exam. While it is not really specific to state law—each state makes and administers its own laws—it covers the areas typically overseen by state regulatory authorities. In order to be fully licensed and active as a securities representative, you will need the Series 63 along with either the Series 6 or 7.

This exam has 100 multiple-choice questions. You will have 2 hours and 30 minutes to complete it, and the passing grade is 70 percent. While study guides, review courses, and online tutorials are readily available, this exam is not very challenging.

Series 65

Series 65 is an exam administered by the NASAA. If you plan to charge fees for financial planning and will hold yourself out as a financial planner, you will need this license. Certain states will waive this requirement if you have demonstrated substantial experience in a related industry or have completed certain advanced designations. You'll have to check with your employer or your state securities administrator to be sure what the rules of your state are.

Completion of the Series 65 exam will qualify an investment professional to operate as an investment advisor representative in certain states. The exam focuses on topic areas that are important for an investment advisor to know when providing investment advice. These areas include subjects such as retirement planning, portfolio management strategies, and fiduciary obligations. The name of the exam is the Uniform Investment Advisor Law Examination. It's also the exam that you will need to pass in order to register as a financial planner.

This exam is 140 questions, multiple-choice. Ten of the questions are pretest questions that do not count toward your grade, and they are not identified among the 140 questions. A passing grade here is 68.5 percent, and you will have 3 hours to complete the exam. Study guides, review courses, and online tutorials are readily available. This exam is very challenging. Because it may be a free-standing exam for planners who choose to become fee-only, registered investment advisors, it covers a lot of ground. You would be well advised to consider a review course for this exam.

Series 66

This exam is administered by NASAA and is the equivalent of the Series 63 and 65 exams. Successful completion of this exam and the Series 7 qualifies you to register as a securities agent and investment advisor. This exam has 110 multiple-choice questions with 10 pretest questions randomly seeded throughout the exam (they don't count toward your grade). A passing grade is 71 percent, and you will have 2 hours and 30 minutes to complete the exam.

Although this exam combines the content of the Series 65 and 63 exams, it is easier in aggregate than preparing for the Series 63 and 65. Study guides, review courses, and online tutorials are readily available. This exam is of moderate difficulty, and a review course is recommended.

Series Exam Failures

Failing any of the series exams will result in substantial delays of your licensing because of mandatory waiting periods before scheduling a retake. You must wait a minimum of 30 days after failing the first exam before your second exam can be scheduled. You must again wait a minimum of 30 days after failing the exam for the second time before you can schedule a third exam. The third time you fail is no charm here. You must wait a minimum of 180 days after failing the exam for a third time before the fourth exam (and each subsequent exam) can be scheduled.

In the Know

The longer it takes you to complete your licensing exams, the longer it will take you to earn a living. Invest in yourself. Take review courses with a goal of passing on your first attempt.

Life, Accident, and Health Insurance

The licenses to sell insurance products are different in each state. Here's the process: you get the licenses you want in your home state of residence, then you apply for licensing in other states where you need licensing after your home state licensing is completed. You will need to be licensed in another state if you are working with a client who resides in that state. It's a real test of your patience; some state insurance departments are so backed up that it could take months to get approved in a different state. Think well in advance about which states you may want licensing in—and get it done early.

The licenses are typically called life, accident, and health insurance licenses. Advisors who decide to make insurance sales part of their practice will typically advise, and sometimes sell, life insurance, annuities, disability insurance, long-term care insurance, and health insurance. In most states, two exams and one license cover it all. In other states, you need two exams and two licenses. Either way, reciprocity among the various states is okay as long as you are in good standing with your home state (meaning your licenses are current and you have met all of the continuing education requirements of that home state). Check with your employer or state division of insurance for your specific requirements.

The exams are multiple-choice and are typically offered at private company testing centers in convenient locations throughout your state. Once again, each state uses a different service—and you'll have to get the details of your exam content, cost, and location directly from your employer or state division of insurance. Like the securities exams, there are a number of ways to study for your exam: study guides, online tutorials, and review courses. Many states even require a formal, live training class taught by a state-certified instructor.

Barriers to Entry

It may sound like a lot of work just to get in the game—and it is. The barriers to entry in the financial planning profession are steeped in licensing and examinations, but that's the hardest part. If you are a reasonably good student with good study skills, you can be finished with all of your licensing within 90 days and still maintain a full-time job. You will, of course, be spending plenty of time on nights and weekends to accomplish this goal. If that doesn't appeal to you, you should rethink this career choice. Many times, you'll have to work more than a regular 40-hour week. There is no requirement to complete licensing within 90 days. If, for family or personal reasons, you can't get it done that quickly, stretch it out over a time period that works for you. A new employer is likely to give you time during normal business hours to get it done. If you are in transition mode, your sponsor or new employer will clearly set his or her expectations regarding time frame requirements.

Your past history could also become a barrier to entry. If you have a criminal background or other personal problems, it will make it difficult or impossible to get hired or sponsored for a licensing exam. Full Federal Bureau of investigation (FBI) background checks are performed on all applicants, along with a complete credit and driving record check. The industry is understandably reluctant to put a person in a position of dealing with other people's money if that person has had a reckless past or significant financial trouble. Don't hide any prior baggage when attempting to get into the industry. Your concealment, when discovered, will cast substantial doubt on your integrity and will typically deny you entry. A regulator or new employer would rather you confront your past issue up front with remorse and hear your personal story—or that you overcame such adversity.

Compared to other entrepreneurial endeavors, financial planning is pretty simple. There are no huge capital or equipment outlays. Your first employer often picks up your education, licensing, and training. It is most often a contribution of your sweat and effort that is required. This may be different if you are adding personal financial planning to an existing business or if you want to be self-employed right out of the gate. It probably isn't wise to attempt to become self-employed as a new financial planner, however. You are likely to need more guidance than you think. I will talk more later in the book about what it takes to add these services to an existing business or to strike out on your own.

The Least You Need to Know

◆ Planners get paid in a variety of ways; fees, commissions, or both are acceptable methods of compensation.

◆ Educational resources are abundant and offered in traditional university and classroom settings or through online study at home.

◆ Testing and licensing is mandatory before any professionals can call themselves financial planners.

◆ Barriers to entry are low, but a background free of any criminal, financial, or regulatory problems is required.

Chapter 4

Charting Your Course

In This Chapter

- Why you should plan your career
- Looking into internships
- Getting what you want from your financial career
- Finding your niche in the financial planning industry
- The growing trend of multidisciplinary practices
- Don't forget your own financial plan!

Most people don't ever take the time to design a career plan. They start a job right out of school, and as long as they are making enough money to do what they like, they stick with it. Statistics about people who love their jobs commonly point to a large majority who really do not. Remember, it is your life and your job—and you have the power to change it to make yourself happier or more wealthy, depending on your objectives.

In this chapter, I'll tell you about making a career plan—one that's designed to meet your personal and professional goals and objectives. We are, after all, talking about a career as a financial planner. Why not start the planning with you?

There are many ways to work in the financial services industry, and now we'll begin to explore some of them. Where you start in the financial services industry is unlikely to be where you end up, however. Some start supporting the industry and end up as financial planners. Some begin as financial planers and end up selling to financial planners. However you begin your financial services career, this chapter is dedicated to helping you find the dream career that will provide you with endless years of joy and satisfaction.

What's in It for You?

This is a good question to ask when thinking about the industry. You have already learned about the effort it will take just to get into the game—now, let's look at some of the reasons why it's worth your while.

When thinking of the benefits to you, first ask yourself what benefits you are looking for. For some, the answer may lie in the intellectual challenge found in changing economic conditions and people's attitudes about money or the ability to become a specialist in a highly technical area of the tax code. For others, it may be the pure personal interaction and thrill of helping families get their priorities in order and making the financial decision-making process clear and simple for them. And for some, it may be the lure of earning a lot of money.

In the Know

If you are married, treat this section as a joint exercise for you and your spouse. It would be far better to know that you both will be happy with what the next few years of your life will be like.

In this industry, you can have it all. You can design your time to fit into whatever life you want. You can have all the fun you want through practicing in an area that you find fun and interesting—or by choosing to only work with clients with whom you enjoy associating. You can plan a lifestyle that's supported by any of the industry or planning companies that are willing to hire you. The best answer to the question, "What's in it for you?" Whatever you want.

Your career satisfaction with financial planning may also be heightened from your ability to shape the future of the industry. Remember, the field of financial planning is fewer than 40 years old and is still evolving. The industry is hungry for new professionals who are eager to help grow the esteem and recognition of the industry. It already is considered a prestigious profession, and that level of prestige will only increase as more and more people discover the benefits of working with a financial planner.

If you are financially motivated, you've come to the right place. There are some financial planners who earn in excess of $1 million per year. Now, don't expect this figure as a rookie—but the most successful planners can get to this level within 10 years with hard work. These most successful financial planners make up the top 1 percent of the industry and are extremely good at relationships and sales. Entry-level compensation for rookie financial planners can be from the mid-$30,000 range to as high as $50,000, depending on location and education. If you are in a company that has a formal career track, expect to get pay increases in excess of the consumer price index (CPI). If your compensation package has any entrepreneurial component or success metrics, you may easily be in the $100,000 range within 10 years.

Finding an Internship

In a nonmedical environment, professional internships are typically three- to six-month temporary jobs. For you as the employee, you get to see the job from the inside out. It may take you several internships to find the job that you really want to pursue. And from the employer's perspective, he or she gets a glimpse of your working ability and can use that to benchmark other rookies or to help decide whether he or she wants to make you a full-time job offer.

There are several ways to go about finding an internship:

◆ **Use your natural network.** Talk to people you know in the industry and see whether they can give you leads to firms that typically hire interns. These may be former college classmates, former employers, parents, family, or friends.

◆ **Attend job fairs.** You can find job fairs for financial planners at many colleges as well as at industry associations. The Financial Planning Association (FPA) frequently holds career fairs at many of the local chapters and also has a devoted career section on its website. Go to www.fpanet.org and click the Career and Practice tab to be connected to the FPA Career Center.

◆ **Check the postings at your college career counseling office.** Even if there are no current postings, the career counselors often know which firms have hired interns in the past and can give you their names and addresses.

◆ **Do your homework.** Look in the Yellow Pages for local business listings and for the major financial planning, investment, and insurance companies. If you call them and say that you are looking for an internship, you may have more success than you think. They really value self-starters and will probably be impressed with your assertiveness to cold-call them. Remember, many of these organizations still look for good sales ability in their new advisors.

To get the internship, you'll need a good resumé and cover letter. If the prospective employer sees a bunch of resumés, he or she will look at your grades and prior work experience as the most important criteria. All resumés begin to look alike after a recruiter looks at so many of them, so your cover letter may be your best differentiator. In your cover letter, let the company know why you are interested and why you think that you have what it takes to be a successful financial planner. Keep your cover letter to one page, single-spaced.

In the Know _____

Avoid internships that offer no pay or only clerical-level experience. Make the experience count. You want experience that will give you a good taste of what working in the industry will be all about.

Compensation for internships varies from zero to an hourly rate that is consistent with the pay for first-year, full-time, new hires. Try to get an internship that's closely focused on what you think you want to do full time. If you are not sure, take the one that sounds most interesting to you—and you'll see how much you like it as you proceed. Ask to speak with last year's interns, and ask them what they got out of the experience and whether they'd recommend that you take the position.

Plan Your Life

A career changer may have an easier time with life planning than a new college grad, but give it a shot. A plan starts with where you are today, where you want to go, what resources you have to get there, and what you'll have to do as you move forward toward your objectives. Another realistic part of planning is to realize that it's not an unchangeable course. Your life plan must adapt to your changing needs and goals.

We'll talk more about life planning—a style of financial planning created by financial planner George Kinder—in Chapter 10. But the process of thinking about your life first and your career second is where you should be right now. Your life shouldn't revolve around your career; your career should fit into your life.

Start with a vision of your desired lifestyle. Are you willing to live in humble quarters, or do you want an upscale downtown residence? Do you drive cars into the ground, or will you want to lease the latest hot model every two or three years? How about family—will there be one? Will you pay for private college, state college, or none at all for your children? Do you like local day-trip vacations to the lake, or would you prefer Lake Como in Italy or South Beach in Florida? While your vision of what is desirable is sure to change as you mature, it's never too early to start thinking.

Will you want to be self-employed someday? If so, this goal may guide you to live more frugally in your early days as a planner. Starting a business requires capital and reserve funds to support your lifestyle while you get your business up and running.

There's no substitute for a solid work ethic in financial planning. During peak demand periods, this discipline will allow you to focus on getting your most important tasks done on time. Are you okay with working 80-plus hours per week—always, some of the time, or never? If the answer is "Never," you may want to avoid becoming a tax professional. It's common for tax professionals to work long hours during the income tax filing season, which ends on April 15. Ask yourself what else is important to you. Do you want to maintain your role as a reservist in the military? Do you want to have dinner with your family every night? Do you want to devote 10 percent of your salary or volunteer one day per week for charitable endeavors?

If you have the courage to bring up these issues at job interviews, you are likely to find a better match with an employer. If you know what makes you happy, you are more likely to be genuine in client interviews and find out what's important to them. Thinking about these factors will help you find the course that is most suited for giving you the career satisfaction enjoyed by millions in the financial services industry.

Being a Top-Notch Financial Planner

Maybe it's a bit presumptuous to talk about being a top-notch financial planner, but you do have that burning desire, right? Top-notch in this sense doesn't necessarily mean a top earner, though—or being tops in some fictitious magazine ranking of the best financial planners. It means top-notch in the eyes of your clients and in keeping with the profession's core objectives of proactive, holistic advice that's always given with the client's best interests in mind.

As people's lives and the financial world that we live in become increasingly complex, there is a big demand for one advisor to be the "go-to" person for the client. In the world of personal finance, clients often have several advisors—such as a CPA, lawyer, insurance agent, banker, investment advisor, Realtor, and whoever else they might need, given their situation. It is fairly common that one or two of these professionals are closer to the client than the others, but all of them generally wish that they were more significant in the client's life.

It's also common for a client to speak with more than one of these advisors about the same issue, looking for corroborative guidance or a favorable second opinion. Unfortunately, what the client frequently gets is conflicting advice or the recommendation to see yet another professional. In fact, some of these advisors—when asked for guidance outside their area of expertise—will give the client three or more names of professionals and tell him or her to interview all of them. This only makes the confusion greater—and a final decision even tougher.

A top-notch financial planner is like a head coach of a professional sports team. With a sports team, there's a well-defined hierarchy: a team owner, a general manager, a head coach, and several assistant coaches. The same hierarchy could be designed for a client. The team owner is the equivalent of the client. The general manager and the head coach would be the financial planners. The assistant coaches would act as all of the other professionals that are needed to complete the client's advisory team.

As head coach/financial planner, you are ultimately accountable to the team owner/client. All decisions and subsequent results will reflect on your abilities. As in a sports team, the head coach does not perform every single job but is accountable for the work of his or her assistants. Some sports teams have dozens of assistants for many specialties: offense, defense, specific positions, conditioning, nutrition, and the list goes on. While you may not need as many assistants as a sports team, you are equally accountable to see that each assistant is towing his or her weight and is contributing effectively to the financial plan and the eventual accomplishment of clients' goals and objectives.

To successfully serve as head coach, you need to be familiar with all areas of personal finance and understand the consequences of one action over another. You should have the authority to recommend to the client who is utilized on the team and to replace or add an additional team professional. In the implementation of plan recommendations—such as the drafting of legal documents or the sale of a business—you should ultimately be accountable for the work of these other professionals. You must be certain that their efforts result in what is best for the client and that their work contributes toward accomplishment of the client's goals and objectives.

While not an easy task, being a top-notch financial planner—or head coach of the client's team of advisors—is a very rewarding role, both financially and emotionally. You get to see a project from its creation stage through completion and have the authority to adapt and change tactics as necessary.

> ### Walking the Walk
>
> I view the role of my financial planner as very similar to the role that I play as a head coach of a professional basketball team. I count on my planner for advice and guidance that will be in my best interests and help my family reach financial goals.
>
> —Jeff Van Gundy, former head coach, Houston Rockets and New York Knicks

Finding Your Niche

Not everyone is cut out to be the head coach, however. Some find it too difficult or simply enjoy another aspect of the financial planning industry. Financial planning needs all types: specialists, head coaches, managers, supporting roles, and people to supply the industry with the tools it needs to mature and grow.

In terms of prestige and earnings capabilities, many of these roles are just as prestigious and financially rewarding. In fact, if you rise to the top of the heap in any of these other roles, you can make more money than many financial planners ever will or become an industry spokesperson.

Some of the leaders of today's largest financial services firms started out as advisors themselves. Some had long, successful careers as top-notch financial planners—while others spent a few years in the trenches of financial planning and went right into firm management. Any knowledge that you gain in the industry will give you greater insight about your options and will help guide you to the right location within financial services.

As a Specialist

A specialist in the financial planning industry can come from two perspectives. First, you can be a financial planner and specialize in a certain type of client, such as corporate executives, small business owners, foreign nationals, or whatever other special situation or natural fit you find most appealing. We'll talk more about specific niches for financial planners later in the book. Second, you can be a knowledge specialist and spend most of your time as a team member to advise your clients only in specific areas such as insurance, investments, estate planning, or taxation.

The insurance professional is always needed but not always welcome to the financial planning team by the client. Insurance salespeople have very low credibility ratings in the eyes of the public; consequently, many clients do not like insurance or the people who sell it. Once you get your training as a financial planner, you realize that insurance is necessary, complicated, and specialized. Perhaps one of the reasons why people prefer not to talk about insurance is because of their lack of insurance knowledge. Most planners have never heard a client complain because his or her deceased loved one had too much life insurance. Similarly, clients will not bemoan the fact that healthcare for their elderly parent with Alzheimer's disease was fully covered because of a long-term care purchase made years ago. Yet millions of people are underinsured—or even uninsured.

Insurance professionals may specialize within the insurance area: corporate benefits, life insurance, annuities, disability insurance, or long-term care insurance. Typically, your career will start as an insurance generalist and may evolve into an area of specialty that you really enjoy. The most successful insurance professionals are well-versed in financial planning and have a broad background or training in other matters of financial planning, such as estate or retirement planning.

Insurance professionals work almost exclusively on a commission basis, although fee-only insurance advisors are emerging. Many states will require separate licensing for professionals who want to practice as insurance consultants who charge fees rather than accept commissions. In fact, most state laws forbid you from serving in both capacities. (I'll talk more about commission versus fee-only planning in greater detail in Chapter 5.)

Investment advice is often another profession where it is common to serve as a specialist. In the investment world, professionals may specialize in mutual funds, U.S. stocks, foreign stocks, small companies, large companies, bonds, real estate, or even specific industries. The larger a client's investment portfolio, the more likely that he or she will have an investment advisor on his or her team.

def•i•ni•tion

Emerging market investments are investments typically made in companies located in countries that are not major economic centers. These could be third-world countries or countries that have undergone major political change, such as South Africa, Vietnam, or the former Soviet Union.

Investing is similar to financial planning in that it's impossible to be an expert in each of the specific areas where one can invest. Most investment advisors are trained to build a diversified portfolio to match the risk tolerance, time frame, and needs of their clients. The average investment specialist can easily oversee others' work and make sure that the client is well-served—even in areas as specialized as *emerging market* investing.

The media creates a lot of noise relative to investments because people love to talk about, read, and watch this enticing area of personal finance. The media is also obsessed with making sure that those investors bypass investment advisors in the search for the lowest-possible cost investments. What the media doesn't publish, however, is that emotions get in the way of the average do-it-yourself investor—and that their total returns are often horrible. The average do-it-yourself investor is moved by headlines and last year's winners, and he or she often buys what worked well last year and not what may do well this year. While not even a professional can guarantee what will succeed this year, the professional is supposed to maintain an unemotional, disciplined approach to even out the peaks and valleys.

> **Walking the Walk** _____
>
> An older client who described herself as a very conservative investor came into my office looking for advice on her 401(k) holdings. She was ready to move them into four different mutual funds offered inside the plan. When I looked at her suggestions, I noticed that she had circled all of last year's winners. None of her selections would be classified as conservative.
>
> —Ted Hintz, CPA, CFP, president Hintz Financial, Portland, Connecticut

Twenty-five years ago, the average investment professional was a stockbroker or commission-based salesperson. Large investment companies trained their advisors how to sell, and investment brokers frequently bought and sold stocks that the home office told them to—period. Today, however, there is a large trend moving toward fee-based investment advisory services where the client pays the advisor along the way—often quarterly. Even the large investment companies have moved in this direction. In this arena, the advice is considered far more objective. If you, as the investment advisor, want to keep your clients in the long run, you'll need to perform according to the clients' needs and expectations.

Estate planning professionals are often also practicing attorneys. While you do not need to be an attorney to plan an estate, you do need to be a lawyer to draft legal documents such as wills and trusts. If you are not an attorney and want to be an estate planning specialist, you need to form close relationships with estate planning attorneys who can implement your plans.

Most financial planning firms will either hire the necessary industry specialists or form close relationships with outside specialists who can support them. As a specialist, you are not limiting your career in any way. Even if you start your career in a specialty firm, it doesn't mean that you'll have to limit yourself to that specialty forever.

As a Manager

The financial services industry wouldn't be as prominent as it is today without great leaders and managers. All companies, large and small, are always looking for talented managers to lead. Some of the larger companies even have specific management trainee programs designed to build tomorrow's leaders. Many companies also value management experience gained in another industry.

Management positions are available in financial planning companies, banks, insurance companies, investment companies, mutual fund companies, and employee benefit and retirement plan companies. While many of these areas are indeed highly specialized, the process of financial planning has been so well embraced that integrating these offerings into the financial planning process has been easy. Many of these specialists were once limited to working only in their core specialties, but over the past two decades, these companies have diversified their businesses into other specialty areas through acquisitions or launching new divisions.

While the industry is rapidly growing, it is also going through a period of mergers and consolidations. Layoffs and downsizing happen here just as well as in any other industry. You may climb the ranks of management in an insurance company—only to find yourself out of work and then working in management for an investment company. As in any other arena of the financial services industry, starting in a management training program doesn't guarantee that you'll be a manager someday.

In a Support Capacity

The financial services industry is supported by a host of other related disciplines—including the media, regulatory authorities, trade and professional associations, educators, and consultants.

Many great careers have emerged from working in a support capacity for the financial services industry. Many of the regulatory authorities date back to the early twentieth century. With all of the new regulations and product advancements over the past century, the need for good regulators has only increased—whether through a state or federal agency or the many private-sector groups, such as the NASD or NASAA. Starting a career in a regulatory environment doesn't mandate any prior financial experience, but a base education or knowledge will probably get you in the door faster than someone who doesn't have those skills. Like many agency and government positions, these are dependable positions where risk of job loss is not great—except for incompetence or other failures.

Many industry associations also want talented people to help grow their association and create value for their dues-paying members. These not-for-profit professional associations have positions available as technical consultants, writers, marketing specialists, administrators, managers, and salespeople.

As a Seller to Financial Planners

The financial planning profession could not do without certain products and services. Some of these include hardware and software, research and other knowledge products, financial products, and memberships. If you want a career in financial services sales but don't want to sell to individuals, the financial services channel would be a good choice.

One of the higher-paid salespeople in the financial planning profession is a wholesaler—a person who represents a financial product that a planner would use to implement a client's financial plan. Wholesalers have a critical role for financial product manufacturers who are looking to gain or improve their distribution through financial intermediaries. Most companies selling their financial products to clients through the financial planning community hire wholesalers. These firms include mutual funds, insurance companies, annuity companies, trust companies, and investment advisors.

Financial planners buy a lot of software, training, and research tools. Sales representatives of these products and services are well versed in the financial planning profession and in the tools needed by a financial planner to be successful. Often, they are knowledgeable with respect to practice management and best practices of planners—which is paramount to creating the value proposition for a company's goods or services.

Multidisciplinary Practices

A multidisciplinary practice is a professional practice that offers in-depth services across more than one professional boundary. A good example would be the combination of a law and CPA firm. It's not very common in the United States today, but this practice has been very common in Europe and other continents for years.

The growing trend now is for professionals—such as attorneys or CPAs—to add a financial services component. Some of the old law firms in the Boston, Massachusetts, area had set up investment advisory divisions decades ago, but it's now gaining popularity in other parts of the country as well. It's the same story for CPA firms, which were once prohibited from acting in an advisory

 Pitfalls

Just because a CPA firm has a good client base does not guarantee its success in the financial services industry. Make sure that the partners are committed to that success and are willing to invest the necessary resources before you join the firm.

or financial planning capacity. The doors opened in the late 1980s for CPAs to offer these services.

Some who have gone in this direction are showing early signs of success. That's no surprise, because these professionals already have many client relationships steeped in trust. It will probably take another 10 or 20 years for multidisciplinary practices to become more commonplace, so career opportunities in this arena will be available.

Your Own Financial Plan

You would be negligent if you didn't start thinking about your own financial plan at this stage of charting your course. As a new grad, you probably have less to plan than a career changer who has a mortgage, a lifestyle, and maybe even a family to support.

A good financial plan starts with where you are today, where you want to be, and what you'll need to earn, spend, and save to get to point B. All plans are simply the starting point in what may be a very long journey. In the case of a new grad, your plan today may be limited to paying off college debt, getting some new wheels, and learning to live on your own while staying within your means.

For the career changer, having a financial plan may be the most important part of your transition. As a new financial planner, you need to be prepared that you may not earn as much as you did last year. You may also have some out-of-pocket expenses in connection with education or licensing. You must be conservative in your earnings projections and estimate a longer time period than you may have thought of—either paring down your lifestyle expenses or living off your savings. You will need a reliable budget and a realistic timeline to achieve positive cash flow. Ask your future employer to help you with the earnings side, but be conservative if your income will be based on how well you do at finding new clients for the firm.

Make sure that you are not left without benefits such as health and disability insurance for any period. Purchase individual coverage before you leave your old job if you anticipate a period without coverage. Disability insurance, for example, cannot be obtained unless you are currently employed. Not having this coverage could cause irreparable harm to you and your family. If you cannot cut your living expenses and do not have the savings to supplement your cost of living, the transition will be very risky.

Do not count on your old 401(k) for living expenses. Not only is that bad long-term planning, but it also could have a costly tax impact plus an Internal Revenue Service (IRS) penalty. Similarly, do not borrow from your home equity during this new profession startup phase. There are two issues with home equity: first, you may not qualify for the debt if you are going through a period of lower or no earnings. Second, once you borrow the money, you owe it back! The monthly payments may be unbearable or even cause you to move if your career in financial planning doesn't work as planned.

A solid plan now will give you a greater chance at success and help avoid financial surprises. You may want to consult a financial planner yourself to help chart this path. This person can give you valuable guidance on your own finances as you get started and maybe even a few solid tips on how to get your new career moving in the right direction.

The Least You Need to Know

- A financial planning career will be challenging because of the complexity of the subject matter, the varying personalities of clients, and our ever-changing world.

- A financial planning career is very rewarding from both a financial perspective and because of the satisfaction you get from helping people achieve their life dreams.

- An internship can give you a good idea of what a particular firm is like or help you decide how you would like to work in the financial planning industry.

- It's common for your career path to change as you grow and learn more about the various specialties and support roles in the financial planning industry.

- Plan both your finances and career now; the benefits will be substantial in just a few short years.

Part  Earning a Living

Finding a great first job as a financial planner could make the difference between early success and keeping your resumé current. Your day-to-day efforts, training and education, and groups you associate with will all help shape your success. Experienced financial planners are often willing to share their experience and ideas with others, so take advantage of that. The life planning movement, the process of helping people live their dreams and visions, is a style of planning that will move your client relationships to a far more intimate level than numbers-only financial planning.

Chapter 5

Get a Job

In This Chapter

◆ How finding your first job will shape your entire career

◆ Choosing the right firm culture

◆ Key questions to ask during an interview

◆ Learn how to interview your prospective employer as he or she interviews you

◆ How to succeed and build lasting relationships

◆ Hitting the "glass ceiling"

Finding employment in financial services is fairly easy. But finding the job that will offer you the challenges, opportunities, and compensation that get you excited to get out of bed every day should be your goal.

In this chapter, I'll explore the many career paths available to someone as motivated as you to succeed in the financial planning industry. Whether you're a technical nerd or a salesperson, there is room for you to grow and prosper. You just need to know what to ask and how the answers you receive will fit into your personal goals and objectives. Compensation structure varies from firm to firm, and here's where I'll teach you what to ask and how to interpret some of the answers.

Finding the right fit for you is merely the first step. You then need to know all the small steps that will show you how to take giant steps toward success. You will learn about the significance of a mentor and how to find out whether you've got a good one. We will teach you about making lasting, good impressions and building trust—which is required for you to progress. The small steps you take today in your first job will build the foundation for your success in years to come.

Finding Your Career Path

Finding the right career path as a financial planner is a little easier once you understand all of the different types of planning companies that exist. You'll then come to realize that there are many different roads that can get you there. It may take a few jaunts down different paths before you actually settle on the right path for you—and that right path will involve a combination of factors. You may be on your way but with a firm where you don't fit in very well. Or you may be on the wrong path and need to approach the planning business from another point of view. Or you may be in a firm that's steeped in an investment or insurance culture when you want to be in a pure planning environment.

The hardest career track to find is one with a pure financial planning firm. Unlike the accounting profession, not many firms in existence today are looking for new financial planning associates in a traditional, salaried job with good career advancement possibilities. While those jobs exist and are becoming more plentiful by the day, they still are not that prevalent. The types of firms that may have this traditional entry-level type of financial planning job may be accounting firms, trust companies, *multifamily offices*, or smaller local financial planning practices.

def•i•ni•tion

Family office is the term used to define a type of practice that serves very high-net-worth individuals and families. These family offices typically offer concierge-level planning and administrative services, from holistic financial planning and tax preparation to bill paying, arranging for domestic services such as home sitting, maintenance, and cleaning, and even booking travel. Essentially, it is the family's business office.

If staying on the pure salary track is important to you from the start, then you may have to consider working for a company that either supports the financial planning industry or sells products and services to the profession. A good example would be a customer service representative at a large mutual fund company or broker dealer. At a large mutual fund company such as Fidelity or Putnam, there are scores of customer service representatives who are generally divided into two large groups: the retail group and the institutional side. Retail deals with customers directly regarding issues such as adding to their accounts, setting up accounts, or ownership and beneficiary information. On the retail side of a large fund company, you'll begin to see what types of issues are important to servicing accounts for individual investors. There's also the institutional side of the business, which typically deals with brokers or investment advisors. On the institutional side, you'll get a feel for the types of issues that advisors deal with on behalf of their clients.

The same holds true for insurance companies, broker dealers, or any other type of firm that supports financial planners. There are typically both retail and institutional departments, and you must develop a fundamental knowledge about financial planning to offer the greatest assistance to your clients. Many of these firms will further invest in your career by paying for your licensing and studies leading to a graduate degree or financial planning designation.

 Pitfalls

Earning a lot of money in your first year as a financial planner is not likely. Make sure that your living expenses are low or that you have a financial cushion to survive the first few years.

If you want to be a financial planner right from the start but cannot find a salaried position in a planning firm, there are still plenty of options. More common than the pure planning job is a position that is entrepreneurial-oriented—where the majority of your success is defined by your business development ability. These types of jobs come from the insurance industry, investment companies, annuity companies, banks, and financial planning firms. Common names such as Ameriprise, Mass Mutual, Prudential, Morgan Stanley, Merrill Lynch, Royal Bank of Canada, and Bank of America are a few prominent companies worth considering. Just about any of the firms like these, large or small, offer entry-level opportunities in financial planning.

Most will offer a base salary or a draw against future commissions. The amount of your draw or base will depend on your experience. Pure rookies can expect a base or draw in the $3,000 per month range. It is common for a draw arrangement to last for up to three years—some less and some more. After the draw or base salary period expires, you are typically moved into a compensation scheme based entirely on your production with no base or draw. Some of the draws are recoverable, meaning that if you do not generate enough sales by the end of the third year, you will owe money back to the firm. Some are not recoverable, and the companies view that as their incentive to select great candidates with a high likelihood of success and to provide adequate training and mentorship that will aid success.

In the Know

You are not likely to find an entry-level job in financial planning through a head-hunter or employment agency. Most employers are not willing to pay someone to find them rookies who may not last that long on the job.

Actually finding the job is no different than for any other entry-level job. You will need a good resumé and a basic cover letter format that is interchangeable for different types of employers. You should attend career fairs offered by local colleges and universities and financial planning associations and talk to people you know in the business. Don't rule out the Yellow Pages and the Internet. Financial planning is a business where self-starters are desired, so reaching out to prospective employers personally with a phone call is a great alternative. The more of your personality that you can pour into your job search, the better you'll do.

Fees, Commissions, or Both?

As you learned in the previous chapter, there are two basic ways that financial planners receive compensation. It is imperative for you to not have any prejudice in the early stage of your career. Both options are perfectly acceptable, and neither makes your prospective employer good or bad.

For those prospective employers whose income is largely derived from commissions, just make sure that they make all of the top product manufacturers available for sale to clients who may need them. What gave commission-based financial planners a bad name was too much focus on proprietary products—products made by them, by their parent company, or by a related company. So if you go to work at Fred's Financial Group, and the Wilma Insurance Company owns Fred's, make sure that Fred's employees are free to sell products made by other insurers. Also, make sure that there is no pressure from management to sell Wilma's products over other companies' products that may be in the clients' best interests.

Do You Want to Be a Fiduciary?

There is significant industry debate over the use of the term "financial planner." That usage may inherently or inadvertently place a fiduciary responsibility upon you, the planner. Some planners want to be fiduciaries; others do not. Some of the large commission-based companies have placed restrictions on their advisors against actually creating financial plans for a client and have asked them to remove any financial planning credentials from their business cards.

Others who accept commissions actually support being a fiduciary and offer disclosure about accepting commissions and the potential conflict therein. The choice of how to practice is yours. But if you want to be a financial planner and choose the route that accepts commissions, just make sure that your firm will allow you to hold yourself out as a financial planner and actually produce written financial plans for clients.

Pitfalls _____

Beware companies that offer financial incentives or bonuses to sell their proprietary products over what may be the best option for your clients. As a financial planner, you have the responsibility to consider the best interests of your clients first and foremost.

Joint Work

In many planning firms where you are responsible for finding clients or your income is solely based on your production, you will be introduced to the concept of joint work. Here, you team up with another advisor to split the duties of the planning engagement and the ensuing fees or commissions generated.

Many new reps make the mistake of not doing joint work because they need the money. Remember: 100 percent of zero is still zero! Doing joint work will add credibility if you choose your joint work partner carefully. Many senior advisors are perfectly content with half the revenues generated from a case that you bring to them. Many clients are also more pleased to see that the team has some depth and experience. It will also give you a higher closing ratio if you have a pool of advisors with different specialties and talents.

Some advisors always do joint work because it is a cost-effective way to delegate portions of the work associated with a planning engagement. You can keep your fixed overhead low because you only pay for what you use—and when you use it.

Small Firm vs. Large Company

Financial planning is still a relatively small industry. But when you count all of the related disciplines, the financial services industry is quite large and makes up a significant part of the world's economy. Depending on your needs, there are advantages and disadvantages to each size firm.

When starting out, some things are more important than others. Training tends to be one of those material needs for rookie financial planners. The big companies have established training programs that have been tested and adapted for decades. They offer university-type settings at remote locations, online seminars, local office sessions, and firm-wide conferences where the learning track is very good. However, the advantage of big companies is fading. Small companies can use training materials developed by independent companies for their rookies or planners at any level. The only question, then, is whether or not your small firm will invest in that training for you.

Your on-the-job casework may be more diversified in a small firm. You may not see as many different types of clients at a small firm, but you are likely to be called upon to serve in more capacities. Where the large firm may have levels of management and experience, the small firm may have only senior planners or the owners to work with you. In this case, these few senior members may delegate a more diverse or challenging set of issues for you to learn about. You are also more likely to learn about small business management in a smaller firm. You'll probably be in close proximity to everyone from the bookkeeper through the owner and will absorb a lot of small business know-how just by observing.

Both small and large firms also realize that rookies, regardless of their age, may not be the best at business development. They will try to pair you up with a seasoned veteran for purposes of making prospective client presentations. In a large firm, you may have many professionals to choose from and can select based on expertise, personality, and style. In a small firm, your choices will be limited—so make sure that you really like the people in the office and evaluate their willingness and ability to help you.

In the Know

The size of your firm may be important to some prospects when it comes to attracting clients. Most will work with you for your credibility and sincerity, regardless of the firm's size.

There should be no material difference in compensation and benefits between the two sizes of firms. Small firms have come to realize that to attract and retain good talent, they need to compete on those fronts. In an entrepreneurial-based small firm, you may actually make more in the long run. The larger firms generally retain a higher percentage of the revenue you generate to pay for their overhead, marketing, and management.

Large firms also have the impression that they are more fiscally stable than smaller firms—which may be true in some cases but not in others. It also may not matter much of the time, because the small firm should never actually hold client funds in its accounts. Some small financial planning practices are actually independent representatives of much larger firms that have substantial financial strength. Also, in most small practices, firms use an independent firm such as Fidelity, Charles Schwab, or TD Ameritrade to hold custody of clients' investments. Clients of these practitioners using a major firm for custody should have as much comfort as they would with any other major investment firm.

Questions to Ask in an Interview

This section is geared toward finding the financial planning practice that is right for you. Your questions probably should be limited to what the first three years on the job are like. This is the most critical period for you and the employer. Also, after three years on the job, you are much more marketable to other firms or have enough experience to open up your own shop, and your issues will be different. It wouldn't hurt you to ask a few more questions about a longer time frame than three years, but most recruiters are realistic enough to know that as a rookie planner, survival and early success should be your priorities.

The following questions should serve as a guide for your discussions. In the interview, it is okay to take notes. After several interviews you may begin to get confused about which employer said what.

- **How have the people hired before me for this job done during their first few years?** How many lasted three years? How have their earnings progressed along this timeline? Ask if you can speak to those people directly.

- **What kind of training program do you offer?** You want to make sure that it meets your expectations and that it is comparable or better than what is offered elsewhere. Ask to see the actual printed training material. Also ask graduates of the training program about their experiences and its effectiveness.

- **What is the firm's expectation of me during the first three years?** You want a clear answer of how your success will be judged in years one, two, and three.

- **Does the firm provide an incentive for me to undertake any advanced studies leading to certification?** The answer will give you a good feel as to whether it's a planning or sales culture.

 In the Know

Make sure that you conduct thorough research on the company before the interview. It will guide some of your questions and will indicate your sincerity by knowing as much as you can about them. If you are matched evenly with another candidate and did your homework, you will probably get the offer.

◆ **Has the firm had any regulatory problems in the local office?** The company is grilling you about your background, so it's fair game for you to be sure that the company and all of its other planners also have clean records.

◆ **Can you tell me about your revenue?** Gross revenue is important, but you should be more interested in the composition of their revenue. You want to know what percentage of their revenue comes from financial planning fees, asset management fees, insurance commissions, and securities commissions. If there are any other lines of business, make sure you find out about those, too. If a product manufacturer—such as an insurance company or mutual fund company—owns the firm, you want to get a specific answer to the percentage of their revenue that is generated from the sale of proprietary products.

◆ **What rewards and incentives do you offer?** Often, planning companies talk about exotic trips that their most successful advisors get to take—sometimes with spouses, for free. Find out whether qualification for these trips is based on overall success or success with a specific company or product line. If the trip is tied to production from a single insurance company or mutual fund, realize that management's first priority is that you sell these products.

◆ **How does the firm assist with business development?** You want to know whether you will be working on firm-generated cases or cases that you find on your own. It is common for many of the firms that hire new planners to expect them to perform an all-out marketing assault on their family and friends. While some of them may, in fact, need advice, they are probably just going to listen to you out of sympathy and because they know that you need the business—not because they are eager to have you as their advisor. Frankly, it is better if you can develop your business without counting on family and friends. It's usually better to not mix personal relationships with business.

In the Know _____

Make a list of the criteria that are important to you. Document your feelings about a particular firm right after the interview. This step will avoid mix-ups and help you decide which firm has the advantage after you've spoken to several.

◆ **What's the working environment like?** Are you one of many rookies who they hire? What percentage of the large group do they expect to survive year one, year two, and year three? Do you assign rookies to teams that have more experienced advisors? The team approach is becoming more common in large firms because it takes the business development pressure off you a little bit and enables you to work with a group of experienced advisors. This approach also stalls any secret plans you have to open your own shop. You will often be asked to sign a non-competition and non-solicitation agreement—meaning that any clients you work with while at the firm are property of the firm, and you are not allowed to solicit them after you leave.

◆ **What is the firm's policy for out-of-pocket expenses?** You can expect that any entertaining you may want to do will be on your own dime, but sometimes these firms will charge you for supplies. Some even charge you for office space, copies, postage, stationery, and company brochures.

◆ **What type of errors and omissions insurance does the firm provide for its advisors, and is there any cost to the advisor for the coverage?** It's not that you are planning to do something wrong, but in this litigious society you don't necessarily need to do anything wrong to get sued. A lawsuit could arise from a case where you are a team member and are only peripherally involved with that client. Complaints against advisors happen, and you just want to make sure that you are covered.

Don't Believe Everything They Tell You

Many times, the person interviewing you is selling you on joining the firm as much as he or she is checking you out. It's okay for you to interview that person just as hard as he or she will interview you.

When the firm's recruiters create a vision for you of a wonderful career and the lifestyle that will follow, they are talking about the most successful of their advisors. The stories of those who failed and why—or what they didn't do right—are often forgotten the day after these people get laid off. Ask them about those who have failed. Ask what the firm saw in them upon hiring and why they think that person failed.

There is still a fair amount of deceit in the interviews by firms that portray themselves as independent financial planners. Many times, these firms have names that sound impressive—like the Granite State Financial Group. They tout themselves as an independent firm, but they are also general agents (GAs) for a large insurance company. Not that being a GA in and of itself is deceitful, but they often significantly underestimate to clients and employment candidates just how dependent their existence is on that insurance company. The insurance company commonly pays their rent, provides payroll services, pays for staff, and provides employee benefits to everyone—including you, the new planner. Commissions from that company are typically much higher than if the firm were to use another company for whom it is not a general agent. The tradeoff is that the insurance company expects most, if not all, of the insurance sold by planners in that office to be their products.

In the Know

If a firm makes you an offer, ask how much time you have to accept. While you don't want to cast doubt in their minds, you do want to let them know whether you have other options and that you are looking to make the right decision the first time.

The term that these companies use to describe your paycheck is often called a financing plan. That's code for the first three years salary. If that paycheck comes from an insurance company, it is probably a financing plan. That means that they are subsidizing you through the survival years in the hopes that you can be part of the small percentage of first-three-years survivors.

This type of arrangement is still very common in the industry and should not be a deal killer for you. You just need to be aware of it and know that regardless of what they tell you in the interview, your success will be judged by how much of the insurance company's product you sell.

You're Hired!

Oh, happy day! You just got your first job as a financial planner. Now, your journey to success can begin. Hopefully you had several interviews and many offers from which to choose—so you can really feel good about your choice. If it is your first offer, though, and you have nothing else in the pipeline, you may have to take it. Once you accept the position, you now have a moral obligation to completely immerse yourself in that position to give you the highest likelihood of success. The firm is making a substantial investment in you, and it deserves and expects dedication in return.

But beware: if you do want to make a quick change or bounce around a lot in the first few years as a planner, it will be harder for you to find another great starting position. Good employers are concerned about stability and investing in someone who they think can be with the firm through their successful years. A previous failure or marginal start to your career will hurt you more than help you. If you have any doubt about liking the job or your ability to succeed, don't take it. Keep looking for a position where you may be better suited for success.

If you ever do decide to change your job in the future, the success you have with previous employers will weigh heavily on what opportunities become available. If you are very successful, future opportunities will find you. If you are marginally successful, you'll have difficulty improving your position anywhere. As large as the financial services industry is, it's also a small world where many of the professionals at different firms know each other—and they can find out about your previous success after only a few phone calls. Some will even ask that you produce a copy of your earnings statements for the past three years to prove the consistency of your success.

> **Pitfalls**
>
> Make sure you read the employment agreement very carefully. Sometimes there is restrictive language limiting your ability to work with clients you have introduced to the firm if you decide to leave. There may also be payback terms for some of the financing that the firm provided.

Making the Right Impression

You can do some simple things to give yourself every advantage and opportunity at success. One is to show up on time. If your workday begins at 8:30 A.M., don't stroll in at 8:35. Get there at 8 A.M. so that you can get your coffee or fruit bowl, engage in pleasantries with your co-workers, read the paper, and be ready for productivity at 8:30. Plan to stay in the office a little later than closing time and avoid extended lunches or other breaks. The same is true for client meetings. When you have a client meeting out of the office, allow extra time for traffic or unforeseen events—and plan to arrive at least 15 minutes early. Bring some technical reading, a cell phone, or a laptop computer with you so that if you're very early, you can be productive during that waiting time.

> **In the Know**
>
> Don't forget about the all-important first impression. Do whatever you can to make it a good one. It's true: you never get a second chance to make a first impression.

Another way to make the right impression is to fully understand what is expected of you—and to do it. Hopefully, you gathered this information during your interview process. If you are still unclear on day one, however, you'd better start talking to other recent rookies—fast. Not meeting the expectations of your employers or clients is the best way to get off on the wrong foot.

Doing what you say you are going to do—and finishing what you start—is extremely important. There are two sides to this issue. First, be careful not to open your mouth without careful thought. By blabbing about things you are going to do when you have no idea how or whether you can do it, you are setting expectations. Your career will not get far if you continue to overpromise and underdeliver. The other side: plan your time accordingly. If you have set an expectation to get a certain task done, take the time to plan exactly what has to be done to accomplish that goal. Start with simple tasks and design a system that you can later use for more significant tasks or projects. This style of project planning and management will be very helpful to you later in your career when you are supervising the work of others.

Showing appreciation is another great way to make the right impression. This is not something that can be faked; you either have genuine appreciation for others or you do not. False platitudes or an empty thank-you will not cut it. To have genuine appreciation, you should understand that everyone is different and that you will never get along with everyone. But everyone has something good going on, and you will need to find the good, recognize it, and appreciate it. As it relates to your career, you don't need to practice this philosophy for everyone walking down Main Street; however, you should for everyone in the workplace—especially for the people who you cannot avoid, such as bosses, clients, or others working directly or indirectly with you. Common courtesies such as please and thank-you can go a long way.

Be helpful to others in the workplace. Everyone is under time constraints to integrate their personal and business lives and to do as well as possible on the job. In the financial services world, collaboration and working with others is mandatory for success. When a co-worker asks for your assistance or professional guidance, try to see how you can help rather than make excuses for why you cannot. Make an effort to be the person people seek out for guidance and help, rather than the one they try to avoid. The tide will turn someday … and you'll need help from someone.

 Pitfalls

Avoid office gossip. This is probably the number-one workplace morale killer. Way too many people want to waste their time complaining about others. If you have a legitimate gripe with someone, have the courage to speak to that person directly—in a respectful way—to let them know what bothers you. It may help them and should make you feel better. Staying out of the gossip loop will always keep you on the high road and project a good impression.

Finding a Mentor

For many successful advisors, finding a good mentor is one of the most helpful experiences in their early days. A mentor relationship usually involves someone who is older and more experienced providing advice and support to—and watching over and fostering the progress of—a younger, less-experienced person. Your mentor will be a teacher, a guide, an advisor, and a career counselor.

There are no formal, paid mentors in the financial planning business. You have to be assigned one, find one by pure luck, or seek one whom you admire. The firms that assign you to a team assume that the senior member of the team will be your mentor, but that doesn't always happen. Maybe you don't particularly like the person, or maybe that senior member treats you like a personal assistant who is only there to help find new clients. Some of the smaller firms also have formal mentoring programs, but you can run into the same issues as with a team.

There is no requirement for your mentor to be a member of the same firm. Some find mentors in their wholesalers or outside coaching programs that are built for the financial services industry. Others find one in their general circles of contacts, family, or friends. Finding a mentor on your own is kind of like asking for a first date. It's relationship-based and starts with reaching out and asking for help. Find people you know and respect, and ask whether they are willing to devote a short amount of time to meeting with you to answer some questions and to provide you with career guidance. During the course of that meeting, if you like the person and the advice that you are getting, ask whether he or she would be willing to meet with you on a regular basis to continue these advisory sessions. Monthly would be great, but quarterly is probably adequate. You should probably seek out more than one sage provider of guidance and advice, however. No one advisor has the key to success locked up in his or her head, and there are many different approaches that work.

Walking the Walk _____

I have had mentors since early childhood. First, they were mentors guiding me through a successful high school and college hockey career. Now, as a financial planner, I have found several seasoned professionals with whom I meet frequently to help me grow and achieve success. It would be far more difficult without guidance from these experienced professionals.

—Sean Condon, TLC Financial Advisors, Plymouth, Massachusetts

Be appreciative of your mentor. You should be willing to buy lunch sometimes or incur travel or other expenses associated with meeting. Thank-you notes are always appreciated, and even thoughtful, caring gifts will help express your gratitude.

The Significance of Trust

Trust is everything in any personal services business. In financial planning, a lot of relationship building happens based on a foundation of trust. Everything that I've talked about in making the right impression lays the foundation for trust—and everything you do throughout your relationship with your employer, colleagues, mentor, and clients is based on that foundation. Without trust, you will go nowhere in the financial planning business.

If your mentor trusts that you will take advice, implement what you are taught, and learn from your mistakes, that relationship will continue to grow. If your employer trusts that you will be everything that you promised in your interviews, you are likely to get more opportunities and the benefit of the doubt when you need a break. If your prospects trust that you will do the right thing for them, they are likely to become your clients. And if you do the right thing for your clients over and over again, they will trust you and be your clients for life.

It takes a long time to build trust and only a short time to take it away. If you make a habit of always delivering on your promises, the people you work with will always consider you trustworthy. Fall short one time, and others will doubt your ability. Fall short many times, and others' trust in you will disappear.

Promotions and Earning More

In a traditional job setting—either as a financial planner or as someone supporting the industry—promotions and earning more money usually follow a well-defined track. It'll be based on your ability to do more valuable work for the firm and to accept greater challenges that the employer feels you can meet with success. You will need the respect of your superiors, peers, and subordinates. Working well with colleagues is a very important part of the equation. Promotions often involve the hiring, training, or supervision of others—and you can't get there if you have a reputation of being a difficult co-worker. Everything you've done in the past can either work for you or be held against you.

The growth of your technical abilities or mastery of your job function is also a big factor. You don't grow in a corporate setting just because you have another year on the job. You should know more, move up to a higher level of competence, and become a better student of your profession. Sometimes, this process requires hours of reading or studying on your own time. You may need to consume evenings and weekends reading trade journals or completing tasks that you just couldn't do in the confines of a normal workday or week. This work may not be too different from college, where you had some friends who never studied and got a 4.0 grade point average—and then other friends who were always studying to barely get a 2.5.

In the Know

Ask for semi-annual performance reviews during the first few years so that you get more frequent feedback on how you are being perceived on the job. It never hurts to learn what you can do to improve halfway through the year. This could have a very favorable impact on your annual reviews.

The larger the firm, the greater the competition for promotions. You will be judged on a scale that puts your efforts and results squarely against those in your peer group. If your hiring group consists of top performers who have immersed themselves in their jobs, you'll need to be right up there with them.

In an entrepreneurial environment, promotions and earning more are purely up to you. In some environments, if you do not earn more and get promoted, you may be asked to leave the firm. In a purely incentive, compensation-based firm, there will be minimum production requirements to stay—but your true growth potential and earnings ability is determined by your ability to attract and retain business.

The Glass Ceiling

Have you ever been in a job where you knew that you had reached your maximum potential in that firm—that there was no room for improvement or promotion? That's called hitting the "glass ceiling." Typically, in the financial planning industry, there is no such thing as a glass ceiling. The sky is truly the limit. However, there are circumstances and jobs in the financial planning industry where you can easily hit a glass ceiling. It can be because of a firm's particular niche, clientele, services offered, or a lack of support.

It can happen in a small firm where you were once hired to be an assistant financial planner. Many times, a small firm is owned by one person who has no intention of growing beyond a few staff members. You can hit that ceiling within three to five years in this type of company. Unless the owner is looking for a partner or is willing to add staff, it is likely that you'll never earn what you could at a larger firm or receive the intellectual challenges of a growing firm that has a steady flow of new clients.

The ceiling can also come at you in a firm that specializes in or practices one type of financial planning. If you start your career in a shop that specializes in retirement plans or estate planning—but you always wanted to practice holistic financial planning—you'll hit the glass ceiling. This may take a little longer than in the small, holistic financial planning practice because there is so much to learn when focusing on a specialty. You can get regular promotions and pay increases in a specialty firm as long as the firm wants to grow.

The Least You Need to Know

- Schedule several interviews in order to explore and understand your financial planning career options.

- Take notes during your interviews so that you can recall what particular firms said and then do a more thorough job contrasting the opportunities.

- Don't jump at the first job opportunity you receive. Offers will vary substantially from firm to firm.

- Mentors offer career advice and guidance to younger, less-experienced financial planners and are especially critical at the beginning for a new employee's success.

- While some jobs may limit your growth in the long run, the industry provides ample opportunity for you to have unlimited earnings and job satisfaction as a financial planner.

- Your ability to build trust with clients, employers, and colleagues is critical in the financial planning industry.

Chapter 6

The First Few Years

In This Chapter

- Starting your career in an insurance agency, with a large investment firm, in a bank, or with a CPA or law firm
- Inside financial planning firms
- Selling services and products to financial planners
- Managing client expectations (and what clients expect from you)
- How to manage your irreplaceable resource: time

The first few years in any career can set the stage for the rest of your life. Finding the right entry point to the financial planning business is a very personal decision, and you need to consider what you are expected to do for the first few years.

In this chapter, you will learn what to expect in the first few years in the financial planning business. Making the right choices and knowing what is expected of you will get you on the fast track to success. While the first few years are fairly similar in many of the entry-level financial planning jobs, there are some unique differences that can make a big difference in your experience.

Good habits developed in the first few years will last a lifetime. Being efficient, paying attention to the needs of your clients, and managing your time properly are all talents that need to be developed. Make them routine, and your first three years will be great and fly right by.

Starting as an Insurance Agent

When starting a career in financial planning as an insurance agent, there are two types of agencies. One is a pure insurance agency that really doesn't offer financial planning. A good example of this type of agency is any large insurance company with agencies that bear its name. Many are primarily property and casualty companies offering perfectly acceptable insurance products with several agencies in most states. They hire financial planners to cover one or more of their agencies primarily to sell life insurance, annuities, and mutual funds to clients of that agency. At this time, most do not allow their planners to charge fees for financial plans or to create comprehensive, holistic written financial plans. The financial products sold to clients are sold in the context of their overall needs, goals, and objectives—but the plan is not the focus.

On the insurance and annuity side, agents are limited in the companies that they work with—and most are subsidiaries of insurance companies. Here, the product sale is the focus. The good news about this type of insurance agency planner is that there are clients. Each agency already has hundreds or thousands of clients, and the planner has a stocked pond of available prospects. The agency managers or owners are also paid incentive bonuses for the success of financial services sales in their agencies. This incentive helps the planner with introductions and sales.

The other type of insurance agency offers and does care about financial planning. A good example is Mass Mutual. Mass Mutual operates general agencies in most states, and many of its salespeople do practice financial planning. The culture of a Mass Mutual general agency is working with high-net-worth investors and small business owners. Not all of the agents are successful in that marketplace, either failing out of the system or simply working with a less-wealthy client. But here, there are usually no property and casualty insurance sales—and the culture supports and allows written, holistic financial plans for a fee.

Unlike the large property and casualty shops, there are no long lists of clients for you to solicit. Rather, there are long lists of products and services for you to offer—but you have to find the clients on your own. Here, your sales and business development abilities will determine your success.

Either way, you will learn a lot about life insurance and annuities. This learning will be delivered in such a way as to fit into the financial planning process at both types of agencies. Both will offer basic training on insurance issues such as income replacement and retirement planning. The agencies with a fee-based financial planning focus will offer deeper training on financial planning matters and issues facing high-net-worth clients. But make no mistake—you are there to sell life insurance for the company that signs your paycheck. The planning types of agencies often have an employee who supports you on technical matters and during the actual production of a financial planning document.

The effort for you in the first few years will be very similar in both settings: a heavy focus on sales and learning. Your revenue from a pure insurance agency is likely to be almost 100 percent from insurance—with very little emphasis on investments or annuities and no income from formal holistic financial planning.

The first three to six months, you'll be absorbed in licensing and training. As I discussed in Chapter 3, the licensing alone is a time-consuming endeavor. Neither type of agency is likely to sponsor you for a Series 7 securities license. Series 6 is usually their preference; that's all you'll need to sell variable annuities, variable life insurance, and mutual funds. At the same time, the office will have some basic training sessions on the risk management side of financial planning. All firms do this differently—some in all-day sessions for a few weeks in a row; others for part of the day, allowing you to work on building a business.

Another big part of the first three years in an insurance environment involves building your client base. Many companies require that you start with an inventory of prospects. They will ask you to document the names, addresses, phone numbers, e-mail addresses, and other pertinent contact information for up to 300 of your personal contacts who you would consider prospects. The sales manager will then oversee your sales efforts to these people in the hopes of trying to get you some business. Many firms will have the sales manager or another experienced agent accompany you to appointments to teach you how to make client presentations.

In the Know

As an insurance professional, you will need to master business development techniques such as networking, asking for referrals, and public speaking. Spend time with your mentor on this task (see Chapter 5), and talk to anyone else who can give you good ideas about how to find prospective clients.

You will spend a lot of time in your car driving from one appointment to another. Unfortunately, that comes with the turf of being a rookie. You need to see people more than they need or want to see you. If you can, try to schedule as many appointments in your office as possible—rather than on the road. An appointment in your office gives you the chance to draw on other resources during the meeting if needed. Also, a client who is willing to drive to your office indicates a stronger interest, and you'll be in an environment far more conducive to doing business than sitting at the client's kitchen table. It is preferable to have the undivided attention of both the client and his or her spouse, if applicable, at a first meeting.

You need to be a voracious reader throughout your career as a financial planner—especially during the first three years. Remember, at the end of year three in the insurance industry, you will be judged by how well you have done as a salesperson. There's a direct correlation in your sales success between your people skills and knowledge of financial planning matters. So, be a good self-assessor and read as much as you can in order to sell more services and products. After a few months on the job, a good sales manager should begin to steer you toward what you need to do for improvement and success.

With a Large Investment Firm

Large investment firms come in many flavors. First, let's talk about a firm such as Fidelity. While there are many different divisions at Fidelity, let's speak about the mutual fund division that deals directly with investors.

Starting with the mutual fund area, your first three years will probably be in a customer service arena. You could be on the telephone assisting customers with servicing issues regarding their mutual fund accounts or on the marketing and sales side of the mutual fund business. While you wouldn't expect any focus or formal training on financial planning matters in either of these capacities, you will learn a lot about mutual funds and how they are used in a financial planning environment. You'll learn about how clients use funds in retirement and trust accounts and how to diversify their portfolios. In the back office, you are usually not able to give planning or investment advice but will learn a lot just by being there. If—after a few years in this capacity—you still want to be a financial planner, you'll have to transfer to another division within the firm or move to another company.

In the Know

Careers in large investment companies can be very lucrative. While you may have good intentions of becoming a financial planner someday, the good pay and comfortable work environment of a large investment company may cause you to reconsider your original intention.

You could also begin your career at a large investment company by becoming a discount broker. An example is TD Ameritrade, which has two distinct divisions of discount brokerage. There's the retail side—dealing directly with clients—and there's the institutional side, dealing with investment advisors. Neither gives out investment advice, but both deal heavily with investors' needs. Here, you will learn about investment choices and how they are used. You'll also learn about the operations side of the business.

Your first three years here will start as a customer service or sales representative—either on the telephone or in one of the investor centers sprouting up around the country. There will be emphasis on investment training and customer service skills but little on financial planning.

While a financial planning track does not exist at most discount brokerage firms today, there probably will be one in the near future. As the baby boomers move into retirement, it appears that those firms that want to capture their assets have come to realize that they will need to give advice. For today, however, a move to financial planning from this vantage point will have to include a new job and company.

The last type of large investment firm that I'll talk about is the traditional firm, such as Merrill Lynch or UBS. These firms have deep roots in investment advisory and offer an active financial planning component. Similar to the insurance entry point, your first three years are consumed with licensing, training, and building your client base. Firms such as these are among the best in the world at training new advisors, and this training usually starts with a two- or three-week intensive off-site program. These firms are so immense and diversified that you could use up the first year just learning about the different divisions and firm resources.

You will often be assigned to a team of advisors. On the team, you'll be exposed to a wide range of client issues and technical disciplines within the firm. Team leaders will also take the business development pressure off you in the first few years by assigning you responsibility for smaller clients who don't really need a higher level of experience. You'll also learn how an experienced advisor markets his or her practice and uses a professional network for referrals and sharing client responsibilities.

> **Walking the Walk**
>
> A career in a major investment firm provides wonderful training with unlimited opportunity for success as an investment advisor, investment banker, or financial planner.
>
> —Carl Chaleff, chairman of InterOcean Financial Group, LLC, Chicago, Illinois

Your ultimate success here is largely defined by your sales and business development success. You are typically responsible for building your own client base and maintaining those relationships as their primary advisor. As the team approach proliferates, even this business development pressure may wane as more successful teams develop the need for permanent planning and service members.

Working in a Bank

Twenty years ago, pursuing a financial planning career in a bank was just not an option. Today, however, banks are emerging as significant players in the financial planning business. There are usually two distinct options in a bank: the branch program, which places financial advisors on the floor of a local branch, and trust departments or private client groups. Most banks will divide the client service based on their investable assets. Clients who have more than a certain amount—typically $250,000 to $500,000 or more—will be ushered to the private client group, whereas people who have less than $250,000 will remain clients of the bank representative. The first three years in these two divisions will be very different.

In a Branch Office

In the branch program, you will be trained on sales and the basics of investing and annuities. Most of the smaller banks will outsource the training and operations of this department. You will work closely with branch managers and tellers and deal with many clients on smaller transactions. There is not much comprehensive financial planning happening at the branch level.

The average client comes to you because he or she is conducting another transaction with the bank, such as opening a certificate of deposit (CD) or obtaining a mortgage. These tellers, branch managers, and customer service reps are your lifeline to new clients in the early days.

Many of the banks are very good at cross-selling customers to another division of the bank. They will stuff notices in checking account and mortgage statements, post signs in the branch, and hold seminars and events to alert bank customers to these additional services. A financial planner in a bank branch can make a lot of money, but he or she is not likely to do much holistic financial planning.

In the Private Client Group

The bank's private client group is often the opposite of the branch side. The relationships are not transaction driven but instead relationship driven. Successful private bankers are actively involved in the financial planning issues in their clients' lives. The first three years in the private client group is all about training and servicing the clients.

There probably won't be as much licensing emphasis in the first year. Many private client groups do not work with commission-based products. Their services are more advisory in nature and fee-based. While some of the group will be fully licensed, that probably won't be you in the first year or two.

Unlike the branch side, you probably won't have much direct contact with clients for the first few years with the private bank—except in a service capacity. Clients will clearly look to the senior members of the group for advice. You will relay messages—maybe even do some of the analysis—but the client will view the senior members of the team as his or her advisors. This experience lends well to a career of servicing higher-net-worth clients.

Inside a Financial Planning Firm

The lines become a little blurry here. Many insurance-based organizations consider themselves financial planning firms. Many of the major investment firms consider themselves financial planning firms. And large firms such as Ameriprise—a hybrid of the insurance and investment firm models—consider themselves financial planning firms. They are all telling the truth: their company goals are clearly to give clients holistic advice in the context of a personal financial plan.

Your first few years at a large financial planning company that also sells products will be similar to life in insurance or investment firms. You are dedicated to licensing, training, and building your clientele. Ameriprise in particular has a terrific training program for new associates that blends selling skills and financial planning.

With large financial planning firms, your success is once again defined by your ability to find and retain clients. While these firms do have some leads from their national marketing campaigns and *orphan accounts* from

def•i•ni•tion

Orphan accounts are accounts developed by advisors who left the firm. Managers will assign orphan accounts to new advisors in the hopes of retaining their business, getting you experience, and hoping that you uncover more opportunities with these clients.

advisors who have left, you are primarily responsible for developing your own marketing campaign and building your business.

These firms will have rather stringent employment agreements, stipulating that clients are the property of the firm. Even your friends and family are clients of the firm. While you are not allowed to solicit these clients to follow you if you change companies, there is no law that prevents them from finding you and asking to work with you. The law is a little fuzzy as to how you can notify your clients of your change in position. Typically, a letter to clients notifying them that you have left the firm to pursue other options is usually okay. Just make sure that the letter has your home or new business address with a contact phone number. Be courteous; thank them for their business and tell them what a pleasure it was to work with them, but do not ask them to work with you in your new location. That is most definitely a violation of your non-solicitation agreement and will give rise to legal action.

If you find employment in a small or regional financial planning firm that is modeled after the large ones, it may be the same drill. But there are currently many financial planning shops that really want to hire financial planners—not salespeople who also want to be planners. Many of these firms are fee-only firms, but some also get involved in product sales. Here, your first three years will be very different.

Training is still a big part of what you need in the first few years—but here, much of it will be on-the-job training and guidance. Your training needs to be supplemented by courses offered by independent organizations or professional associations. In these firms, you are likely to have many tasks and gain broad experience. Financial plans need to be analyzed and written, and this task involves learning how to use financial planning software and spreadsheets for analysis. There may be an investment analysis system or software that you will learn and use. There will be writing, too, when you prepare client memos and recommendations.

In these types of firms, your success during the first three years is usually defined by your technical ability and time efficiency. The more you learn and the better you become at analyzing client situations and developing recommendations, the better your promotions and responsibilities will be. You will not likely be in a sales position—except to serve as a persuasive voice urging clients to implement plan recommendations that they are slow to accept.

> **Walking the Walk** _____
>
> Many of the investment advisors using the TD Ameritrade Institutional platform are small businesses that practice financial planning. I see a growing number of these firms adding staff financial planners to their employee roster.
>
> —Joe Saunders, Fidelity Investments, Boston, Massachusetts

With a CPA or Law Firm

CPA and law firms are the latest to enter into the financial planning business. Most of them do not hire rookies unless the practice is mature—probably within a larger firm.

The first few years here may be similar to a trust company or private bank environment. There will be very good on-the-job training that will be supplemented by in-house or third-party formal course work. You'll generally work with a more sophisticated client from a financial needs perspective and assist with the core practice of the firm. In a CPA firm, you may do tax returns for your clients. In a law firm, you may do trust and estate tax returns, estate planning projections, or some estate settlement work.

In these environments, there will be a new twist to how your early success will be defined. Both CPA and law firms have employees track their time spent on client matters in minute detail and bill their clients based on the time expended. The result is called billable hours. Each firm will have a different goal for new associates, but asking for 1,800 to 2,000 billable hours per year is not uncommon. If you do the math, that means 40 hours billed for 45 to 50 weeks per year. After you count holidays, vacations, and training, you realize that there is a built-in expectation of working overtime. You may get some slack for the first year or two, where they'll allow fewer billable hours because of training—but after the first couple of years, billable hours rule.

Efficiency and quality of work will also be a big factor for you. Just because you track your time and have time sheets showing 50 billable hours in a week doesn't mean that it is all collectable. You may have spent five hours on a task that management thought should be completed in two hours. In this case, the firm is not likely to bill the client for the entire five hours and will write off the other three. So, management will actually track another component of your billable hours called net realizable fees, or hours. Here, the firm will see just how many of your billable hours will turn into fees that are actually collected from clients.

Your technical abilities and analytical skills will be a critical part of your first three years. Your supervisors don't expect too much from you in the first six to twelve months, but after you've been through a few cases and training sessions, you'll be expected to take the case and run with the basics. You will need to demonstrate an ability to learn and apply that knowledge in a practical setting. You will also need people skills to work with other professionals—and, gradually, directly with the firm's clients.

In the Know

One challenge during your first three years in CPA and law firms is building trust. Not client trust—clients already have trust in the firm's core service. You need the trust from firm partners and senior associates. These firms are so scared of losing a client for their traditional work that they are sometimes reluctant to refer their accounting or legal clients to the financial planning division for fear that you'll mess up the relationship. You will need to build confidence among the firm's associates and partners that you will do a great job with their financial issues—and won't jeopardize the entire client relationship.

Selling to Financial Planners

Some sales roles require no knowledge of financial planning; others do. Clearly, both would command a good personality and ability to sell. Financial planners buy lots of things for their practices, and you could sell software, mutual funds, annuities, insurance products, outsource services, publications, advertising, memberships, educational services, and lots more.

Depending on how technical your sale is, you may be able to hit the road instantly. If it is memberships to one of the professional associations or training materials, you can get right into it. But if it's financial planning software, you will need to understand the planning process and have complete knowledge of the competitors' software products' advantages and disadvantages.

The first few years of a nontechnical sales role will involve getting known and becoming respected by the planners in your territory. This result comes from exhibition at seminars and trade shows, making a lot of phone calls, and driving thousands of miles. You'll be asking for orders all the time and will be judged by your boss—by meeting or exceeding quotas that will be set for you. You'll get to use your creative side to try new ways to get the attention of a time-limited professional. By year three, you should be well known in your territory—getting referrals from planners to others who may benefit from what you have to offer.

In a more technical sale, you will probably spend the first three years inside the company supporting the outside salesperson. You'll be scheduling appointments for the outside salesperson, handling service calls from planners, and assisting with marketing activities such as trade shows or promotions. At the same time, you will be expected to learn the technical side of your product and how it fits into the financial planning business.

Your success will be determined by the successes that you've helped create for the outside salesperson and by the feedback that the firm receives about your telephone assistance. A successful salesperson in a technical role usually makes pretty good money. If you want to move up into an outside sales role, you'll need to have geographic flexibility. Because these are such coveted jobs, the person in the territory that you want may not be ready to leave—so your opportunity may come up somewhere else, requiring you to relocate in order to stay with the company.

Great Expectations

In any new career, you are full of enthusiasm. You expect to love your job, to find great success from both a financial and fulfillment perspective, and to build a lifestyle that matches your ideal vision. As a financial planner, you need to now come up with a tactical plan to make your enthusiasm work for you and to keep you enthused as you progress in the business.

Without the right level of enthusiasm and confidence, finding success is not possible. This is the first half of the equation; the other half is the enthusiasm of your audience. Most new clients may be excited about creating a plan to reach their goals and objectives. The tough part is keeping their enthusiasm high as you progress though a process that may seem slow and detailed. This can be accomplished in the early stages of a financial planning engagement by understanding and helping set expectations. Managing expectations is one of the most valuable things you can do to maintain long-term, successful client relationships.

What Clients Expect from a Financial Planner

Clients expect that you will care about them and treat them the same as you would treat your—or your mother's—financial plan. They don't expect to be sold products because you need a paycheck or because you're under pressure from your boss. They expect that when they buy a product, it's the same one that you would buy for yourself—and that you've surveyed alternatives and concluded that it's the best product available for their needs. They also expect that this product will fit into their lifestyle, budget, and time frame and that it will help them reach their financial goals and dreams.

Clients expect that you will be available when they have a question. It may be as simple as returning phone calls on a timely basis or replying to e-mails within 24 hours. You also need a mechanism to let them know when you are not available, such as by changing your voicemail greeting or setting an e-mail out-of-office reply. Giving them your cell phone number is a sincere way to show your availability, but even that may not help if you are in Europe. It also means having an alternative source for them to speak with when you are not available.

Competence is something that you may take for granted, but it is high on the list of client expectations. They don't expect you to know everything, but they do expect that you'll know what you are talking about when giving advice. "I don't know" is a perfectly acceptable answer for a client as long as it is followed up with "I'll find out" or "Here's how we can find the solution to that situation." They don't want you to experiment with their personal finances.

They expect that the relationship will be proactive and holistic. They want you to consider all factors and related consequences before you advise. They expect that you'll care enough about them to be proactive when something in their financial lives needs attention.

Clients need you to be a good communicator—speaking with them in language they can understand and avoiding industry jargon or technical terms. Clients want to hear from you on a regular basis—sometimes just as a check to see how they are doing or to let them know that things are going according to plan. And when things are not, that's when they want to hear from you most. When their investments are not performing, get on the phone and set up an appointment. They will sincerely appreciate your concern and efforts to inform them and will listen to your suggestions for improvement. They also want to see you, face-to-face, on a regular basis. Each client is different. Find out at the start of the relationship how often your clients would like to come in for a review of their financial situation.

Pitfalls

Surveys show that clients leave financial planners for a number of reasons, but the reason most often cited is a lack of contact or communication.

What to Expect from Clients

The planning relationship is a two-way street. You have the right to set expectations of clients. Some of them are non-negotiable, such as your need for complete and accurate financial information. You cannot do your job or be held accountable for your advice if you do not have complete and accurate information. This means both financial and other information, such as health or children's education goals. If a client has an inheritance coming or an elderly parent who will need support, you will need to know.

Under the category of personality or relationships, expect each client to be very different and to approach the planning relationship in his or her own unique way. Most will be anxious or nervous when you meet for the first time. People are more private about their financial situation than they are about anything else, and you need to gain their confidence in the first 10 minutes of the first meeting for them to feel a little more at ease.

Expect clients to have different goals and objectives. It's not a time for you to judge; rather, you need to listen and understand to see whether you want to work with these clients and can help them.

Pitfalls

Not setting client expectations about the relationship invites disappointment. Be clear about how you work, and lay out the ground rules for a successful long-term relationship.

You can expect that clients will read newspapers, magazines, or other professional newsletters and ask you questions about what you are or are not doing for them. Expect intellectual curiosity from clients about their most prized and personal information.

Some clients will not always take your advice too easily (or may not follow your advice at all). Sometimes it is painfully obvious to you that a certain goal cannot be achieved—but the client just ignores you and continues on the same path as before. Expect him or her not to receive the memo where you are clear and explicit about the inability to accomplish a certain objective unless the client alters his or her actions. That's one of the tough parts of the job, but you have to do it.

You can expect clients to work within the parameters or style that you have stated. For example, if you do not do house calls or will not meet on a weekend, you have the right for the client to live with that expectation.

Time Management

Managing your time is a critical component to success as a financial planner. Good time-management skills developed in the first three years can spell success a lot more quickly and benefit you for the rest of your career.

As your career progresses, your time-management system will also need to evolve. I'll talk more about time-management evolution as your career progresses later in the book. But there are certain basic elements that should never change.

Maintain a good calendar. The old-fashioned date book will work, but in this age of affordable technology, it is short-sighted not to use a Palm Pilot or personal digital assistant (PDA)/cell phone combination that will synchronize with your computer. If you use an electronic medium and back it up with a computer, it will serve you a lot better than a lost or destroyed date book. These systems will also enable you to store all of the contact information that you'll need for clients, colleagues, and whoever else you want to include. This is great for efficiency and organization. When you are starting out, organization is a good habit to form. When you advance in your career and have assistants or others who need to access your calendar, the electronic medium is a lifesaver.

In the Know

Poor time-management skills will cost you money and client relationships. A Blackberry or other combination phone/organizer may cost you at least $200 but will help you save money and make money by being more efficient with phone calls, e-mail correspondence, and appointments.

Block time on your calendar for important things that you need to do every day—tasks that you will not let anything interfere with. You may want to block out an hour for returning calls or making outbound calls. This is something that you'll need to do every day, so make it consistent and routine. Not returning calls is one of the worst things you can do, so make the time. You may want to block out time to exercise or to spend with your children or spouse. After learning that one of the most critical factors in most new financial planning jobs is to gain new clients, you should block out time every day devoted to implementing your business development strategies—whether it's daily lunch meetings, breakfast meetings, sending letters, or time spent on the telephone.

Avoid playing extended games of telephone tag. Try to set telephone appointments instead of leaving and retrieving several messages. This is easier to do if you or the people you are calling have an assistant who can book the phone appointment.

Set boundaries for clients. Most professionals such as doctors or dentists have very rigid time boundaries that help keep them on track. You, as a financial professional, need to do the same thing by letting your clients know when they can expect to speak with you or see you. If you refuse to work weekends or want sacred vacation time, make that clear. If you do not want to be called at home, say so. In the first few years, this is difficult because you often need new clients more than anything else. But compromising your desires early may be a tough habit for clients to break and could make you unhappy with your career choice. Stick to your time boundary decisions.

Use time budgets for meetings or for preparing financial plans. Taking on an engagement is your primary goal during your first three years, but making sure that you have accurately estimated the time to complete the job and blocking out that period to get it done is important. If you have a say in the pricing of an engagement, this could be the difference between making money and losing money.

Use assistants wisely. Delegate whatever you can. You may not have your own personal assistant during the first three years, but you may have some access to a helper. Work smarter and devote your time to those tasks that will give you the highest return from your hour. For example, if you are sending letters, maybe you can hire a student to stuff the envelopes?

Use whatever technology tools you can afford. A good example is a service called Copy Talk (www.copytalk.com), where you call a toll-free number and dictate. Within a few hours, that dictation shows up in your e-mail inbox ready for your edits. It's perfect for follow-up memos that you can dictate while driving or from home at night. This can be a great time saver and help you get your follow-up correspondence out in a timely manner. For $50 to $60 per month, if this service helps to get you one client, the whole year's cost may be recouped.

The Least You Need to Know

- ◆ Success in your first few years will be impacted by where you start: in an insurance agency, with a large investment firm, in a bank, or in a CPA firm.

- ◆ Working inside a financial planning firm can span from entrepreneurial firms where you are responsible for your own business development to firms where you are hired to support the firm's clients with no business development responsibility.

- ◆ Selling to financial planners is a great career choice for someone who wants to be involved in the industry but not responsible for working with individual financial planning clients.

- ◆ Planners and clients need to be clear about the expectations to and from each other to ensure a long-term relationship that is satisfying for both.

- ◆ Managing your time effectively is critical to your short- and long-term success as a financial planner.

Chapter 7

Credentials and Designations That Count

In This Chapter

- The significance of credentials
- The confusion created by so many choices
- How to decide which credentials are right for you
- Obtaining the most well-known credentials for personal financial planners: CFP and ChFC

There are many reasons why the financial planning profession is overwhelmed with so many credentials. It isn't a bad thing to have so many choices. After all, financial planning is such a broad and pervasive topic that no one designation can make you an expert in all of the subject areas.

It does, however, give lots of clients and prospective financial planners pause and confusion. Is one credential better than another? Do you need another designation? Is this planner better than that one because of the letters after his or her name? I'm a smart guy; why bother with credentials, anyway? I'm in this business to make money, not to go back to school.

In any business endeavor, all top achievers seek to gain the respect of their colleagues, clients, and prospective clients. When you least expect it, the time you take early on to study and become credentialed may make you more successful. Studies have shown that advisors who have credentials, as a group, earn more than those who do not. It could mean the difference between getting your dream client or the best job of your life. This chapter will help you decide whether you should get one and which credential may be the best for you.

Who Is Checking, Anyway?

As inventors and creators of *designations* market their courses of study, they begin to create awareness through a two-pronged approach. First, they target potential credential holders. Second, they target the audience who is supposed to want to hire those credential holders.

The relevance of any *credential* will always be in the eyes of the beholder. That said, you should start to think about whom your beholder is. Of course it starts with you, and I'll talk in detail about you and your choice in the next few pages. But think about the outside world. Think about those who will begin to judge you the instant that they lay eyes on your business card or signature at the bottom of a letter or advertisement.

def•i•ni•tion

For the purposes of this book, the terms **credentials** and **designations** are used interchangeably. What you want from any credential or designation is knowledge, esteem, and respect—something that clients, prospects, and other professionals will look favorably upon. Other terms used to denote such achievements are certificate holder, certificant, specialist, designee, licensee, and certified.

Prospective Clients

Prospective clients care about any designations you may have because no one wants to work with someone who appears to be untrained. They view your credentials as a sign of competence. True or otherwise, their first impression is inclined to be a bit more favorable if you have at least one credential.

Employers

Some jobs simply have a credential as a bare minimum requirement for qualification. For example, it is not likely that you'll ever be the director of financial planning in a large financial institution without the Certified Financial Planner (CFP) designation. Your role as the director is to provide leadership and inspiration to the rest of the department. CFP will not be a credential requirement for an entry-level job, but if you are one of many candidates vying for the position, the designation will give you a strong lead going into the interview stage.

Vendors

A vendor in the financial planning industry is a person or company that supplies a product or service needed by a planner to carry out his or her duties. A vendor could be a mutual fund company, an insurance company, a software company, or a publisher of knowledge products. Believe it or not, some manufacturers of financial products—like insurance or mutual fund companies—are somewhat exclusive. They really don't want any old Joe to represent their products—especially if their products tend to be very sophisticated or difficult to understand. These vendors will often look to your credentials as a reason to appoint you to sell or represent their products or services. The credential can also serve as a mitigating factor if they see other reasons, such as prior regulatory problems that may otherwise cause them to deny your ability to represent their products or services.

Regulators

A regulator is someone who works for a government agency or licensing body and is charged with enforcing the laws governing fair practice of the license or profession that he or she regulates. Regulators may look at your credential as a double-edged sword. Like a vendor, it may help you get approved in a certain state or for a specific license if you have a designation. Certain states even have designations as minimum requirements to obtain a given license. The other side of the sword, however, could crop up during an investigation or complaint hearing. With a designation, you may be held to a higher standard if the regulator knows that you should have known better by virtue of your training and experience.

Walking the Walk

Media professionals usually insist on our recommending credentialed professionals for interviews or expert appearances.

—Jim Farrell, president, PR First, Hanover, Massachusetts

Media and Public Speaking

At some point in your career, you may be approached or even have an interest in getting some publicity from the media. Whether that's a quote in your local newspaper, a spot on the evening news, or a guest appearance on a radio show, the media will be very much interested in any of your credentials. As a public speaker, your audience usually doesn't know who you are. In most cases, the audience will be easier to engage if you have credentials that evidence that you have pursued advanced studies.

Lenders

If you decide to go out on your own, you may need to borrow money to lease an office and the equipment to furnish it or to buy software through installment payments. Your credit score and any collateral that you may post will be the most important parts of the qualification process. But the lender will also want to evaluate your business plan and assess your odds of success. A lender may see you as having a higher likelihood of business success and repaying the loan on time if you have invested your own time and money to obtain a professional credential.

Alphabet Soup, or Designations That Matter?

As you can already tell, the world cares about training, designations, and credentials. Now you also know who is watching and why designations are important. The downside is that our clients and prospects are confused because there are so many new and different designations.

In addition to the confusion, the alphabet soup game may be somewhat misleading to your clients and prospects. Some designations offered are nothing more than an eight-hour study program regarding a particular product or service. Others are very detailed educational programs with a very narrow area of expertise. If you're a new advisor, you should not disguise your inexperience by using such designations. They may be used appropriately if you intend to specialize and offer advice on that specific topic and not otherwise hold yourself out as a holistic financial planner.

Do your homework to see whether the curriculum is adequate and whether any other professionals or designation holders feel that the designation is worthy of your precious time. If you already have a broader-based designation such as CFP or Chartered Financial Consultant (ChFC), such specialty designations may be more valuable to you and your clients.

In the Know _____

Don't waste your time with a designation or credential that has no meaning to your prospective clients, that doesn't enhance your genuine thirst for knowledge in the industry, or that doesn't enhance your competence in a meaningful way to your clients.

Later in the book, I'll address advanced designations. While some of these credentials may be lesser known, don't confuse them with mere selling tools. Advanced designations can be extremely valuable, especially if your client needs specialized assistance in a specific subject area. But even advanced designations have less meaning and usefulness unless you've covered your bases with some of the more popular and well-known base designations. You can't even get some of the advanced designations unless you meet the prerequisite of a core designation first. At this stage of your career, get the basics and consider a specialty designation after you've demonstrated some success in your endeavors.

Not many clients know how to judge competence and genuine care. This is particularly true in an area as complicated as personal financial planning, where the public is vulnerable because of what it does not know or understand. Designations without merit that offer a false sense of client confidence are bad for the industry. A client who was once soured by an incompetent advisor hiding behind some unknown designation may never trust a financial professional again.

Pitfalls _____

Don't believe everything that providers of specialized designations tell you. Only devote your attention to those that are offered by reputable organizations with a meaningful educational track—delivering the benefits that you and your clients need.

Which Ones Are Right for You?

By now, you can already tell that it may be a good idea for you to eventually earn more than one designation. To no one's surprise, neither will anyone else who cares complain about your multicredentialed business card. Even those who have a natural head start—such as CPAs, attorneys, and professors—should go ahead and get a planning-related designation. The actual curriculum for any of the core designations that I will address is terrific for anyone wanting a career in financial planning. It will also give even the most seasoned technician the added new perspective of seeing the world from a planning point of view.

Your mentors and employers should be good sources of guidance in helping you choose which credentials to pursue and how to get started. A good employer may even offer reimbursement for successful completion, but please don't let that prevent you from going forward. This is one of those areas where you must invest in yourself—even if no one else is willing.

Because you are striving for success as a personal financial planner, you should start with one of the two designations that favor the broad spectrum of personal financial planning: CFP and ChFC. Let's take a closer look at both.

Walking the Walk

I have been a practicing CPA for more than 25 years. About 6 years ago, we added personal financial planning as one of our service offerings. I thought that because of my practical experience, I really didn't need a designation in financial planning. I was wrong. Obtaining the CFP designation gave me a much better planning perspective and greater ability for my clients.

—Thomas Morrone, CPA, CFP, North Haven, Connecticut

Certified Financial Planner (CFP)

Rapidly becoming the designation of choice for personal financial planners, the Financial Planning Standards Board has granted use of the CFP credential to more than 52,000 professionals in more than 20 countries.

The CFP is a difficult and time-consuming designation to obtain, but the educational program is outstanding and the visibility is growing. The CFP Board continues to reach out to the public to educate people about the benefits of financial planning and to attract outstanding candidates to the profession. For these and a host of other reasons discussed in this book, the CFP designation should be your first choice of designations for success as a personal financial planner.

To obtain the CFP designation, candidates must complete a six-part process:

1. Complete the education requirement.

2. Pass the CFP certification examination.

3. Meet the experience requirements.

4. Adhere to the code of ethics and professional responsibility and pass background check.

5. Pay certification fees.

6. Receive authorization to use the CFP credential and all associated trademarks.

Education Requirements

The education requirement is very comprehensive, covering a huge amount of subject areas. The education qualification for the CFP exam can be met in any of three ways.

The first way is to complete a CFP board-registered education program. There are more than 285 academic programs at colleges and universities across the country from which to choose. These programs include credit and noncredit certificate programs, undergraduate, and graduate degree programs. They use various delivery formats and schedules, including classroom instruction, self-study, and online studying.

In the Know

Many CFP board-registered programs also offer in-house educational programs for individual companies. For a complete list, visit www.cfp.net/become/programs.asp.

Any of the educational programs will take you between seven months and two years. Obviously, the seven-month program is intense and will consume a majority of your time. You can also stretch the education over a longer time period if you wish—or if you have other commitments that will prevent faster completion.

The costs to complete any of the educational programs will vary. Complete self-study courses can be obtained for as little as $2,595. You can also enroll in a program as expensive as one of the accredited universities offering undergraduate and graduate degrees in personal financial planning. These programs of study usually consist of 10 courses that may cost from $500 to $2,500 per course, depending on the institution. Neither is necessarily better than any other; it really depends on your experience and learning preferences.

The second way to fulfill the educational requirement is to apply for challenge status. Certain academic degrees and professional credentials fulfill the educational requirement and allow you to sit for the CFP certification examination. These include the following:

- Certified Public Accountant (CPA)—inactive license acceptable

- Licensed attorney—inactive license acceptable

- Chartered Financial Analyst (CFA)

- Doctor of Business Administration

- Chartered Financial Consultant (ChFC)

- Ph.D. in business or economics

- Chartered Life Underwriter (CLU)

The third way to satisfy the educational requirement is to request a transcript review. Certain industry credentials recognized by the CFP Board—or the successful completion of upper-division college courses—may satisfy some or all of the education requirements set by the Board. A good example may be a Master's degree in taxation. If taken from an accredited institution, this degree may satisfy both the taxation and estate planning educational requirements.

The CFP Certification Examination

The licensing examination itself is quite rigorous, with a relatively low passing ratio. Many recent sittings for the exam produce passing ratios in the vicinity of 50 to 60 percent. That's a good thing! You wouldn't want a designation that is so easy that everyone who sits for it comes out a winner.

The CFP certification examination is designed to assess your ability to apply financial planning knowledge to real-life financial planning situations. By passing this exam, you demonstrate that you are at the appropriate level of competency required to practice financial planning.

To develop exams that reflect the current practice of financial planning, the CFP Board conducts regular job analyses by reviewing the typical tasks performed by planners and assessing the knowledge and skills needed to perform these tasks. Valid job-related exam topics are developed and exam questions written by task forces that include practicing financial planners and financial planning educators. The exam questions are subjected to a rigorous review by the CFP Board's board of examiners and subcommittees of content experts composed of practicing planners and educators. Each question is answered——and assessed——by practicing financial planners.

Typically, new legislation and changes—such as tax law changes—will not be tested on the exam until six months following the date enacted.

All questions on the CFP certification examination are presented in a multiple-choice format. There are two primary types of questions:

- ◆ **A brief fact or scenario.** Enough facts are given to allow the tester to answer from one to six questions that follow. These questions are worth two points each.

- ◆ **An extensive case scenario.** After reading each scenario, you will be asked to answer 10 to 20 multiple-choice questions. Typically, there are three case scenarios and three corresponding sets of questions on each exam. Each case question is worth three points.

In the Know _____

You can download or view sample exam questions at www.cfp.net/become/ examquestions.asp. The sample multiple-choice questions provide you with an understanding of question format but should not be used as a practice exam or indicator of exam preparedness.

The CFP certification examination will test your ability to integrate knowledge from all of the CFP Board's specified topic areas. Questions may focus on discrete topics or may require knowledge of several topics. Each exam attempts to achieve a distribution of the topics based on the target percentages shown for each category.

The topic list for the CFP certification examination, based on the 2004 Job Analysis Study, is the basis for the CFP certification examinations. To take a look at the topic list, refer to www.cfp.net/become/topiclist.asp. Each exam question will be linked to one of the topics, in the approximate percentages indicated, following the general headings in the link. Questions often will be asked in the context of the financial planning process and presented in an integrative format.

The CFP certification examination is scheduled to last 10 hours over a day and a half and is held three times a year, generally on the third Friday and Saturday of March, July, and November. The exam is a pencil-and-paper format and consists of one four-hour session on Friday afternoon and two three-hour sessions on Saturday. More than 50 exam locations are available around the United States. Exact location sites are not secured until after the application deadline so that all applicants can be accommodated. Information about exact exam location sites is provided to applicants approximately one month prior to the exam date.

The fee for the CFP certification examination is $595 and must be paid in full by the application deadline. Provisions for refunds and conditions of forfeiture of fees are highlighted on the Certified Financial Planner Board of Standards website: www.cfp. net/become/exam.asp.

In the Know

To pass the test, you will need to master a financial calculator. Exam questions will require your knowledge of calculating internal rates of return, and periodic and unequal cash flows. This information is not easy stuff and is almost impossible without the calculator. Mastering a financial calculator will take you between 8 and 20 hours, depending on your experience. Do this at the beginning of your studies. Once you pass the exam and are in practice, you'll probably never use the calculator again—thanks to the financial planning programs on the market.

Review Courses

Most successful exam candidates will take a formal review course prior to the two-day exam. While you shouldn't be learning anything new in the review course, it will highlight those areas in which you may need extra work to pass. A good instructor can also give you helpful test-taking hints and a heads up on the most important areas of the exam.

When selecting a review course, there are many factors to consider. Some questions to think about include the following (from the CFP Board of Standards):

- Does the provider possess the organizational and financial resources to carry out its program on a continuing basis?

- Is a CFP certificant involved in the development and maintenance of the course material, and do key personnel have the backgrounds to develop and maintain the course?

- How do candidates sign up, receive materials, ask questions, or access faculty members? Does the provider have a written complaint policy/procedures?

◆ Are there policies of exclusions or exceptions of eligibility?

◆ Does the provider have a discount or free enrollment process for candidates who may need to retake the exam?

◆ What is the cost of the course and materials? When are the dates of course availability? What is the cost of updates (if any)?

To access a list of review course providers, please visit www.cfp.net/become/reviewcourse.asp.

Pitfalls _____

When preparing for the CFP licensing examination, you should not take it lightly. Most failing candidates cite lack of preparation as their primary cause for failure. Take a formal review course, even if you are a great student with years of planning experience. The cost of a good review course will be less than $4,000.

Experience Requirements

Because the CFP certification indicates to the public your ability to provide unsupervised financial planning, the CFP Board of Standards requires you to have some experience in the personal financial planning process. However, the CFP board recognizes the variety of situations and circumstances in which people participate in the financial planning process and has developed a work experience requirement to account for this factor.

Qualifying experience must fit within one or more of the six primary elements of personal financial planning:

1. **Establishing and defining the relationship with the client.** This element includes explaining the issues and concepts related to the personal financial planning process. You must specify the services that you or your firm will provide and clarify the client's and your responsibilities.

2. **Gathering client data, including goals.** Data gathering includes interviewing or questioning the client about various aspects of his or her financial resources, obligations, and expectations. During this process, you will need to determine your client's goals, needs, and priorities; assess your client's values and attitudes; and determine the client's time horizons and risk tolerance. In addition, you will collect applicable client records and documents.

3. **Analyzing and evaluating the client's financial status.** This process involves analyzing and evaluating client data such as current cash flow needs, risk management, investments, taxes, retirement, employee benefits, estate planning, and/or special needs.

4. **Developing and presenting financial planning recommendations and/or alternatives.** Financial planning recommendations should meet the goals and objectives of the client and reflect his or her values, situation, and risk tolerance. This process includes presenting and reviewing the recommendations with the client, working with the client to ensure that the plan meets his or her goals and expectations, and revising the recommendations as necessary.

5. **Implementing the financial planning recommendations.** This process involves helping the client put the financial planning recommendations into action and could include coordinating with other professionals, such as accountants, attorneys, real estate agents, investment advisors, stockbrokers, and insurance agents.

6. **Monitoring the financial planning recommendations.** Areas to be monitored or reviewed include the soundness of the recommendations and the client's progress. This process also involves discussing with the client any changes in his or her personal circumstances, evaluating changing tax laws, and making recommendations based on new or changing conditions.

Candidates must complete three years of full-time experience or the equivalent part-time (2,000 hours equals one year of full-time) if they have a Bachelor's degree from an accredited U.S. college or university. Without the degree, five years of full-time experience is required. Note that after January 2007, candidates without a Bachelor's degree in any subject would have to complete their five years of experience before January 2007.

Experience may be gained up to 10 years before or up to 5 years after the exam date. If your work experience is not completed within this time frame, your candidacy for CFP certification may be terminated. A one-time, three-year extension may be granted on a case-by-case basis.

You will prove your experience for certification through the completion of a formal application, references from employers, and letters from clients.

Chartered Financial Consultant (ChFC)

To obtain the ChFC designation, candidates must pass the educational component and demonstrate the completion of the experience and ethics requirement. To maintain the designation, holders must maintain ongoing continuing education and ethics requirements.

The ChFC designation is offered through The American College in Bryn Mawr, Pennsylvania. The American College is well known for many prominent designations in the financial services industry, and two in particular have a focus on life insurance matters: LUTCF and CLU.

- The LUTCF program provides high-impact sales training for new life insurance agents and experienced agents looking to fine-tune their sales skills. To earn the designation, you must pass five exams plus an ethics for financial services professionals exam. More than 65,000 professionals hold the LUTCF designation.

- The CLU designation is widely recognized as the highest level of study in the life insurance industry. While there is clearly a life insurance focus to the designation, its curriculum is detailed and broad enough to also satisfy the educational requirement for the CFP certification exam. Since 1927, more than 94,000 individuals have earned this designation.

The Education Component

The educational material covered in ChFC is very similar to what is covered in training for CFP plus two additional elective courses. Completion of the ChFC designation also satisfies the educational requirement to take the CFP certification exam.

The comprehensive education may be obtained from textbooks, CDs, DVDs, online, or live instruction at The American College.

The curriculum consists of six core courses and two elective courses. The core courses are as follows:

- Financial Planning: Process and Environment (you should take this course first)
- Fundamentals of Insurance Planning
- Income Taxation
- Planning for Retirement Needs

- Investments

- Fundamentals of Estate Planning

Your elective courses are as follows (choose any two):

- The Financial System in the Economy

- Financial Planning Applications

- Estate Planning Applications

- Financial Decisions for Retirement

In the Know

To learn more about the ChFC designation and other designations offered by The American College, visit www.theamericancollege.edu and click "Programs of Study."

To enroll in the program, there is a one-time admission fee of $110. Each course then carries a $535 tuition fee. Discounts may be available for membership in the National Association of Insurance and Financial Advisors (NAIFA).

Examinations

When you register for a course, you actually select the exam period in which you wish to take the exam. The exams are offered at a Pearson VUE exam center. Pearson VUE is a provider of computer-based examinations-on-demand and located in more than 4,000 testing centers in more than 150 countries.

The Experience Requirement

To be granted the ChFC designation, candidates must complete the experience requirement. Three years of full-time business experience is required. The three-year period must be within the five years preceding the date of the award. An undergraduate or graduate degree from an accredited educational institution qualifies as one year of business experience. Part-time qualifying business experience is credited toward the three-year requirement on an hourly basis, with 2,000 hours representing the equivalent of one year of full-time experience. Activities described in the next few paragraphs meet the required business experience qualifications included in the ChFC certification process.

For insurance and health-care professionals, field underwriting and management—including sales and service activities, supervision and management of persons involved in sales or services, or staff support of persons in these activities—will qualify along with company management and operations in positions involving substantial responsibility.

For those with financial services and employee benefits experience, client service and related management—including direct contact with clients, supervision and management of persons involved directly in the process of providing financial services or employee benefits, or staff support of persons in these activities—will qualify.

Financial institution management and operations in positions involving substantial responsibility will also qualify.

Other experience that counts toward the three-year requirement includes university or college teaching of subjects related to the entire American College curriculum on a full-time basis at an accredited institution of higher education. Government regulatory service in a responsible administrative, supervisory, or operational capacity may also qualify.

Professionals involved in activities directly or indirectly related to the protection, accumulation, conservation, or distribution of the economic value of human life will also qualify. These include the work of actuaries, attorneys, CPAs, investment advisors, real estate investment advisors, stockbrokers, trust officers, or persons in other similar occupations.

The Least You Need to Know

- The CFP or ChFC designation provides credibility for you to prospective employers, clients, regulators, and media outlets.

- Start with a well-known and professionally respected core designation like CFP of ChFC, both of which favor the broad spectrum of personal financial planning.

- Pick a course of study and a program that suits your learning preferences.

- Don't underestimate the preparation time for the required exams.

- Don't waste time with unknown or easy designations.

Chapter 8

A Day in the Life

In This Chapter

- Setting a routine to fit everything in
- Selling yourself or your ideas on a daily basis
- Developing powerful, inspiring client meeting skills
- Your involvement in your client's investments
- The role of research and diligence
- Staying current and doing a good job for clients

The job title of "personal financial planner" has a nice ring to it. It's prestigious, fun, and can give you a sense of providing much-needed help to people who you care about. But what exactly does a planner do all day?

In this chapter, I'll talk about getting you into a groove that will make you happy and find you the greatest success. You will learn about some of the basic tasks surrounding the financial planning job that really define who you are and what you do for your clients. You can't possibly be very good at all of it, so I'll talk about how you can work with others to stay on top and deliver the most rewarding experience possible for your clients—and your business.

Your Routine

Have you noticed that even the best professionals have an established routine before they engage? Golfer Phil Michelson envisions each shot going right where he wants to land it. Baseball sensation Nomar Garciaparra goes through that ritual of adjusting his gloves and tapping his toes on the ground every time he steps into the batter's box. TV host Oprah Winfrey starts each day on a positive note with gratitude and wondering how she will make a difference in the lives of others. Maybe you'll never be as famous as any of these superstars, but you can start by developing a system that will make you as good as you want to be.

The most successful financial planning professionals create a routine that fits into their lifestyles and gets developed into their personal winning formula. A combination of time management and focusing on what matters most is a key ingredient to success in financial planning. Some never really create a routine, and go through their professional careers led by voicemails, e-mail messages, and whatever else pops up that day. These planners tend to be less successful.

Some routines are very rigid yet broadly diversified. Each day includes time for exercise, family, spiritual activities, socializing, and work (of course). Some will break down their work time into categories such as those developed by The Strategic Coach founder, Dan Sullivan. Dan created The Entrepreneurial Time System, which suggests that entrepreneurs essentially have three different types of days:

◆ **Focus days, when you work on anything that is revenue-generating or specifically the most valuable activity that you can do for your business.** For most planners, that would be meeting with clients or generating work for client-related situations. Focus day activities are high priority and the best use of your time.

◆ **Buffer days, when you do everything else that is not a focus activity.** Buffer activities may include continuing education classes, sales and marketing activities, or reviewing industry publications.

◆ **Free days, when you're completely free from any work activities in order to rejuvenate and relax.** In Dan Sullivan's world, a free day where you check your e-mail or return calls is not a free day. His definition of time off is time that's completely devoid of any business activity to obtain maximum rejuvenation.

Dan maintains that a balanced week includes some of each, unless of course it's an entire week of free days—vacation!

Everyone's routine will be different, and yet each of us must do the things that define us as financial planners. Whether your day is rigid, where you only do certain things on certain days, or you do a little of each activity on any given day will be determined by how many assistants you have (or don't have) and what makes you most effective.

Sales and Business Development

Sales and business development is something that you'll be doing nearly every day as a financial planner. The first type of selling that you'll have to do is getting a client to hire you. When you first start out, this process can be nerve-racking. After you've got a couple hundred meetings under your belt, this will be even easier than doing the planning itself. You may be selling over the telephone, live in the conference room, or in a room of your local library packed with 25 people who are eager for you to teach them about financial planning. You are selling the potential for a long-term relationship—one that is dedicated to helping them with their financial issues through the good and bad times. A good sales professional will ask great questions during this process and listen to his or her prospects to learn what is important and what he or she hopes to accomplish in a planning relationship.

> **Walking the Walk**
>
> Selling is not a four-letter word. It is a process where you are discovering the needs of your client and putting the best solution in front of them. The selling part is seeing that they do what is right for them and what they need to do.
>
> —Bill Murray, CEO, Winning Inc., Norwood, Massachusetts

After a planning relationship begins, there will be many more times when you will need to use your skills of persuasion—in other words, sales ability. Believe it or not, although clients confide to you what is important and why they hired you, there are some recommendations you will make that a client just does not want to implement. You will find situations after you have had a client tell you that he or she wants to educate children and have a financial contingency plan if one of the two family breadwinners should pass away prematurely. Obviously, the answer here is to acquire enough life insurance to accomplish that objective. Sometimes you will get a client who is looking for another solution where one may not exist. You will need to remind the client of his or her goals and objectives and let the person know that either removing that objective or implementing the only solution available to them is best. If the client still refuses to take your advice, you will need to either have him or her sign a disclaimer acknowledging the refusal to follow your advice or ask him or her to consider withdrawing from the engagement and state your reasons in writing to the client. Whether you sell the insurance or not, it is your obligation as the financial planner to explain to the client why he or she needs to implement this recommendation to achieve the objective.

You may need to sell a client on hiring or replacing one of the other advisors. A common area where you will encounter this task is estate planning. Some clients may want to use some cheap Internet do-it-yourself will service or may already have a family lawyer. You will need to be clear that you are not going to endorse a do-it-yourself Internet document preparation service and be accountable for the documents that result. Similarly, the family lawyer may be the attorney they used when they bought their house or for some other non-estate planning issue and may not be well versed in estate planning matters. Even a basic will or trust could pose a problem for someone who is not familiar with those documents. It would be your job to sell the client on finding competent counsel or to notify him or her in writing that you cannot be accountable for the work of a nonprofessional in this area.

As the financial planner, you may be the first person to ever oversee the client's entire financial situation. In that role, you are often able to judge existing advisors or recognize huge gaps where professional guidance is needed. Don't be shy about standing your ground when a client needs to replace an existing advisor or find another who can become a nice complement to the planning team. As in the life insurance area or the incompetent estate planning attorney, disclose your findings in writing and attempt to get the client's written acknowledgment of your advice to fix it. This paper trail is simply good practice and may help defend you in the event of future problems.

Another type of selling you will do is classified as business development. You may be meeting with the CPA of a good client and want to explore ways that you may be able to help each other grow your business through referrals. It could be a center of influence, such as a Realtor or mortgage broker who is working with people who may benefit from a relationship with a financial planner.

Client Meetings

As a financial planner, you will spend many hours each week in client meetings. You will meet with your clients one-on-one, with other advisors, or maybe even with other members of the client's family. The frequency, duration, and participants involved in a meeting will often depend on the complexity of the case. Let's break down the meetings with clients into three types.

The Initial Client Engagement

The initial client engagement may consume as few as three meetings or as many as ten. Regardless of complexity, the first meeting should always be about the client's interview. Here, you get to know the client—and he or she gets to know you. You want to mutually decide whether there is common ground and the right personalities to develop a long-term relationship. In this meeting, you want to set expectations, what you expect from a client, and what he or she can expect from you (as I discussed in Chapter 6). Resist the temptation to give advice during this first meeting. You'll run the risk of misguiding the client because of not having all of the facts or not completely realizing the client's' goals and objectives. Sometimes you will even discover in a subsequent meeting that the client and his or her spouse have different objectives or concerns. Ask specifically whether either spouse has his or her own feelings or agenda to address and that he or she may contact you separately if there is anything to be discussed in private. Should any issues arise that would appear to raise a conflict of interest, the planner would either raise the issue with both or advise one of the spouses to hire another advisor.

After the first meeting, you begin to gather data and get to know the details of your clients' financial lives. You'll learn how much they make, what they spend, how much they owe, what they own, how much their holdings are worth, and how everything is owned. With all of this data, you will begin to analyze their current situation in light of their time frame, risk tolerance, and goals and objectives. After analysis, you will begin to construct a plan.

While the complexity of a case will determine how many client meetings you will need for reviewing findings and going over recommendations, no meeting should last more than two hours. Unless your client is a rocket scientist with a very high threshold of pain, clients usually cannot absorb more than a few topics and meetings lasting more than an hour and a half. In simple cases, you may be able to discuss three or four major areas of the client's plan in less than an hour. In complex cases, you may spend three meetings just creating their estate plan or discussing options surrounding the continuity of their business and hold more than 10 meetings total. Do not rush the plan. You are developing a long-term relationship, and the client needs to know that you care enough to craft a solution that is personal and meaningful to them.

On the other hand, some clients are natural procrastinators and will drag on a decision as long as you will let them. Over time, you'll learn to recognize the difference between a procrastinator and someone who is carefully weighing his or her options. Either way, you must bring the engagement to closure. The best way to accomplish this task with a procrastinator is to simply put your final advice in writing and let him or her know that the planning process is complete. Let your client know that it is in his or her hands to take action and that you'd be happy to assist with implementation.

Pitfalls

Financial plans are built to be implemented. Do not allow clients to waffle over decisions forever. This will take you uncounted, unpaid hours of excess time and may expose you to liability should some adverse situation arise while the client is thinking about your advice. Make sure that your advice is in writing, dated, and acknowledged as received by the client.

Meetings with Other Advisors

As the planner, you are responsible for the overall success of the plan. The client's success can easily become out of control if you are not careful to closely review the work of other professionals. Many planners will give advice to be implemented by another professional and will refer the client to that professional to implement a part of the plan.

While that professional may be very good at what he or she does and you have seen his or her work before, there is a risk that some of your advice gets lost in the translation from the client to the other advisor. It is best if you invite that other advisor to your conference room to meet with you and the client to supervise the meetings. This way, you can be sure that his or her service is consistent with the goals of the plan.

In the Know

Building strong relationships with other professionals has two immediate benefits for your business. First, you are giving your clients the best possible advice. Second, it will showcase your talents to another professional who may have an occasion to refer you to one of his or her clients.

Being present at meetings is the first part of working with other advisors. Beyond that, you must review the other advisor's work carefully to make sure that it fits in with the plan.

Over time, you can expect the client to develop a relationship with some of the other advisors you have brought onto the planning team—and meetings will naturally occur without you present. Make it clear to the client—and to the other professionals—that you are acting as the head coach and that you expect to be copied on all correspondence and planning discussions that impact your work.

Review Meetings

These meetings are the most important when it comes to retaining client relationships. The most common reason why clients leave advisors are because of no phone calls or follow-up review meetings. Just like an initial engagement, a review meeting may take one hour or multiple meetings. The purpose of review meetings is to review the original goals and objectives and to see whether the planning recommendations are on track. Sometimes the goals and objectives change, the client's circumstances change, or the recommendations need to be altered to accommodate changing conditions. Like any other planning meeting, try to schedule meetings for no longer than an hour and a half and end any that drag on for two hours.

Letting your client know at the outset of the planning that there will be review meetings is an important part of setting expectations. Some clients will want to see you annually; some quarterly. It depends on the complexity of the situation. If your firm is managing a client who has a sizable portfolio, it would be common for that client to want to see you quarterly. In a simple situation, once a year may not even be necessary.

A secondary benefit of regular client reviews is that your business will grow. This is how clients will reveal additional assets from an inheritance or bonus check that they'd like you to invest—or they'll refer you to someone just like them who can benefit from what you do.

In the Know

Find out just how much of your analytical work the client wants to see. Some planners go over every excruciating detail of the planning and decision making, only to bore their clients to tears. Ask specifically whether they want to see all the details or simply want your recommendations.

Doing the Planning

Some part of your day will actually be spent in the trenches of analysis and plan development. Ironically, this is what clients pay for—but it's in the meetings where they get their comfort. Lousy planners who have great people skills can make their clients feel great—and great planning technicians who have lousy people skills can have uncomfortable and uneasy clients who are always looking for another advisor. Needless to say, it is imperative to develop great technical skills to be successful in the long term.

Doing the actual financial planning can be the most time-consuming part of the planning engagement. You will need to analyze all of the data and the data backup. For example, it is not enough to simply know how much insurance your client has. You need to know what type of insurance the client holds, who is the carrier, what is that carrier's financial health, what the client's alternatives are, and how much insurance he or she needs. Be sure to dig deep and evaluate every detail carefully. Get help from another person in your office (or even another firm) if necessary.

The same will be true with the client's investments. It is not enough to know how much your client has invested. You need to know whether what the client is holding is appropriate for him or her specifically and whether there are alternatives that may either perform better or fit his or her risk profile or time frame a bit better. Maybe the client is holding investments that are way too costly and are dampening any potential returns. To accomplish this analysis, you will need software or Internet-based tools that provide independent analyses.

You will perform financial projections using a financial planning software package or spreadsheet that you develop. You will need to project the consequences of the client's current actions and the consequences of your proposed actions. Your client will want specific guidance for issues such as how much he or she should save for a child's education or how much he or she should put into a 401(k) account to be able to retire by age 67. Although you will couch these recommendations with the phrase, "It depends," the client will still want to know. "It depends" is based on the earnings of your savings or investment, the rate of inflation for college or basic living expenses, or your health and ability to work and continue saving. This is another reason why having reviews at least annually is so important.

In the Know

The first few financial plans will take you more time than you anticipate. It won't be until you've done about a dozen or two that you'll gain efficiency and will be able to complete a plan in a reasonable or budgeted amount of time.

There is one exception to having great technical skills: building a planning team with great technicians. Your firm may provide you with the technical talent to assist you, or you may do joint work with other professionals who have the expertise you need.

Managing Money for Clients

Financial planning is about much more than investments, but clients always want to talk about those. Investments are more fun to talk about than death and taxes and are more readily understood by the average nonprofessional because of all the media coverage.

A pure planner looks at client portfolios from the planning perspective, rather than getting involved with managing them. They will work with clients through the details of their risk tolerance and whether they need yield or growth from their portfolios. They don't give advice on which holdings to keep or sell or offer comments on the performance of a specific stock or money manager. Clients of these types of planners will either manage their portfolios themselves or hire a professional money manager.

On the other hand, many advisors are quite active in their clients' investment portfolios. Asset managers have in-depth experience and interest and actually do portfolio management, whereas asset gatherers oversee portfolios and manage the managers.

Pitfalls

Greed sometimes gets the best of some planners. Greed can come into play when selling investments that maximize commissions or taking on too many clients where you don't have enough time to adequately service their investment needs. The best way to make money in the investment area is to retain clients for the long term. You must be fair and attentive to your clients.

The Asset Manager

Some financial planners have significant experience in the investment business and also want to manage assets for their clients—which is a lot more work than many think. To be an asset manager for your clients, you would need to analyze existing holdings, research investments to see what you want to hold, build portfolios that are in line with your clients' needs, re-evaluate the holdings on a regular basis, prepare performance reports for clients, and make trades to *re-balance portfolios* or accommodate future changes. In addition, you will need to leave time for other financial planning matters and meet with clients.

If your firm provides extensive support and delivers many of these required tasks, then maybe you can be an asset-managing financial planner. But if you plan to open your own practice (or already have), you will need to make some steep investments in staff, technology, and research to do as good of a job as a dedicated investment professional.

def•i•ni•tion

Portfolio re-balancing is the process of selling some holdings and buying others to bring the portfolio back to its desired allocation of holdings. As certain positions grow and others decline in value, the portfolio strays from the original allocation and needs to be brought back into line with the client's objectives.

When you have just a couple dozen clients and less than $25 million in assets that you are managing, you can manage money and be a financial planner. But when you reach 100 clients and greater than $25 million in assets, you will hit the wall. You'll spend as much or more in tools and people as you would to outsource the management—and you'll still have to deal with issues such as staff turnover and rising overhead. Also, your investment performance will be compared to the best money manager in the world. For a small practice, you are fooling yourself that you can be a great asset manager and a great financial planner beyond the first few clients.

The Asset Gatherer

Asset gatherers are financial planners who oversee portfolios in greater detail than a pure financial planner—but not as detailed as an asset manager would. Sometimes these planners are called managers of managers, and they're rapidly becoming a financial planning trend. With the improvements in technology and increasing investment complexity calling for specialty expertise, a planner can effectively oversee the work of professional managers in a very cost-effective manner.

def•i•ni•tion

One **basis point** is equal to ¹⁄₁₀₀ of 1 percent. Conversely, 50 basis points are equal to one half of 1 percent. 150 basis points are the same as 1.5 percent.

The client may pay a little more for this type of service as it relates to the investment portion of his or her plan—but not for the overall management and planning services combined. If the client were to segregate the financial planner from the asset manager, he or she would pay separately for both services. The asset manager commonly charges between 75 and 150 *basis points*, and pure planners either charge by the hour or fixed fees.

The asset gatherer financial planner will add between 50 and 100 basis points to a discounted money manager fee of between 50 and 100 basis points and have a blended fee of between 100 and 200 basis points. Most money managers make their services available to advisors for a discount because they do not spend time directly with the clients. The asset gatherer financial planner is responsible for the client relationship and integrating the investment strategies chosen for the client's financial plan. The overall cost to the client is not a significant premium when you factor in all of the other financial planning services you will offer.

As an asset gatherer, you will be responsible for consolidated performance reports, researching the manager's performance and comparing that to similar managers that you may utilize, make re-balancing moves, and decide on the client's overall asset allocation. In addition to your work as the gatherer, you will be accountable as the client's overall financial planner.

Whereas the asset manager financial planner may have to be involved in day-to-day investment decisions, the asset gatherer financial planner will be less concerned with day-to-day fluctuations. You will still need good technology and access to client positions around the clock to answer clients' questions or just to have current information. You will not need to worry about whether a certain stock or bond should be sold today or bought tomorrow.

Research and Diligence

Research and diligence are two very important areas for financial planners and can consume a large part of many days. Your clients count on you for expert guidance, and they expect that you will make your judgments based on a review of the many alternatives available in the marketplace. Our world moves so fast that what you believe is the best solution today may not be the best solution tomorrow.

You will perform research on investments, mutual funds, investment managers, insurance companies, insurance products, software products, banks, lenders, and whatever else your clients want you to research for them. Planners for the very wealthy may find themselves doing research on charter jets for clients' personal and business travel. You simply could not do a good job for your clients without a good part of your week devoted to research.

Your research will be done on two specific levels: general and personal. On a general level, you need to know what companies, products, or services may suit your client's preferences and your style of practice, ethics, or basic requirements. You can eliminate certain companies or products from future analysis in this high-level review. Your second level of research is personal and requires diligence. It's more specific and detailed and may relate to a specific client situation. Diligence involves reviewing any specific contracts, the backup or supporting information behind the company's claims and assertions, and then comparing their offerings to competitive products or services.

For example, if you are a financial planner and your client needs $1 million worth of term life insurance, it is negligent to just recommend company A because that's what you have to sell or that's what you own yourself. Term life insurance is available for a specified period of time. You can buy annual renewable term life insurance in which the premium rises each year and is renewable until the stated age in the contract. You can buy term life insurance where the premium is guaranteed for a period of years, such as 5, 10, 20, or more. It, too, is often renewable after the guaranteed term, but typically at a much higher rate.

With the dramatic changes in the life insurance business over the past 10 years, term rates are now cheaper than ever before. As a result, you must see who is most competitive today. The competitive analysis is a moving target based on many factors—first of which may be pure cost. But you must ask, "Cost under what conditions?" If your client is a marathon runner who has never been sick a day in his or her life, maybe company A is most cost effective. If your client is overweight and has a family history of heart disease and cancer, maybe company B is most cost effective. And if your client is buying term insurance today, knowing that he or she will convert it to a permanent insurance product down the road, then company C may be most cost effective.

A permanent life insurance product is designed to last for your entire life. It has much higher premiums than term life insurance in the early years but will often accumulate a cash surrender value. In the long run, if you are sure that your client will need life insurance for his or her entire life, permanent life insurance may be the lowest cost through your client's life expectancy.

Another component of competitive analysis is the health of the insurance company. It would not be good if your client has bought insurance from a company that is in terrible financial condition just because the premium appeared lower. You can find information on the financial health of an insurance company from its annual reports or from independent companies such as AM Best, Standard and Poor's, Moody's Investor Services, or Weiss Ratings.

In the Know

Whether you perform research or diligence yourself or have it done by another professional, financial planners are required to provide reasonable care. Reasonable care means that you are giving your stamp of approval to the research and diligence, whether you did it yourself or not.

While all states have laws to protect insurance company solvency, some companies do fail. Historically, these companies have been taken over by other companies—and all policies that were issued were honored. But what can happen is that the contract will change. Rates can go up, and the contract is no longer that competitive. If your client is still healthy, you may start all over again and look for another option. But if your client's health has worsened, finding a new policy may not be an option.

Beyond research, you will need to perform some diligence on many matters for each client you encounter. Diligence involves looking beyond the obvious or the sales pitch and digging a little deeper to verify or corroborate your research. A good example would be selecting an estate planning attorney to draft your client's estate documents. A good recommendation from another professional is a fair start. A good personal interview with the attorney is a good next step. But deeper diligence may include an interview with some of the attorney's previous clients, checking on the state licenses, checking for complaints or lawsuits against the attorney, and a review of some of his or her legal documents.

Staying Current

You will devote time each week to staying current. Because this is such an important part of the job, you may want to formally schedule an hour or more each day just to read—either in the morning, at lunchtime, or in the evening. It's best done on a regular schedule so that you don't fall behind.

There are literally hundreds of trade magazines that come out monthly (see Appendix C for a sampling). One of your first tasks may be to peruse them all and decide which ones you want to read regularly. There are ones focused on financial planning, insurance, investment advisory, securities, accounting, taxes, retirement plans, baby boomers, and just about any topic related to financial planning.

Then there are the dailies that are always full of information related to your job as a financial planner. Publications such as *The Wall Street Journal* or *Investor's Business Daily* are good places for breaking news in the world of personal finance. These publications also give you the advantage of seeing what your clients are reading.

In the Know _____

Staying current could be a full-time job in and of itself. You may form a small group of professionals and assign certain areas, publications, or websites to each one—and in turn, they will be responsible for reporting their findings to the group.

With Technical Issues and Changes

You may get some of this knowledge from daily newspapers or monthly magazines, but often you'll need more detail—more frequently than monthly. For legal or other broad changes, there are publishing companies that are completely dedicated to publishing current and very detailed news related to financial planning. Good examples are CCH, formerly known as Commerce Clearing House, and Thompson Publishing. CCH and the Thompson companies have a wide range of technical financial, tax, and estate planning material updated daily.

While technical issues may not require daily attention, don't delay when the need arises. Clients expect you to be aware of breaking news and changes that affect their personal financial situation.

You will always run into situations in client cases where you are treading on new ground. Just like with breaking news, clients expect that you'll do your homework and give them well-founded answers—not guesses. If your firm does not invest in some of the research services for financial advisors, you can find them in any good business library. Some of the professional trade organizations also have decent research services on their websites or through their knowledge provider websites.

With Industry Trends and Best Practices

Most financial planners are fairly conservative in their judgment. This can be a challenge when you are in a profession that is still evolving and creating rules and standards to equal the major professions of law and accounting. You need to stay on top of trends and best practices.

The dedicated practitioner will take time from his or her week to do this through a variety of mediums. (I'll discuss joining associations and continuing education in the next chapter.) The best ways to stay current on trends and best practices is to look for material on this topic and to ask other professionals their opinions and discover how they are doing things.

Two of the best sources for trends and best practices come from Bob Veres and Horsesmouth. Both offer subscriptions to websites and electronic newsletters that give fantastic information to keep you in step with the best practitioners in the country. For $299 per year, the Bob Veres's website (named Inside Information—www.bobveres.com—is full of just that: inside information about the financial planning business. For $189 per year, www.horsesmouth.com gives you valuable insight into practice management and industry trends. Both are fantastic and will give you a free trial look.

Practice Management

Practice management is defined as working on your business to do things better that will make you more valuable to your clients and make your days more productive. The financial planning industry's best and brightest practitioners are always thinking about practice management.

While not an everyday activity, it is something that you can't ignore until a problem flares up. And that problem is often just a symptom of the bigger situation. For example, if a client tells you that he or she didn't understand the quarterly investment performance report, that is probably not the first time that one of your clients felt that way. The problem isn't your client—it's probably the report. A good practice manager will examine the report in light of the client's concern, then ask other clients about their opinions. After you gather enough information, you should have a clearer picture of what your clients want to see each quarter and then change the report so that it works better for all of them.

Another practice management issue would be to look at your first client meetings each month. How many did you have? How many became clients? Did you handle each meeting substantially the same? Is your closing ratio adequate to achieve your business development goals? If not, what can you do differently to improve it?

Many successful planners will survey their clients. This is actually something that should consume a lot of time during each week. Rather than doing an annual or bi-annual survey, it is better to survey a few clients each week or month. This will give you the time to follow up with each client for personal feedback. With your personal involvement, the clients will know how important it is to you that they are satisfied. From this feeling of sincerity, you will receive honest and valuable feedback.

The Least You Need to Know

- ◆ Developing a routine to better manage your time and focus on what is important will make you a better financial planner.

- ◆ Business development must be a part of your daily routine if your goal is to always improve and grow your practice.

- ◆ Your style of dealing and communicating with clients in meetings will make or break you.

- ◆ The initial financial planning engagement is where you will get to know the client well and be able to build the foundation for a lifelong relationship.

- ◆ Ongoing client review meetings are the best way to see if anything has changed in your clients' lives and to make them feel comfortable with all of the work you do for them behind the scenes.

- ◆ Block out time every day to stay current with industry news and trends.

Chapter 9

Getting Better with Time

In This Chapter

- Choosing the club or association that's right for you
- Learning from other financial planners
- Expanding your knowledge with continuing education
- Increasing your skills and opportunities
- Going beyond the core: advanced and specialty designations
- Attending industry events that are worthwhile

In this chapter, I'll take you to the next level of success as a personal financial planner. A combination of whom you associate with, what advanced knowledge you choose to pursue, and which educational forums you attend will shape your future. You can't live in a vacuum as a financial planner. You must keep on top of trends and changes and increase your knowledge to properly serve clients and grow your business.

There is no shortage of professional associations to join, advanced designations to earn, and professional meetings to attend. After absorbing the material in this chapter, you'll know what the best planners are doing—and what you should be doing—to take your financial planning business to the level of success that you have envisioned.

Joining Clubs and Associations

Because the majority of today's financial planning practitioners are in a small-practice environment, professional associations and trade groups are a vital part of your existence. They are places where you can meet like-minded people, learn about ways to improve, and take advantage of beneficial educational sessions. Each has a long list of member benefits, from discounted services and affiliations, publications for members, and great websites loaded with information to help you. Some are even offering meeting-place–type services for practitioners looking to buy or sell a practice or post job opportunities.

In the Know

Membership in any financial planning professional organization is tax-deductible and a great way to network and learn from those who have more experience.

There are many groups to choose from, and while each one has its strengths, you can't possibly belong to all of them. Each organization has membership requirements—some as simple as paying dues. The financial planning business can be a lonely environment, especially for the small practitioner. You should investigate the various organizations and join one (or more) that best suits your needs. (See Appendix B for contact information.)

The Financial Planning Association (FPA)

The FPA was created in January 2000 by combining the International Association of Financial Planners and the Institute of Certified Financial Planners. This organization is for financial planning practitioners and offers three main member benefits:

- Continuing professional education
- Access to the latest information and trends in the financial planning business
- Networking

You join the national organization and then join your local chapter for a moderate increase in dues. Each chapter is somewhat autonomous with respect to what it offers its members. Most regional chapters have regular meetings that typically focus on educational sessions. Some meet monthly for two hours; others meet quarterly for half-day sessions. Most also have an annual one- or two-day event featuring top speakers from all around the country.

The FPA also does community outreach within its chapters to spread the word about financial planning. There are workshops, career days, and a financial literacy campaign to help the public learn about the benefits of financial planning and hiring a professional financial planner. Most chapters offer a pro bono service for those who are desperately in need of financial advice but cannot afford to hire someone— including low-income households, welfare recipients, cancer patients and their families, and members of the U.S. Armed Forces.

Membership dues are $295 per year for national membership, with annual assessments for local chapter memberships ranging from $10 to $100 per year. A reduced rate of $145 is available to students, including those who are enrolled in a CFP course of study—no matter what age. The local chapter dues are not required but are strongly recommended; these assessments are needed to operate your local office. The national FPA shares a small amount of your annual dues with its local chapters, so that small extra fee you pay for local chapter membership is a critical component of the local budget.

In the Know

The FPA is the most vibrant of all professional financial planning organizations. Its members are typically passionate about financial planning, and the quarterly or monthly meetings are packed with good content and networking opportunities.

National Association of Personal Financial Advisors (NAPFA)

NAPFA is the nation's leading organization dedicated to the advancement of fee-only comprehensive financial planning. Similar to FPA, NAPFA touts high ethical standards and comprehensive financial planning. The main differentiation is compensation. NAPFA members may not accept commissions and only receive compensation that is paid by their clients in the form of a fee.

The core values of NAPFA are what differentiate it from any other professional financial planning organization. In particular, their core values dedicated to practicing holistic financial planning advice in a fee-only environment and complete disclosure are what make the difference. NAPFA members are required to provide clients with an explanation of fees and complete disclosure of conflicts of interest. This sounds simple, yet no other professional trade group requires complete disclosure of compensation. For this reason, along with its other core values, NAPFA is well recognized among media looking for source information and clients seeking fee-only advisors.

Full membership in NAPFA is $475 per year. Financial services affiliate memberships are available for fee-only asset managers, fee-only insurance advisors, or fee-only estate planning attorneys for $350 per year.

National Association of Insurance and Financial Advisors (NAIFA)

NAIFA is one of the oldest associations of financial professionals in the United States. It was founded in 1890 as the National Association of Life Underwriters—and back then, life insurance professionals dominated its membership. Today, there is a more diverse group of members in NAIFA, but it is still primarily comprised of insurance-focused members.

The vision for NAIFA is to protect and promote the critical role of insurance in a sound financial plan and the essential role provided by professional agents and advisors.

NAIFA member benefits include creative sales and marketing ideas, networking opportunities, skills and sales training, and industry legislative representation.

Membership dues vary by region but are in the vicinity of $350 to $400 per year (which includes membership in your local chapter).

Society of Financial Service Professionals

Founded in 1928 by the first graduates of The American College, the society's mission is to promote professionalism among its members through high-quality continuing education and the maintenance of high ethical standards and conduct. While many of its members have earned a designation or degree from The American College, the society is a separate and independent organization.

Society members are credentialed financial service professionals who provide financial planning, estate planning, retirement counseling, asset management, and other services and products to clients. Members reflect a great diversity of financial practitioners from fee-only financial planners and estate planning attorneys and accountants to asset managers, employee benefits specialists, and life insurance agents.

The society is the only professional organization in the industry that requires its members to be credentialed or to actively pursue one of these widely recognized financial service designations or degrees: CEBS, CFA, CFP, ChFC, CLF, CLU, CPA, CPC, CTFA, Enrolled Actuary, JD (licensed), a graduate degree in financial services (MS, MSFS, MSM, MBA, Ph.D.), REBC, or RHU.

Membership dues are approximately $340 per year, including both national and local chapters. There are 50 percent discounts for retired or disabled members and associate memberships. An associate member is someone who is currently pursuing one of the required credentials.

Estate Planning Councils

An association called the National Association of Estate Planners and Councils (NAEPC) is a national organization that consists of regional and local chapters. In Massachusetts, for example, there are six regional estate planning councils. Each council opens its membership to attorneys, CPAs, CLUs, CFPs, and trust officers. In addition, many councils admit professionals from other disciplines. The objective of the estate planning councils is the development of all aspects of estate planning.

While the estate planning councils are the most specialized professional organizations, their membership may be the most diverse. The meetings are a good venue for networking and learning from professionals in all of the membership categories.

In addition to being a member from a qualified profession, you need to be recommended by two existing estate planning council members in order to join. The member benefits include networking and education. Meeting schedules vary based on your local chapter but come in many varieties, from lunch meetings through half-day and multi-day venues. Dues also vary widely from chapter to chapter. You can expect dues to range from $50 to as high as $250.

Pitfalls

Don't join too many associations at once. In order to maximize your benefits, you will need to attend the meetings and read their newsletters, magazines, and websites. If you spread yourself too thinly among your memberships, you'll get little out of many groups instead of potentially getting much out of one.

American Institute of CPAs—Personal Financial Planning Division (AICPA-PFP)

While the AICPA is clearly an association dedicated to the CPA profession, it actually has a vibrant and valuable personal financial planning division. While you do not need to be a CPA to join, you must at least work for and be sponsored by a CPA firm member. Base AICPA membership is required to become a member of the personal financial planning division.

If you are a CPA or practice financial planning within a CPA firm, this membership is worthy of your dues and time. There is good technical information in the form of monthly and quarterly newsletters and a terrific website at http://pfp.aicpa.org/. The PFP section of the AICPA website is available to members of the PFP division only. The PFP division website has material from practice tools to a very detailed technical section. There are also several conferences each year where you get a good discount as a member of the division.

Million Dollar Round Table (MDRT)

Founded in 1927, MDRT provides its members with resources to improve their technical knowledge, sales skills, and client service while maintaining a culture of high ethical standards. The mission of MDRT is to be a valued, member-driven international network of leading insurance and investment financial services professionals and advisors who serve their clients by exemplary performance and the highest standards of ethics, knowledge, service, and productivity.

In the Know

While there may be many MDRT members who also practice financial planning, the membership is dominated by life insurance professionals. This group is ideal for planners who want to specialize in insurance matters.

Membership in MDRT happens by qualification only. This organization is dedicated to life insurance professionals who may or may not also be financial planners, and the qualification has to do with income. You need to produce a minimum amount of life insurance premiums or commissions each year to qualify. The minimum qualification for 2007 is $75,000, of which 50 percent must come from certain insurance-related products. MDRT's website, www.MDRT.org, contains all of the details regarding qualifying business and amounts.

MDRT is a forum for the exchange of sales ideas, techniques, and practice management suggestions among agents. The annual meeting and other educational opportunities are designed to offer members new insights into the business to increase their success.

Membership dues are $450 per year. There are two higher levels of membership—which of course require even a higher dues amount and a higher amount of revenues or insurance premiums to qualify.

Learn from Other Planners

Learning from other financial planners is a great way to see what is happening in the real world. While most planners have had similar training and live with similar codes of ethics, everyone still has unique styles and methods. What works for one person may not work for you (and vice-versa).

The financial planning community is s group of caring, sharing people. In an industry dominated by small practices, hearing the specifics about how one advisor handled a situation and how another may have handled it differently is experience that you cannot get by staying within the four walls of your firm.

In this area, being shy will not help you. You need to reach out and ask questions of the advisors in your professional association. Most are remarkably friendly, knowledgeable people who are willing to help you out. If the person you ask cannot help you, more likely than not he or she will refer you to someone within the group who can. Most of the professional organizations hold networking events specifically for the purpose of getting to know your fellow practitioners. You should create time in your schedule to attend these events.

Some learn from other planners through the formation of study groups—professionals, typically no more than six, who get together on a regular basis to share ideas and help each other improve. Some groups are comprised of local practitioners and meet on a monthly basis in a neutral location or rotate the meetings from one office to another. Others are groups comprised of planners from all around the country, meeting in locations picked by the members. Each type often invites guest speakers, assigns specific topics to members for group discussion, and shares best practices.

The formation of a study group happens when one person takes the lead and invites a group of people together. The leadership of your group is critical, especially in the first year. Until everyone gets comfortable and has a good handle on the benefits and what to expect, a good leader can keep the meetings moving and valuable.

Continuing Education

Just because you are now licensed as a CFP or CFC doesn't mean that you know all there is to know. Those designations are just the beginning of your lifelong commitment to learning in the financial planning profession.

Required Continuing Education

There are two types of required continuing education (CE). The first is informal, which is required for you to stay current on new laws and issues affecting your practices and clients. While there is no official rule requiring this education, you have a moral obligation to your clients to be current and to have your advice fit within the context of changing regulations or conditions. Any oath that you agree to upon obtaining a designation will also make it part of your ethical responsibilities to your clients.

The second type is continuing education required by your designation, professional credential, or license. CFP and ChFC each require 30 hours every 2 years to maintain your license. They also require that at least 2 of those 30 hours are in ethics training.

Holders of a CPA, insurance, or securities license also have CE requirements. Many of these are set by the particular state and vary. It's common for CPAs to need 40 hours every two years. For insurance, it does vary widely—but you will need approximately 30 hours every 2 years. For securities, there are annual requirements that are set by your broker dealer under the guidance of the National Association of Securities Dealers (NASD) and tri-annual requirements set directly by the NASD.

Not just any course qualifies as official continuing education, however. The licensing authority must approve most courses to be sure that they have merit and sufficient content to satisfy the continuing education requirement. Some advanced designations also qualify as satisfying the CE requirements for the base designation. There is some overlap in that one course may qualify for CFP, ChFC, CPA, and insurance CE—but don't take that for granted.

Pitfalls

Beware of free continuing education workshops. While many offer great content and CE credits, there are just as many that are merely sales pitches for a particular company or product. Do your homework. Find out as much as you can about the agenda of a free workshop before you attend.

Desired Continuing Education

Desired continuing education is when you voluntarily seek a deeper understanding of a specific area or methodology. For example, life planning—the subject of Chapter 10—has many different training courses available, from two-day workshops through six-day workshops. Practitioners often enroll in these workshops because they are driven to learn about and master the topic. Many of the life planning workshops, for example, also qualify for required continuing education.

Master's degrees are not required, but many financial planning practitioners will seek a Master's degree in taxation, business administration, or financial services. Some even decide to attend law school to round out their formal training.

Your desired continuing education is where you can pursue your passions. It is time that you are taking to invest in yourself for enjoyment or improvement. If you are looking for an area in which to specialize, use this educational time to see what areas have the greatest appeal to you. As you'll see once you are in the business, you will be solicited to attend conferences and workshops nearly every day.

Increasing Your Skills and Opportunities

Some say the two go hand in hand: increase your skills, and you will increase your opportunities. This may be a logical thought pattern, but it's not a guarantee. If you end up loving a certain specialty and decide to sharpen your skills in that area, don't forget that you still have to let the world know about it and close the deal. You need to alert your clients of your new abilities, tell your referral sources, and maybe even begin prospecting in a new way or in different circles. Just like the early days as a planner, you can decide to pursue the opportunities and get your skills as you go along.

You should always compare opportunities in light of your capabilities. Sometimes the opportunity is huge and your capability is low. In these cases, you must assess whether the opportunity can wait until you build the capabilities or whether you need to use your entrepreneurial skills to acquire the capabilities as soon as possible. If the opportunity is not time sensitive, get the training and pursue it when you are ready. If the opportunity is time sensitive, go to plan B. Of course, you can't become an expert overnight—so you really need to see who possesses that capability today and see whether there is some joint-venture possibility.

If your situation is the opposite—where your capabilities are substantial and the business opportunity is not that great—either pass on it or delegate it to someone else who is looking for opportunities like the one in front of you.

You may see an opportunity in the area of business succession. Business succession means creating a continuity plan for the business should the current owner/manager pass away, become disabled, or simply want to retire. Thanks to the baby boomers, this area means a substantial opportunity for financial planners. Your attraction may be due to the large numbers of business-owner boomers who need the help and because the case size tends to be a bit larger and more complicated. Business succession cases often involve life insurance and benefits, retirement plans, management succession,

Pitfalls

Many planners waste countless hours pursuing opportunities where they have no capability and building capabilities for which they will not develop opportunities. Think carefully about both before you invest hours and money for something on a whim.

and estate planning. This is an example where the opportunity is not time sensitive. If you devoted a couple of years to master this market, you'll do fine. The earliest boomers are in their sixties and just beginning to think about these issues now.

On the other hand, you may have good capabilities in this area from personal experience. Perhaps your family had a business and you learned from what they did right, wrong, or didn't do at all. This experience may give you a burning desire to provide the guidance to see that others get it right. In this case, create a targeted marketing campaign—and go for it.

If you feel confident in your ability to market yourself for a specific service but don't quite have the skills to be an expert, you can do a few things. You can team up with one or more experts in the field. In business succession, for example, there are attorneys, CPAs, and life insurance professionals who specialize in this area. Another solution is to team up with another experienced planner in your firm and do joint work. You find the cases, and the other planner will be responsible for case design. After a few cases, you'll get to know more and realize where you need more training to further develop your skills.

The same may hold true for lots of other opportunities. There could be opportunities right under your nose that you could seize if you had the skills. A good example would be a financial planner in a bank. As I discussed in Chapter 6, banks have both a retail division and a private client group for small-business owners or wealthy families. You may see the need for a retirement plan specialist in your bank. Clients there may get good financial planning service, but you notice that all of the small-business clients have their retirement plans serviced by other firms. You may have also noticed that these other firms are always lobbying the clients for their personal financial planning business, as well. In this case, you would be well advised to speak with a supervisor or department head in the bank to ask whether the bank would be willing to market these services to clients. The bank may even be willing to invest in your training to develop these skills.

Advanced and Specialty Designations

Beyond the core designations that I told you about in Chapter 7, there are advanced and specialty designations that will help you as you progress in your career. The purpose of these designations is to deepen your broad financial planning knowledge base or to gain in-depth expertise in a specialty area. Another benefit of any specialty designation is that it will provide you with the continuing education hours necessary to satisfy a core designation licensing requirement.

Specialty designations are generally shorter courses than core designations but are not less difficult. If you have had some practical experience in the subject matter, the designation will be easier. If it's an area where you want to learn to create your capability, you will invest more time and will have to study harder.

Chartered Financial Analyst (CFA)

This course of study is really intended for asset managers and financial analysts. If your planning career takes you in the direction of managing assets for clients, rather than being an asset gatherer, then this designation is for you. It is a very rigorous and detailed training track that takes three years and a minimum of 250 hours of study time to complete. There are three parts to the examination and training process, scheduled one year apart from each other.

To fulfill the entrance requirements for the CFA exam, you must either have a Bachelor's degree, be in the last year of your Bachelor's degree, or have relevant work experience or a combination of work experience and education equaling four years. You will be asked to sign statements of professional conduct and candidate responsibility and be prepared to take the exams in English.

To become a credential holder, you must pass all three parts of the exam, meet the work experience requirements, enroll in the CFA institute, receive your approval to use the credential, and maintain your status. The work requirements are four years of acceptable work experience, which you can obtain when you're enrolled in the program. The work experience requirement mandates that you spend at least 50 percent of your time related to the investment decision-making process.

The cost to enroll in the program is $760 and includes part one of the exam. By the time you are finished with all three exams, total fees will be in the $2,000 to $3,000 range (including textbooks and review courses).

In the Know

This designation is heavy on analysis and math. It is a great credential for a money manager but probably a bit more than most financial planners need.

Chartered Retirement Plans Specialist (CRPS)

The CRPS program is specifically targeted at professionals who design, install, and maintain retirement plans for the business community. Because of ever-increasing client demand for financial advisors who are knowledgeable in the administration of retirement plans for businesses and their employees, there is nearly unlimited professional growth opportunity for planners who specialize in meeting the changing needs of companies and small-business owners.

The College for Financial Planning offers this designation. Enrollment and study guides will cost between $680 and $994, depending on the options that you choose. The basic is simply enrollment and course material, and the most expensive includes a financial calculator and online courses.

Certified Employee Benefits Specialist (CEBS)

CEBS was established in 1977 through a partnership of the International Foundation of Employee Benefit Plans and the Wharton School of the University of Pennsylvania. The International Foundation, the largest educational organization in the employee benefits field, is responsible for the overall administration of the program. The Wharton School, one of the preeminent business schools in the United States, oversees academic content and standards. No other employee benefits or compensation program provides the opportunity to gain knowledge and insight through such a broad university-based curriculum.

The CEBS program offers you the opportunity to earn designations in three distinct areas of specialization: group benefits, retirement, and compensation. Earn a designation in each of the specialty tracks—and, at the same time, receive credit that will qualify toward earning the CEBS designation—which now carries an eight-course requirement (six required courses plus two electives).

In the Know

This designation is terrific for a planner who is choosing to specialize in corporate benefits such as compensation packages, group benefits, and retirement plan design. You will need a natural and substantial flow of corporate clients to maximize this knowledge.

Study options for CEBS include online, formal classroom training, or independent self-study. There is no time limit for earning the CEBS designation. Exams are administered year-round through computer-based testing. Most CEBS candidates are working professionals who take two or three exams a year.

Master of Science in Taxation (MST)

This track is a bona fide Master's degree and is only offered through accredited universities with a business focus. It is intended for those who want to be tax professionals. Most graduates from the program are affiliated with an accounting or law firm and practice exclusively in the tax area. But a financial planner with a desire to focus on taxation can also benefit from this specialized degree.

Most programs are exclusively focused on taxation and comprise about 10 specialty courses. After you have completed the required courses in individual, business, and estate and gift taxes, you will be allowed to choose electives that can further develop any particular tax specialty that you'd like to pursue.

Certified Senior Advisor (CSA)

The CSA designation is intended for advisors who wish to focus on the lifestyle and financial needs of senior citizens. The Society of Certified Senior Advisors offers this designation. It is intended to give you a broad-based knowledge of the health, financial, and social issues that are important to seniors. Topics include Social Security, funeral planning, senior housing, Medicare and Medicaid, long-term care, ethical marketing to seniors, business ethics with seniors, and more topics of concern to senior citizens.

The exam can be taken after a three-day training course or after up to six months of self-study. Your enrollment and course materials for the CSA designation cost between $1,195 and $1,395.

There are three requirements for renewing your CSA designation. You must complete the annual renewal statement, submit the annual renewal fee of $195, and fulfill the CSA's continuing education requirement of 18 CSA CE hours every three years.

Chartered Life Underwriter (CLU)

The CLU designation is offered through The American College in Bryn Mawr, Pennsylvania. It is widely recognized as the highest level of studies in the life insurance profession. Since 1927, more than 94,000 individuals have earned this distinction—enabling them to present a wider range of solutions for the life insurance needs of individuals, business owners, and professionals (including income replacement, estate planning, and wealth transfer). In addition to increasing their clients' financial well-being, CLUs average a higher income than their insurance professional peers who don't have a designation.

The curriculum for the CLU designation includes eight courses. Five are required for all candidates, and three are electives from a choice of seven courses. You may study for the exams through self-study, online, DVDs, or live classroom training on campus at The American College.

You must complete all eight courses within five years of enrollment. Three years of full-time business experience is required—with 2,000 hours constituting full-time for those working part-time. The relevant experience requirements for the CLU designation is the same as those previously discussed for the ChFC designation.

Candidates must abide by the code of ethics and complete 30 hours of continuing education every 2 years. The CLU designation is a great choice for financial advisors wishing for a deeper understanding of and specialization in the concepts and applications of life insurance.

Industry Events and Workshops for Seasoned Veterans

As you get settled into the business, you'll wonder how everyone selling a workshop got your name. Invitations for seminars and workshops will arrive daily. There are some, however, that are particularly good and always stimulating—even for the most seasoned practitioner.

The FPA National Conference

This three-day conference is held in various locations throughout the country each year in the early fall. There are educational sessions for the beginner through the most advanced planner. Several simultaneous sessions are offered on a variety of topics to have the broadest appeal. There will rarely be an hour where there isn't more than one course that you'd like to attend. This is a huge conference with more than 3,000 attendees from many countries. Beyond the classroom, it is a great opportunity to meet and speak with your peers about practice, professional, or industry issues where you want to gain another perspective. With conference fees, hotel, and airfare, this annual event could cost you between $2,000 and $3,000.

In the Know

Although the cost of attending these conferences and meetings may appear prohibitive—airfare, hotel, and tuition—the benefit to your clients and business will be more than worth it.

The FPA Annual Retreat

As the name implies, the FPA annual retreat is a more intimate setting than the national conference, which is often held in a relaxing, almost vacationlike location. The four-day workshop is designed for developing relationships with fellow planners who are there for shedding old ways and creating space for new ideas.

The retreat is focused on practice management, new ideas, and self-improvement rather than just technical knowledge. FPA touts this retreat as being as much about connecting and conversation as it is about advanced education and pushing the boundaries of financial planning. Attendance for this event is limited and often sells out completely. With conference fees, hotel, and airfare, this annual event can cost you between $2,000 and $3,000.

AICPA-PFP Conference

The AICPA-PFP conference is intended for CPA financial planners. Membership in the AICPA or being a CPA is not a requirement for attendance, however. As you may expect, this conference has a heavy technical focus and is centered on issues facing CPA firms and CPA financial planners. It is typically held in a warm-weather location in early January of each year, and will cost between $2,000 and $3,000 for conference fees, hotel, and airfare.

The Heckerling Institute on Estate Planning

This annual event is the grandfather of all advanced estate planning conferences. Held in early January at the University of Miami School of Law in Florida, it is the gathering where all of the countries' top estate planners are present.

The conference is a five-day event with many diverse sessions offered on very specific areas of estate planning. Attendees of Heckerling often come year after year and see it as a way to catch up on what is new and anticipated for the estate planning profession for the coming year. Attendees are a broad and diverse group. The program is designed for sophisticated attorneys, trust officers, accountants, insurance advisors, and financial planning professionals who are familiar with the principles of estate planning. This event will cost you between $2,000 and $3,000 for conference fees, hotel, and airfare.

Morningstar Investment Conference

The focus of this three-day conference is solely on investing. Held annually in the Chicago backyard of investment research giant Morningstar, this conference features presentations from mutual fund managers and industry leaders.

The fee for this conference is $695, plus hotel and airfare. In addition to the investment conference, Morningstar holds a users forum for users of their investment research and analysis products. The users forum covers advanced content and hands-on experience for participants to enhance their knowledge of asset allocation and portfolio construction.

The Least You Need to Know

- ◆ Joining a professional association helps you network with other advisors and offers you continuing education on topics needed by planners.

- ◆ Building on your skills allows you to effectively serve clients in more areas and increases your opportunities in the financial planning business.

- ◆ An advanced designation affords you greater credibility and delivers the education needed to work on more sophisticated matters.

- ◆ Choose continuing education courses that add to your base of knowledge and help you better serve your clients.

- ◆ Learning from your peers from association meetings or study groups is as important as learning in the classroom.

- ◆ There are many financial planning industry-sponsored educational and networking events that give you an opportunity to meet planners from around the world and learn new ways to serve your clients.

Chapter 10

The Life Planning Movement

In This Chapter

- ◆ Creating a life-centered financial plan
- ◆ How life planning enhances client relationships
- ◆ How to be your client's skillful ally
- ◆ Implementing the life planning process
- ◆ A lifelong relationship
- ◆ Questions and concerns for the life planner

Life planning is not just an approach—it's a discipline with a methodology, a skill set, and measurable benefits. With baby boomers realizing that they may live a lot longer than their predecessors, along with a generational difference in how the retirement years are viewed, the need for the kinds of conversations and planning offered by financial life planners is becoming urgent.

For perhaps the first time in history, we are witnessing a significant wave of people who expect to live well past the age of 65 and who want to live a rich and meaningful life in those extended years. Because money is an important part of that vision, the financial life planner is the ideal professional to facilitate the critical—even courageous—conversations that need to occur before effective planning can take place.

For the financial planner, the life planning approach transforms the professional practice into an opportunity to meet regularly with clients with whom there is genuine caring, trust, and commitment. You can participate in the evolution of their life stories, be the catalyst for positive and inspiring changes, and serve as a wise ally through all the unexpected changes of an unfolding life. Planners find their own work life enriched, deepened, and alive with meaning and purpose. In this chapter, you will learn that planners can model for their clients the basic message of life planning: that one can have both money and meaning in life.

What Is Life Planning?

The creation of a life-centered financial plan focuses on the client and is designed to help him or her establish financial well-being as well as a meaningful life. In order to create a comprehensive financial plan, the advisor must first get to know the client. This task, of course, includes gathering all the relevant financial information: investments, account statements, legal documents, tax returns, and so on. But even more importantly, the advisor also needs to gather personal information from the client such as goals, aspirations, dreams, and values. The management of money assets is then guided by what is most important for the client to accomplish in living a richly meaningful life—and the financial plan is structured to support the realization of those life goals.

def•i•ni•tion

> **Life planning** is the process of working with clients on understanding and achieving their life dreams and visions. The financial part of the plan then puts the dollars with sense, and a financial road map is built on why, when, and how to achieve those visions. Practicing financial life planners simply define life planning as "financial planning done right."

The process of getting to know the client in this deeply personal way is what has been called *life planning* or *financial life planning*. Some say that it is simply financial planning done right. It is planning that clearly focuses first on the human being who has financial assets, rather than on the assets themselves.

Money touches every aspect of our lives. It can act as a facilitator for accomplishing our most significant goals, or it can seem to be the greatest obstacle to living the life we envision. Decisions about money and finances are often highly emotional as a result—particularly when they arise as a result of either experiencing or planning for painful life changes such as death, divorce, disability, job loss, or natural disasters. Every advisor has had client meetings where emotions ran high, but few have had any training on how to assist the client through these difficult life transitions. Training in the skill set for being effectively present with highly emotional financial discussions and decisions is the other primary feature of the life planner, along with guiding clients through exploring goals.

Clients assume that you are completely focused on their needs. The life planning process brings this assumption into the spotlight and clearly demonstrates your concern for their issues, dreams, and vision. The life planner serves the client by guiding the comprehensive planning process to include what is most exciting, most challenging, and most potentially painful—while riding the waves of feeling generated by the engagement with confidence, competence, and empathy for the client.

George Kinder is recognized as the father of life planning. He is the author of two books on the subject: *The Seven Stages of Money Maturity* and *Lighting the Torch* (see Appendix C). George defines financial life planning as follows:

> Life planning is the art or the human side of financial planning. In life planning, we discover what the deepest and most profound goals of a client are through a process of listening and inquiry. Then, using a mix of professional and relationship skills, we resolve the obstacles to these goals, create a plan, and guide the client to the accomplishment of these goals in the most efficient and fastest way possible.

By merging meaning with money, life planning allows individuals and couples to review value and purpose in their lives—to assess whether their current lifestyle is as rich within as it is without. Incorporating meaning, passion, and purpose into a life design becomes the dream of midlife—a dream that is often blocked because of money issues or concerns. In the life planning relationship, the advisor is able to help the client not only unearth the profound and meaningful dream but also to devise a strategic financial plan to make that dream a reality.

Walking the Walk

... a hunger wells up for a greater depth of meaning and value in the activities of our everyday lives ... the search for meaning in whatever we do becomes the universal preoccupation of the Second Adulthood. It is rooted in a spiritual imperative that grows stronger as we grow older.

—Gail Sheehy, from "Life Begins At 60" (*Parade* magazine, December 11, 2005)

It's All About the Relationship

The CFP Board of Standards—the organization that sets the highest standards for professional training and performance in the field of financial planning—conducted a 2004 General Market Consumer Survey. It found that the most highly ranked considerations for selecting a financial advisor included, in order of importance:

1. Trustworthy (93 percent)

2. More interested in meeting needs than selling products (91 percent)

3. Someone who listens (90 percent)

Then, the priorities shift to:

4. Good performance record (89 percent)

5. Expert in his/her area (88 percent)

Clearly, financial planning clients are looking for more than analytical skills or market expertise. They want a relationship with someone who they can trust, someone who listens to them and their needs, and who helps them accomplish their goals. They also want their advisors to be knowledgeable, but that is a secondary concern.

A New Path for Continuing Education

The CFP Board took the finding of this survey to heart and added life planning and client relationship topics to their list of topics and programs that are available for continuing education (CE) credit. With this addendum, the Board recognizes that truly professional financial planners need skills for the human relationship as well as a high level of financial expertise.

Beyond your base CPF or other technical training, you need to devote the time to perfecting your client relationship skills. While the CE topics approved by the CFP board will assist you, a deeper reading and training of client relationship issues is recommended and discussed later in this chapter.

Communication Style and Client Trust

In 2006, Susan Galvan was a member of a life planning consortium that conducted a further study, funded by a grant from the CFP Board and in partnership with the Financial Planning Association. The study, titled "Specific Elements of Communication

That Affect Trust and Commitment in the Financial Planning Process," used survey data from 554 planners and 128 of their clients to examine the relationship between specific communication tasks, communication skills, communication topics, and client trust in and commitment to their financial planner and the financial planning process. Results provide support for planners taking a life planning approach to the content of planner-client discussions. Communication skills that are significantly correlated with client trust and commitment are identified, providing an empirical basis for best practices in the financial planning process.

Among other findings, the paper notes that planners need to develop trust, and that there must be a mutual level of commitment between planner and client. The report also emphasizes that clients feel it is a financial planner's job to uncover client values, priorities, attitudes, and beliefs.

In other words, it's all about the relationship once we speak of trust and commitment—which, in turn, depends on how the planner goes about making the client the center of the planning engagement, rather than the money. Your client communications cannot be scripted or canned. They must be genuine and caring or else you will not achieve the level of trust you need for a long-term relationship. The quality of the relationship is also strongly influenced by the relational skills and methodology employed by the planner in the financial planning process.

Although all of us have relationships, very few of us have ever been trained in the skill set for creating and sustaining relationships that generate strong levels of trust and commitment. The financial life planner, as differentiated from the financial advisor, has had that training and is effective in applying those relational skills to the life-centered financial planning process in order to most efficiently integrate life goals and values with money goals and values.

Walking the Walk

At the Kinder Institute of Life Planning, we learned early on that the collaborative relationship is essential to a successful financial life plan. During training, participating financial planners first experience themselves and then observe in their fellow planners that financial life planning is not just a self-help project. It is, in fact, rooted in a relationship of trust and commitment on both sides. It is only with the skills, wisdom, and experience of a knowledgeable ally that clients can both envision a life truly worth living *and* develop the practical financial and personal road maps to make that vision a reality.

—Susan Galvan, cofounder, Kinder Institute of Life Planning

The Skillful Ally

A basic tenet of the life planning approach to financial planning is that planners must have "walked their talk." In other words, a life planner must have been through the life planning process personally and be living his or her own life plan before offering this service to others. This brings both integrity and authenticity to the life planning engagement. Having been through the ups and downs of forging a vision, values, and a plan for a meaningful life, the planner knows how to skillfully empathize when necessary, challenge with sensitivity, brainstorm exuberantly, and strategize effectively.

From a client's perspective, the journey to a fulfilled life is one that inspires as much anxiety as excitement at various stages. A skillful ally is one who understands these mixed emotions and can help the client move with them and through them to the accomplishment of their most significant goals or even dreams.

Life Planning Training

While there are now several books on financial life planning, there is one training program that offers a five-day intensive practicum on the topic. This is the program offered by the Kinder Institute of Life Planning. In this program, participants will develop their own life plan and observe other peers who are deeply involved in the same process. You will learn a reliable and necessary methodology for navigating the interactions with the client. In addition, training in specific skills related to communication, listening, deep goals discovery, partnering, and so on is integrated.

While some planners have worked in a manner similar to life planning, there is a competency and a confidence that only comes with experiencing a training process as well as being mentored, observed, and coached.

Walking the Walk

Overall, I think the week was awesome. The concept of life planning and the Kinder EVOKE model are perhaps the most powerful models I've ever seen for planning. My biggest insight during the week was that every financial planner/stock broker/insurance agent talks and plans from the head—they talk about why their approach is the smartest/best/most efficient, etc. The life planning approach that Susan and George teach is planning from the heart—a much different approach. I have had four new client meetings since the meeting, and all four are moving forward—and I think that much of it is because of this difference.

—Jason Maples, CFP, Colorado (attending the Kinder Institute of Life Planning program)

The Whats and Whys of Client Goals

The skillful ally can reassure the client that knowing how to reach goals is of far less concern that what those goals are and why they matter so much. By focusing first and foremost on the what and why—while letting go of the how temporarily—the strategic ally can help the client clarify the vision, identify the inner and outer obstacles that block the realization of that vision, and develop effective strategies to begin moving toward the accomplishment of the vision. In this process, the "how" comes at the end of the process rather than the beginning—where it tends to bring all hope, all movement, to a sudden halt.

The Life Planning Process

The life planning process parallels the traditional financial planning process—but with some differences. Both involve a series of meetings, a thorough review of the financials, goal-setting, and a final plan.

In life planning, knowing the client takes priority over any problem-solving for the first few hours—unless there is an urgent financial matter that must be addressed immediately. The initial meeting is one of listening to the client's concerns, needs, interests, expectations, and even dreams. While the planner mostly listens—with only rare comments or clarifying questions—the client has a chance to air all relevant concerns not only about money and finances but also about the circumstances that inspired the appointment in the first place.

By listening carefully and closely to the client's monologue, the planner is able to note issues where emotions surface, potential obstacles to the financial plan, and perhaps behavioral patterns and history. For the client, being heard without interruption, judgment, advice, or storytelling alleviates anxiety and inspires a tentative trust in the planner. At times, you will recognize red flags that indicate that the client is not appropriate for life planning. According to George Kinder, red flags for poor life planning clients include a history of anger with planners, overconsumption, an imperious or suspicious attitude, and a history of legal claims and lawsuits.

In the Know

As with all systems and processes in your office, a well-documented process for life planning will add efficiency and consistency to planning engagements and allow you to grow your business.

Designing the Dream

The next phase in the life planning process is discussion of the client's deepest goals and desires. These are discovered through questionnaires and discussions. The aim here is to help the client recognize and articulate what matters most and then to affirm that dream or value as the centerpiece of the financial plan. At the Kinder Institute, this process is called "lighting the torch." This process releases a burst of energy, characterized by excitement and inspiration, that moves the client to willingly address any potential obstacles, financial or otherwise, and resolve them in order to fulfill the dream.

Resolving Obstacles

Working with the client to identify and resolve both internal and external obstacles is the third phase of the life planning relationship. Internal obstacles include emotions such as fear or anxiety, doubtful or negative thoughts, and naïve beliefs about money or the likelihood of accomplishing profoundly important goals. External obstacles may include financial considerations, reactions of a spouse or other close family members or friends, health issues, time pressures, and so on. Most often, the final solutions to these obstacles are discovered by the client—following the skillful assistance of the planner in opening up possibilities, choices, and strategies during a collaborative, creative brainstorming process designed to help the client get "out of the box."

In the Know

The life planner stays continually aware of the truth that the client is the expert on his or her own life while the planner is the expert on how money and financial decisions may interface with the client's life choices.

Depending on the number and complexity of the obstacles to be resolved in order to gain momentum toward accomplishment of the goals, this phase of the planning relationship may continue over a period of time as scenarios are researched, explored, or tested. Lifestyle choices might be very significant—perhaps with a decision to downsize in order to realize a more meaningful goal, such as a new educational path or a career change.

An important consideration in this phase of the life planning engagement is how to integrate the significant goals and dreams of both spouses when working with a couple. One of the internal obstacles may well be that following their individual dreams of freedom will lead them onto separate and diverging paths—and that individual fulfillment may come at the cost of the relationship. The role of the planner here is to be confident that a shared path to the future can indeed be forged—a journey that will allow the partners to support each other in finding fulfillment. Again, most often the resolution of this potential dilemma comes from the clients themselves—rather than from the planner—as they commit themselves to being there for each other to accomplish what matters most.

Once the obstacles have been resolved and final choices made, the life plan is now clear and the financial planner takes over to integrate the life plan with the best financial strategies to ensure both implementation of the goals and prudent management of resources. This is the phase where all of the planner's financial skills and experience come into play to forge the final financial life plan.

Living the Plan

The final phase is the execution of the financial life plan. In this phase, the planner becomes more of a coach—staying in contact with the client through the accomplishment of the action steps that each has committed to implement. Your new role as a coach will help the client stay on track with frequent reminders of the inspiring goals that have been established. Often, new internal or external obstacles arise as steps are taken to execute the plan—and so the collaborative relationship continues until the goals are achieved.

In the Know

Don't keep your clients guessing about when they will hear from you again. Once you have completed the initial plan, schedule regular follow-up appointments to review how well the plan is going.

A Relationship for Life

Because life has a way of happening to all of us, the implementation of the financial life plan is not the end of the story. Having established a relationship of mutual trust and commitment—and collaborated to find the most efficient and timely path to the accomplishment of the client's most important life goals—both planner and client are now working toward a relationship for life. This bond will become the primary resource for working through transitions, sudden life changes, new goals as they emerge, significant financial impacts, and whatever else becomes influential in terms of the planning relationship going forward.

The Ongoing Need

The importance of having this ongoing relationship of trust where life's most significant events and aspirations—financial and otherwise—can be deeply explored and resolved can't be underestimated. Where else can clients find a skilled professional and strategic ally who is not approaching their life issues from a numbers perspective? The thrust of life planning is toward a fulfilled future, not a fractured past. Only the financial planner can effectively have these conversations with clients, because inevitably the financial considerations must be taken into account.

Natural Points of Change

At every phase of life—about every decade or so—it may be important for clients and the planner to come together to reflect, reconsider, and reorient in terms of new values, life goals, time management, allocation of resources, and so on (in addition to other sudden shifts or transitions that may appear along the way). The planner should recognize that life is an ongoing process of growth and development, and the enlightened decisions and choices of one stage may in fact become the obstacles to be resolved at the next stage.

This is perhaps the deeper meaning and dimension of being clients for life. And it implies that each phase, change, or transition is best navigated within the framework of a relationship of trust and commitment with a skillful ally who knows the client's entire story.

Practicing Life Planning

A financial planner who is drawn to the life planning approach needs to decide whether life planning is just another menu item or the basis and framework of the entire financial planning engagement. These questions raise a chorus of corollary issues for planners: How do I get paid for this service? How much more time will it require? What will be the benefits to the bottom line? How will it affect referrals? What about the percentage of assets under management? Will I get bogged down in emotional swamps that drain time and energy? Since I already do some of this work, do I really need specific training? Why do I need a life plan for myself?

Time and Money

When life planners take these questions one at a time, the first concern is usually how to get paid—and that is closely linked to the second concern: how much time will be required for this kind of planning engagement? Life planners are compensated in a variety of ways: fees for assets under management (AUM), fees for the creation of the plan, retainers, and commissions. Many rely on a mix of these options—perhaps charging a specific fee for the creation of the financial life plan and then transitioning to either AUM or a retainer to continue the relationship for life.

With practice, most planners find that the life planning approach is, in fact, far more efficient than a numbers-only financial planning engagement in that it gets right to the heart of the client's most profound desires and thus ensures execution because it is ultimately the client's plan. The typical life planning process takes three to five meetings of one-and-a-half to two hours each. Depending on the complexity of the finances and extent of assets to be managed, the fee for creating a financial life plan starts at around $2,500 and goes up from there. Some planners include their planning services as part of their remuneration from the assets under their management. For clients with less sophisticated financial needs, it takes just a few hours to go through the entire process. There is no single right approach; each finds what works best within the context of his or her practice.

Pitfalls _____

Do not abandon the life planning process as you stumble through your first few engagements or find a client who is not receptive to the process. Once you master the process, your delivery and efficiency will improve.

The Benefit to Your Business

The benefits to the bottom line are directly related to increased referrals and a greater percentage of assets under management—in addition to client retention. Clients feel so well served by the life planning approach that they encourage friends and family to also benefit from this service. Because of the degree of trust that is established, many clients bring 100 percent of their assets to the financial life planner. Client retention is something already discussed as clients literally become "clients for life."

Emotional Roadblocks

One concern often voiced by planners who are new to the life planning approach is becoming entangled in emotional situations where they don't have either the skills or the inclination to get deeply involved. While emotions often surface regarding money and life issues, training is available to give planners the tools they need to successfully navigate these emotionally charged circumstances without being pushed into the role of therapist (learn more at KinderInstitute.com or MitchAnthony.com). Emotions are normal responses to human events and situations.

With an effective skill set, the planner can competently manage emotional moments in a way that allows the client to be heard, to receive empathy, and to move on. When people meet with a financial planner, they know the terms of the engagement and that they are not talking with a psychotherapist—so there is no expectation that the planner should be able to provide anything more than warmth, empathy, and listening without judgment. Just that kind of presence is generally all that is needed.

Your clients need to know that a generous experience of having money and meaning in life is not only possible but also achievable. Of course, it all depends upon what each of us decides we must have to be fulfilled and content—a decision that is most skillfully and productively reached in collaboration and partnership with a financial life planner.

The Least You Need to Know

- Financial life planning is the process of drawing out your client's deepest desires and making those the centerpiece and purpose for creating and following a financial plan.

- Life planning helps to foster a trusting, caring client relationship.

- Life planning helps you focus on what is important to your clients and in turn often builds client relationships for life.

- Rookie life planners are often concerned that their clients will not appreciate the process and won't pay for the service.

- You can implement life planning immediately after you have been trained and understand the process.

- The first life plan you do should be for yourself. It is difficult to be genuine and appreciative of the process if you have not done it for yourself.

Part 3

Be Your Own Boss

Owning your own business is a realistic goal as a financial planner. Some good foresight, surrounding yourself with great people, and developing a business plan and sound marketing and communications plans will all increase your likelihood of building a great success story. Improving a business is like watching grass grow. If you sit there and watch it, nothing happens. But if you look back over a period of time, it needs mowing again. Take the time to work on your business regularly, and it too will grow.

Chapter 11

Going Out on Your Own

In This Chapter

- ◆ Deciding whether to own your own business
- ◆ When to make your move
- ◆ The importance of developing a good business plan
- ◆ Learning from these common mistakes
- ◆ Licenses you will need
- ◆ Meeting regulatory requirements

Owning your own business isn't for everyone, but it's a real possibility as a personal financial planner. Once you get the basics down, build a clientele, and gain a little capital and momentum, there are few barriers to entry.

There will be bumps in the road—some anticipated, others unexpected. You will wear many hats as the boss, clerk, financial planner, marketing representative, and salesperson. Everything falls back as your responsibility. You will make mistakes—plenty of them. But now more than ever, learning from your mistakes can be your best source of growth.

In this chapter, you will learn from the mistakes of others before you and see how to successfully launch your own financial planning business. Your new business plan, business structure, and licensing requirements can all be completed before you actually turn on the lights. The first year is the toughest. If you plan properly and minimize the surprises, you'll be on the road toward living another American dream.

Why Go Out on Your Own?

If you're an advisor in an established practice or a large firm, why would you look to change something that is apparently working? You are making money, have control of your destiny, and are on a track toward what many would consider success. So ... why bother? Independence, flexibility, control, value, ownership, culture, location, and fun are just a few of the reasons that immediately come to mind. Second to the great American dream of home ownership is the dream of owning your own business.

Many financial planners are already owners of their own businesses. In fact, the industry is just starting to break out of the cottage industry category after only 40 years of existence. Because so many of the jobs in the planning industry are incentive compensation only, you are pretty much already in control of your earnings destiny. But it is more than control over how much money you can make that brings out the ultimate in entrepreneurial spirit.

Making the Decision

The hardest part of making the break is the decision-making process. Like many entrepreneurs, your urge to move forward will drive you to dream, talk, and ask questions. You will dream of the day when you can see your name as the firm's name. You will talk to colleagues who have made the bold move before you and to those who chose not to make that move. You will ask questions—of your spouse, accountant, attorney, and industry leaders—looking for encouragement and recommendations on what to do and what not to do. It can be a very confusing time that can last for years.

Start this decision-making process by thinking about where you are now and where you want to be in 5, 10, or 20 years. Analyze what you like about your current situation and what you would do to make it better if you could. Also, think about what you don't like about your current situation and what you would

In the Know

Talk to others who have made this leap before you. Members of the many great professional organizations are very happy to share their experience with you and guide you through this decision-making process.

eliminate. Sometimes these liberating moments of visualization are all it takes to make the decision. But for the analytical types—those who are really intent on fact-finding and follow-through—you'll need to have answers before you dive in.

You need to think about your resources, too. What are the tools, systems, assistance, and services that you receive in your current firm? Can you replace these, or can you live without them? Much of it depends on the type of practice you have built and the expectations of your clients. The good news is that in this technologically driven, outsourced business environment of the twenty-first century, there is little that you can't reproduce or outsource—even for the smallest of startup financial planning businesses. (Many advisors start out with an office in the home to avoid overhead. Chapter 12 talks more about this topic.)

Evaluate your clients and your ability to attract new clients. You should tell a few of your better clients about your plans to start your own business early in the process. You may be pleasantly surprised at the encouragement and willingness to follow you or their impression of just how important your old firm environment is to their satisfaction. Be prepared, however, to tell them why it would be in their best interests for you to be on your own. Being very clear about what's in it for them will increase the number of positive responses you receive. Assure them that they will receive the same or better service and tell them why.

 Pitfalls

Beware any employment agreements that may preclude you from taking or suggesting that clients leave the firm that you are currently with. The larger firms have litigated and fought intensely against advisors who have solicited clients against the terms of their agreements with the firms.

Your centers of influence and referral sources are probably a big reason for your success as a financial planner as a member of another firm. You must ask them about their thoughts of you as an independent business owner financial planner. Would they still see you as someone they would continue to refer new clients to? Would your being on your own cause them to alter the flow of referrals, either more or less?

The Challenges and Risks

As the famous bumper sticker says, "Stuff Happens." So—be prepared. To make this move, you have to be a bit of a risk-taker. Some of the challenges are the same for a new financial planning business as for, say, opening a music store.

You will need to register your new business in the town where you plan to open up shop. In a small town, there may be only one person who does this—and if they are on vacation or out sick the day or week you want to register, there comes challenge number one. It's not a big headache, but a headache nevertheless. Other typical small-business challenges are simply related to the fact that you now have to do all of the things that someone else used to do for you. Printing business cards, paying the bills, getting phone and Internet hookups, and knowing that there is no one above you to ask for help.

The largest risk that you'll face is failure. Failure typically comes from being under-capitalized, or not having enough money saved for correct startup. I'll talk in greater detail about capitalization later in this chapter. But for now, just make sure you know that you can't do this on a shoestring budget. The other risks include some things you won't know about until you get there—and others that you should be able to anticipate.

If you come from a larger firm, you can anticipate that you may have restrictive agreements from soliciting your clients. That doesn't mean that you can't set up shop—it just means that you can't directly solicit your clients from moving to your new firm. It will be up to you to publicize your new business in such a way that these clients will not have to search high and low to find you—and that they will do so. There is nothing in your agreement with the firm that would restrain free trade and prevent these clients from finding you and making the change to your new firm. Depending on your agreement, a friendly announcement letter alerting them that you have left the old firm, without a solicitation, may be permissible.

Pitfalls

Expect the worst to be said about you to your clients after you leave. Some office managers will fabricate stories of legal problems, ethical concerns, and financial problems. Some will say that you have left the industry and moved to another part of the country. This situation often brings out the worst in your former colleagues.

Another risk may surprise you a bit. Remember your colleagues from the old shop and all of the after-work parties and good times you had? Throw them right out the window after you've left. They will solicit your clients like a pit bull going after a bone. Sometimes the stories that they'll fabricate about your departure will be untrue and infuriating, so expect it. You may even find that office managers will offer bonuses to the remaining advisors who reel in the largest number of your former clients.

Another risk is you. First, your ability to act as a business owner must be assessed. Maybe you think you've got what it takes, but don't just assume that because you are a good financial planner, you'll be a good business owner. Your skills as a business owner need to include dealing with adversity, managing people, and honing your leadership abilities. In Chapter 13, I'll talk about knowing your strengths and your weaknesses. Modern management theory suggests that you can maximize your success by focusing on your strengths. But it also says that you can't be horrible at your weaknesses, either—even if you intend to outsource or hire based on those deficiencies.

Another risk associated with you is your health and ability to work. Health is a big concern for you as the chief cook and dishwasher of your new firm. So do not even think of starting on your own unless you have practiced what you preach as a financial planner. Be well protected with health, disability, long-term care, and life insurance. Be sure to have your own personal or family financial life plan complete before you get started. Agreement with your spouse or significant other will help you through the startup phase and during any unforeseen bumps in the road. If your new business startup has significant overhead right out of the gate, consider disability overhead insurance that will pay the salaries and other overhead while you are recovering or trying to sell the business.

Other factors may inhibit your ability to work the rigorous hours of a startup business owner. Do you have a family? Family issues may inhibit your ability to put in the time. Make sure that everyone in the family is well covered with all of the basic insurances. The loss of a spouse is devastating enough without the pressure of trying to run a new business. Now, compound that as a single parent along with the loss of a salary and child-rearing assistance—and you're in trouble. Make sure that both you and your spouse have adequate life insurance to cover you to hire help in the event that you need to do so.

The Rewards

Just like rented cars and apartments don't get the same love and affection as the car and the home that you own, neither will someone else's business. The pride of ownership instills confidence and almost forces you to give it your best, on all fronts, each and every day.

Until recently, planners rarely thought about the value of their businesses. But in recent years, a whole new breed of planners has popped up—and they are actually interested in acquiring small practices. A focus on creating value was thought about only for your clients, but now it is clear that as any other business owner would think, the value of a planning practice must be considered.

You can now control the culture that you create, the products and services that you offer, the firm's pricing schedule, and where you locate this business. If you don't want more than a two-mile commute from your house, then have it your way! If you want to offer fee-based financial planning and your prior employer only offered commission-based planning, go for it.

The ultimate reward you are probably looking for is financial—but that can't be your primary purpose. If some of the other rewards I have already mentioned don't really turn you on—and it's all about the money—think again. You have to love everything else about being a business owner to make the financial rewards work for you.

Some of the early financial rewards will come in your payout rate. As an employee of a larger firm, you are probably getting about 30 to 50 percent of the revenue that you produce for the firm. As an independent, you'll easily raise that to 65 percent—and maybe even as high as 90 percent if you still need a broker dealer or plan to sell insurance products. Payout rate will vary depending on a number of factors. It will vary based on the services you receive, the volume of business you transact, and the products you sell.

Walking the Walk

As a financial advisor, you don't spend the percentage rate of your payout or your contract level. You can only spend the net revenue. When looking for a broker dealer or insurance brokerage partner, make certain you find one that brings value to your practice beyond a high percentage contract. There are firms that will partner with you to keep your overhead low by absorbing significant and costly services; this will greatly enhance your net revenue as a personal financial planner.

—Tim Ash, president, Ash Brokerage Corporation, Fort Wayne, Indiana

If you plan to go the fee-only route and will not be receiving commission compensation from any products or third parties, you'll actually keep 100 percent of what you bill clients. Now, that doesn't mean your net revenue will be 100 percent. Of course you will have expenses in connection with the generation of those revenues.

While the gross revenue bump is a good thing, it is possible that your net revenue will drop in the first year or two. The best advice is to keep your overhead as low as possible when you start out and only add overhead as your business will allow.

When to Make the Move

The time to make the move is when the list of things that you would change or eliminate significantly outweigh the benefits you receive. There is great danger in making the move too soon—and equal peril in waiting too long.

Anytime you are limited or restricted in choosing to do what is right for your clients is an immediate signal to move. All firms will change the rules from time to time because of what is in the best interests of the firm and its shareholders. You and your clients may be secondary—but most firms know that in order to benefit their shareholders, they need to keep clients and their advisors satisfied.

Pitfalls _____

Timing is everything. Move too soon, and the startup ramp may be too steep. Wait too long, and it may be too difficult to extricate yourself and your clients. Be thinking about this from day one in the business if it is a part of your long-term plan. That will help you recognize when the time is right.

As you grow as a planner, you'll settle into a style or maybe even a specialty that may or may not be well supported by your firm. Sometimes the culture that appealed to you as a rookie just doesn't fit your style as you mature as a financial planner. These situations clearly indicate that it is time to move from those firms, but don't let these feelings misguide you into thinking it's time to go out on your own. It could be the first sign—but not the only sign. Look around at other employment opportunities in addition to planning what it may be like to start your own business.

Do you have enough clients and gross revenues to become an effective business? Can you make the move and afford to start a business? The best you can do is to make an educated, informed decision. Every business needs a plan, and if you made it this far, now is the time for your first plan as a business owner.

A Preliminary Business Plan

Many businesses limp along forever without good business plans. Others are phenomenally successful with a lot of luck and no plans. But any competent business consultant will tell you that without a business plan, your odds of a catastrophic failure at some point are much greater.

A preliminary business plan is just that: your first try. A business plan is not something that is bound in a pretty binder and sits on the shelf to prove to some outside party that you have one; rather, it is the road map to your success. It should be a breathing, living document that provides clarity for you and for anyone who works for your organization. It should also be changed as you mature and grow. It needs to adapt to changing environments and situations that may differ from the day that you create the plan.

The business plan can provide valuable guidance to both new and existing employees to guide their actions. It will also give them insight into how to best help you get to the goal line. If you are a really good manager, you will have incentive compensation arrangements tied to tasks that must be performed in the implementation of your plan.

Ready to Start?

To begin your business plan, you will need a place where you can go without distractions. If you have employees at the office or little children at home, neither of these will work. Either give your employees the day out or select a comfortable off-site location where you can be creative and think. Block out an entire day just to plan. You may finish in half or three-quarters of a day, but plan on the whole day. If you finish early, your reward can be an afternoon with your spouse, pampering at a spa, or doing whatever else makes you feel good.

Consider holding this meeting with a facilitator or consultant. Especially if this is your first time with the business planning process, a good facilitator can really add value. Continue this process and review your plan quarterly the first time you create one, then at least annually as your business matures.

Mission and Vision

Mission and vision, a starting point for many business plans, are as important for the one-man band, new business as they are for major public companies. Some say it is more important for the small business because it will help prevent distractions and keep you, the owner without a boss, focused. You can ask yourself every day, "Is this task helping my business accomplish its mission and achieve its vision?"

Your mission is a brief statement that tells clients what you stand for, how you help your clients, and why you are in business. It will help serve as the guiding light for you and your staff regarding how you want to conduct business. Your mission statement should inspire you and be something that you can turn to when you need a lift and some encouragement. The mission statement might read something like this: "Our mission is to guide our clients through the financial complexities of life while managing their financial resources with prudence in an objective, caring environment."

The vision for your firm is about what you want it to become—not what it is today, but rather a picture of your future as vividly as you can construct it. That vision should be so clear to you that your subconscious grabs hold of that vision and automatically causes you to behave in a way that draws you toward the vision.

In the Know

Don't keep your mission statement a secret. Publish it in firm newsletters and let your clients know. Many successful firms even frame it and hang it in many places around the office to reinforce the message.

It may sound like dreaming, but develop a clear picture in your mind of the vision for your firm. Where do you want to be? What will your company look like? What will you do with your day-to-day functions? Think of the vision for your firm like the box of a jigsaw puzzle. Have you ever tried to put together a puzzle without a vision as to what it should look like upon completion?

Goal Setting

Unless you write your goals down, you'll never accomplish them. Studies have shown that those who have written goals achieve them faster and with greater consistency. Whatever it is that you wish to accomplish with your business should be written down and kept in a conspicuous place so that it's always in the front of your mind.

A few rules about goals:

- **Make them specific.** Generic goals such as "I want to grow my business" or "I want to take more time off" are not specific enough. How much growth? How many days off? Also, document why you want to achieve any of these specific goals. The "why" will trigger your deep emotion and remind you why you need to focus on the daily tasks needed to reach the goal.

- **Make sure they are measurable.** If you can't quantify or measure your goals, you'll never know for sure whether you are on track or achieving your objectives. You will eventually want employee assistance with goal achievement, so measurements will help them know how they are doing without you needing to tell them. If you have goals relating to client satisfaction or numbers of referrals, you'll need to develop a scorecard just to define success.

◆ **Make your goal achievable.** Don't be unrealistic and set yourself up for failure. On the other hand, you don't want to set goals that are way too low just so you can pat yourself on the back.

◆ **Set a time frame.** To set a realistic time frame, look at your history. Evaluate how long it took you to get from point A to point B, and work within those parameters. You may accelerate your time frame a bit because of your experience and resources. You should also break your time down into smaller increments and set short milestones to accomplish the tactics that you know you need to complete in order to meet your goal. For example, if you want to add 12 new "A" clients this year, and you know that you'll need to meet 36 new prospects to find them, make a goal of meeting at least 3 per month. If you've got some months that are heavy with vacations and holidays, know that you'll need to have more meetings during other months to compensate for your time off.

Capital Required

According to the Small Business Administration, one of the most common reasons that small businesses fail is the lack of proper capitalization. We're talking not enough money to even make a go of it. In your financial planning business, even if you are successful at keeping your overhead low, you'll still need a fair amount of money to start the business.

There is always a drought of revenue for the first few months. It isn't automatic that the day you open the doors, revenue will begin to flow. You need to send forms to clients authorizing the transfer of their accounts to your new firm. This process alone may take you several months. Some clients will be away; others will simply ignore the mail; and some will not want to join you at your new business.

There are a number of startup expenses. You've got to form the entity, register the business, print business cards and stationery, rent an office, build a compliance manual, and buy or lease equipment and lots of other things (see Chapter 12 for details on setting up shop). You need to quantify as specifically as possible all of the costs that you'll incur to get the business off the ground. It could take weeks to finish this task. You may need to meet with sales reps, shop for prices or financing, and learn what options you have before committing to something that you'll later regret. Consider working with an accountant or banker.

In the Know

Think about arranging a line of credit or home equity line in advance of needing it. Qualification may be difficult if you apply during a period of an income decline or startup phase.

You should also have a nest egg for the unexpected. You should have at least six months of living expenses to see yourself through the unknown. You could get sick; your building could become flooded; or some other natural disaster could keep you from your office for months.

Cash Flow Expectations

If there is one thing that you should not do, it's being overly optimistic with regard to your cash flow expectations. In fact, do yourself a favor and expect less than you collected last year as a member of another firm just to be safe.

Be conservative in your revenue projections. Revenue projections can be extremely volatile if based upon unknowns, such as your marketing success or assumptions about growth of client assets due to market performance.

Common Mistakes

Every business owner makes mistakes; the key is to learn from them and not repeat them. According to the U.S. Small Business Administration, 50 percent of small businesses fail in the first year—and 95 percent fail within five years. There are no specific statistics for financial planners, but hopefully you will take this information to heart and plan your business startup as well as you do your clients' financial lives ... and be part of the successful minority.

Poor Management

You are a financial planner, not necessarily a business manager. Have you ever set up a system for client billing, collecting receivables, mail merges, or hiring staff? If yes, then you probably don't need to worry about poor management. But if not, then you need to be very aware of this reason for business failure.

You can't become a great manager overnight, but you can surround yourself with great management pretty darn quick. In the early stages of planning your expenses, interview and hire people who can help you with day-to-day management. If you look hard enough, you can probably find a retired person or someone who is raising a family and has excellent skills for managing your small business. You may even hire someone to help you hire the right people if you've never done that. It may be a bit too detailed for a small business startup, but *Topgrading: How Leading Companies Win by Hiring, Coaching, and Keeping the Best People* by Bradford Smart (see Appendix C) is one of the best books you can find on the topic of surrounding yourself with the best people.

Low Sales

Lower sales than expected really crush the undercapitalized business startup. If you're not a sales professional but rather more of a planning technician, make sure that you have a good marketing and sales strategy that can be implemented by someone else. If you think that low sales are even a remote possibility, then be extra careful to have very little overhead.

Right Business, Wrong Reason

You may have chosen the right profession for you—but perhaps the reason you went out on your own was not a good one. Among the wrong reasons that are business killers: you did it because you thought that you would make a killing. Another may be that you thought you'd have more time for your family or for other personal pursuits. Unless you have a huge staff from day one, this reason may not be good, either. At least in the early days of being a business owner, don't be surprised if you are working nights and weekends regularly. Many small business owners start out this way and never break from it.

Perhaps you thought that you'd never have to answer to anyone else again. Not likely. As a financial planner, you'll always have to answer to regulators and clients. Furthermore, if you are a member of a broker dealer or are selling as an independent insurance agent, you'll have to do things their way.

Spending Too Much

Maybe you don't need that huge mahogany desk or the expensive Oriental rug in the waiting area. Blowing your budget in the startup phase can be a fatal blunder. The same could be said of salaries, so consider outsourcing or hiring part-time employees before you hire a staff you will not need until your business grows.

Sometimes your startup goes well—so well, in fact, that you decide to expand too soon. Try not to confuse your early success with your ability to expand your business rapidly. You would be better off, especially in the early stages, to grow the slow and steady way.

Lack of Planning

There's a saying about people and their financial planning failures: "People don't plan to fail; they fail to plan." The same could be said about your financial planning business. You didn't start with failure in the forefront of your mind. How embarrassing would it be for a financial planner to fail? Follow the chapters in this book very carefully, and create a plan for success.

Will I Need More Licenses?

More likely than not, you will need more licenses as you go out on your own—although your required licenses will depend on the type of business you are trying to build. As a fee-only planner, the only license you'll need is the Series 65 or 66. You should already have that license by this stage in your career. But if you do not, remember that the Series 66 exam is easier to pass than the Series 65 and gives you the same privileges (see Chapter 3).

If you are going to be selling securities products that will pay you commissions, you may need to obtain supervisors licenses. The National Association of Securities Dealers (NASD) and Securities and Exchange Commission (SEC) are very strict about supervision, and a securities supervisor needs a separate license just for that. A big part of a broker dealer self-policing effort comes in the form of supervising the activities of its registered representatives. A registered principal must review that representative's client correspondence, both incoming and outgoing. All e-mail must be retained and reviewed. All advertising and solicitations must be preapproved. All transactions need to be reviewed. Each broker dealer has a written compliance and supervision manual that is well over 100 pages. These spell out exactly what the compliance review requirements are for the firm and for any registered principal.

It is possible for the broker dealer's home office to provide you with a registered principal who is responsible for supervising your activities. Some broker dealers have geographical limits and size limitations. They will not supervise your office if you are more than a specified distance from the home office or have more than a certain number of registered reps in your location. Each firm sets their own numbers with respect to distance and size of office.

 In the Know _____

Try to get these licenses while you are still with your existing firm. Some will let you; others will not. If your firm will not, you can still study and prepare for the licenses so you are ready to sit for the exam as soon as you start on your own.

If you do plan to grow your business and are interested in maximizing its value, you would be better off becoming an office of supervisory jurisdiction (OSJ) and being your own supervisor or OSJ manager. You are held to higher regulatory standards and are responsible for the supervision and activity review for every licensed registered rep in your office, including yourself. But it is worth the extra effort. It doesn't actually have to be you to assume the role; it can be someone you hire. You should still obtain the additional licenses. With the proper licenses, you will never be held hostage by an employee who decides to leave.

Your business is more valuable to a third-party buyer as an OSJ manager, rather than having a manager from the home office. It is also easier for you to change broker dealer firms or sell your firm in the future if you have an OSJ manager on-site.

Series 24

Series 24 is the general securities principal exam and entitles the holder to supervise and manage branch activities. Before taking the Series 24 exam, you must have your Series 7 license. The Series 24 exam is administered by the NASD and includes topics such as corporate securities, investment banking, *REITs*, trading and market timing, sales supervision, customer accounts, and regulatory guidelines.

def•i•ni•tion

A **REIT** is a real estate investment trust. REITs come in many varieties—both publicly traded and non-publicly traded. REITs are intended to offer clients a way to diversify their portfolios into professionally managed real estate without needing to be a landlord.

The Series 24 exam is composed of 150 questions. Students are given 210 minutes to complete it. The test is composed of four-option multiple-choice questions and is computer-based, although no special computer skills are required. Students are provided scratch paper, a pencil, and a simple calculator at the testing center. Students must receive a score of 70 percent or better to pass.

Series 26

Series 26 is the Investment Company/Variable Contracts Limited Principal Exam. This exam qualifies an individual to supervise the sale of investment company products (mutual funds) and variable products by limited representatives who hold a Series 6. This license is limited and not recommended for someone who wants to build a holistic financial planning practice. You will be precluded from selling REITs, tax-free college savings plans (529 plans), and stocks or bonds. A Series 6 or 7 is required to sit for the Series 26 exam.

The Series 26 exam is administered by the NASD and is composed of 110 questions. Students are given 150 minutes to complete the multiple-choice exam, which is computer-based (but no special computer skills are required). Students are provided scratch paper, a pencil, and a simple calculator at the testing center. Students must receive a score of 70 percent or better to pass.

Series 53

Series 53 is the municipal securities principal exam. While not many financial planners will be active municipal securities traders, some will invest client assets in tax-free municipal bonds. Recently, however, with the popularity of tax-free college savings plans (also known as Section 529 plans), more planners are sitting for the Series 53 exam. 529 plans are considered municipal securities and require a Series 7 to sell them (and a Series 53 to supervise these trades).

This exam is for individuals who supervise the activities of municipal securities representatives. The Series 53 exam is administered by the NASD and consists of 100 questions. Students are given 180 minutes to complete the exam. The test contains multiple-choice questions and is computer-based, but no special computer skills are required. Students are provided scratch paper, a pencil, and a simple calculator at the testing center. Students must receive a score of 70 percent or better to pass. You must have a Series 7 or 52 to sit for this exam.

Series 9

The Series 9—a supervisor's license for options trading—is another license to put in the "Not Likely" column for a financial planner. Not many planners trade options, but some use *option contracts* as a hedge against volatility in underlying stock positions.

The New York Stock Exchange (NYSE) and other self-regulatory organizations require its members and employees to pass this qualification exam to become registered to supervise the purchase and sale of options. The NASD administers the Series 9 exam. It is a 90-minute, 55-question exam dealing with the regulation of options. You must score at least 70 percent to pass and become eligible for registration. Series 7 is a prerequisite for this exam.

def•i•ni•tion

An **option contract** is a security where an investor buys the right, but not the obligation, to buy or sell a security at a specified price.

Your Firm's Regulatory Requirements

If you are offering financial planning services for a fee or investment advisory services for a fee instead of a commission, your firm may need to register as an investment advisor. If you intend to offer these services—but as a part of another advisory firm—there will be no registration requirement on your part. You, along with your Series 65 or 66 license, will be an investment advisor representative of another registered investment advisor firm.

If, however, you want to be more autonomous and independent, you will need to register your own firm as a registered investment advisor. At this time, the rules require that you register with either with your home state or the SEC. If your total assets under management are under $25 million, you will become state-registered. If your total assets under management are greater than $25 million, you will register with the SEC. Registration of investment advisory firms is a fast-growing area of practice as advisors migrate to fee-based investment advice and fee-only advising. There is talk among the regulatory authorities of changing the registration thresholds to higher numbers for SEC registration. Visit www.sec.gov for the latest news.

Dealing with registration and compliance for the first time can be difficult and time-consuming. Hire a consultant to help you through the forms and process to save time and to do it right the first time.

The Least You Need to Know

- The decision to start your own business should be based on a business plan. A solid plan will increase your odds of success.

- Making your move to business owner should be based on your vision, resources, and ability to attract new clients.

- Having adequate capital and cash reserves for maintaining your lifestyle during the startup phase is mandatory to avoid stress and failure.

- Have clear, written goals for a greater likelihood of achieving your vision for success.

- Avoiding the common mistakes of new financial planning businesses will save you time and money, and help you achieve a satisfactory level of success sooner.

- Proper licensing and staying in compliance with the complicated regulatory structure becomes your responsibility as the owner of a financial planning business.

How to Set Up Shop

In This Chapter

- ◆ Choosing your location
- ◆ Behind the scenes business basics
- ◆ Essential equipment for operation
- ◆ Creating a professional image

You've done it. You've crunched the numbers, explored the pros and cons of going out on your own, developed a comprehensive business plan, and made the decision to hang out your own shingle. But the due diligence must continue, for there are a number of things to consider before you pass out those business cards. What type of insurance do you need? Should you retain an attorney? How should you choose from the proprietary financial planning software available? What type of collateral literature do you need to send the right image message?

Going out on your own does have its appeal, but keep in mind that by choosing this option, you've essentially created a double whammy. Not only are you starting a business from scratch—you're also developing yourself as a professional practitioner.

How positive an impact you have on your clients' lives may be the bottom line to a career as a financial planner, but also important is the way in which you conduct business. That includes where you operate from, the service professionals you retain, and how you get the word out that you're in business.

Location, Location, Location

As someone who is likely fiscally prudent, you may want to save some cash during the initial startup years of your financial planning practice by operating from a home office. However, the "image consultant" in you recognizes that perception and success often go hand-in-hand. That old saying about "dressing for success" can also apply to your chosen office space.

In addition to the type of office you have, the actual geography is something to consider. You do have the option of having an office close to your home, but perhaps more important is an office that is close to where your clients will be. It doesn't have to be smack dab in the middle of a major city, but in the middle of a major business area of an upscale office park may be important. You need to factor in the perception and the reality of the types of clients that you will attract. Some clients may be put off by office space that is obviously very expensive, and others would want to know that your business is successful enough to afford the best.

Cost is also an issue. You shouldn't be too frugal but will need to spend money on other areas that may be more important, such as staff and technology. Remember that the actual cost of the office is only one of many expenses that you'll encounter—so don't blow your budget on rent alone.

In days past, the only location options for a startup financial planner were either a home office or a costly rented space. Today, there are many other options to consider—so let's explore your choices.

In the Home

Working at home is cost-efficient, and the only commuting you'll have to do is to a client's location. You may also save on wardrobe expenses, because when you're working at home you can dress in sweatpants if you like. But there are a few important principles to keep in mind when creating a home office. Adequate space and privacy, good lighting, a high-speed Internet connection, and an area that can be expanded if necessary are vital components.

You need separate phone lines and a separate voicemail/answering machine for when you are not at your desk. Many at-home professionals also make extensive use of a cell phone. You'll still need a separate business line for calls that may need better quality than a cell line—and to send or receive faxes.

Working from an area that is somewhat isolated from the main living quarters is also advisable to avoid distractions. And remember, it is one thing to work from a home space if you are a staff of one—but you must consider the comfort level of any associates you retain. You need to provide a practical working environment, regardless of the limited number of hours your employees may keep. If you plan to see clients at your location, take care to create a comfortable meeting place where clients feel relaxed discussing personal information.

Pitfalls

Working from home for the first time can present challenges that you've never encountered. Make sure that you set ground rules with the rest of your family so that you have uninterrupted quiet time and a productive work environment.

Sharing Office Space

If you're operating on a startup shoestring budget and must remain home office-bound—but you occasionally require a more upscale location to meet clients—consider the shared office space concept. Also commonly referred to as serviced office space, business centers, executive suites, and even virtual offices, this approach is less costly than an office rental or lease.

How it works is fairly basic. This turnkey alternative to the long-term rental can typically be contracted for as short a period as three months. Depending on the location and cost, a shared office usually includes basic amenities such as access to faxes and copiers, the use of office furniture, and of course conference and boardrooms. Premium services, such as personalized telephone answering, high-speed Internet connections, and mail delivery are also normally available for a price. The shared office option can also act as a marketing tool for the newly anointed financial planner. You can choose to share your space with professionals in related but noncompeting practices, thereby creating a networking opportunity for you and your virtual officemates.

Another option in sharing space is to rent an office or two from an existing professional. It is common for new financial planning businesses to rent a portion of an office from an existing law or accounting firm. Because of the long-term nature of many commercial leases, most professional service firms must build future growth into their office plans and will have excess capacity in their facilities. This, too, has the dual possibility of networking and sharing clients with the firm that becomes your landlord.

Make sure you look at all of the costs associated with a shared office environment, however. The use of conference facilities may cost up to $50 per hour. If you use your conference room for four hours per day, you'd be better off just renting an office yourself.

Renting Office Space

Maybe you have an adequate budget to invest in your business or are off to a running start with a solid roster of clients. For whatever reasons you decide to go the rental office space route, keep a few things in mind. Don't overestimate the amount of space you'll need. The rule of thumb is you'll need about 250 square feet per employee. That estimate includes waiting areas and a conference room. You'll need more if you want to have a kitchen facility or a nicer conference room. But you must take the future into account when deciding—recognizing that your needs may grow along with your practice. Ideally, you may find a landlord who will offer you the option of moving to a larger (or smaller) space in the building, should your needs change. If you do take more space than you actually need at first, maybe you can find another practitioner to sublet some space from you to defray a portion of the cost.

Take a long, hard look at a few spaces before making a commitment. It would be wise to engage a professional commercial real estate broker to help you. Generally, your cost for space will not be any greater if you are represented by a professional. They know the landlords, the local market, and the types of deals that you can strike. In a commercial lease, everything is up for negotiation. Rarely will you find an office that you can use in as-is condition. There will be paint, carpet, wiring, signage, and maybe significant alterations needed. A good commercial Realtor can let you know who should be paying for what and how that relates to the rent you should pay. A Realtor will also save you a lot of time and not take you to areas or buildings that are not in line with your expectations.

In the Know

Hire an attorney to review any lease before you sign it. There may be some language that seems standard but may bind you in a way that may surprise you if you want to make improvements later or change the signage.

Basic Business Essentials

Going into business requires much more than a desire to be your own boss. Regardless of whether you're the star of the show or the leading character in a cast of many, you need to have the right infrastructure in place. With the appropriate basic, yet vital, business essentials taken care of, your fledgling operation will run more smoothly—allowing for more time to spend on what really matters: building a reputable financial advisory practice based on your hard-earned credentials and sound advice.

Business Banking

You might be tempted to adopt a mix-and-match approach to banking when you first open your doors as a financial planner, especially if you're working from a home office. But of all people, you should know better. If you're going to run a business, then be prepared to run it seriously. It never pays to mix personal and business banking, and here are a few reasons why.

You're operating a business, not a hobby—and that's precisely the message you'll need to deliver to the Internal Revenue Service (IRS). You'll have an easier time relaying that message if you set up a separate business account with your banking institution of choice. Remember, going into business should be a money-making proposition—not a money-losing one. If you mingle your business with personal banking accounts, chances are good that you'll miss a number of potential business deductions. Also, separate business statements provide for a clearer audit trail. And down the road when your business grows, you may require financing to move to a bigger operation or take on additional staff. The longer period of time that you've held a business banking account, the better chance you'll have of obtaining financing. If you incorporate or form a limited liability company (LLC), it is even more important to have separate bank accounts from the first day you start the business.

Now, let's go back to that all-important aspect of perception. It looks more professional when clients make out a check to your practice's name, rather than to your personal name.

> **In the Know**
>
> If you are affiliated with a broker dealer, you may be able to use some of its cash management services and avoid the need for a traditional bank account entirely. Cash management services offered by brokers offer the same benefits as banks—except for lending services.

So how do you choose the right small business banking account? It's homework time again. Small business banking options can be quite varied, both in features and fees. If you've had a good relationship with the institution where you conduct your personal banking, talk to the folks there about business account choices. Also ask other practitioners about their choice. You may also receive good guidance from your attorney or CPA. And remember, fees incurred by a business account are totally tax-deductible as an expense—and while you should look for the lowest fees you can find, this is something you must do. So don't squabble over nickels.

Business Insurance

Several types of insurance are required, depending on the size and scope of your business. The most important is professional liability insurance—also known as *errors and omission* (E&O) insurance. If you are carrying a securities license and are registered with a broker dealer, you must have E&O insurance. Most broker dealers will have a group policy that is optional or even mandatory. If you are not securities-licensed, there may be no higher authority requiring you to have this coverage (except for your business common sense). If you sell insurance products, most carriers will require proof of coverage with minimum coverage limits before they'll allow you to represent their products.

Factors to consider when choosing your E&O insurance will include the premium, deductible, and services included. Some policies will cover financial planning and exclude tax preparation. Others may include both and exclude insurance sales. Make sure that the policy you choose covers you, your firm, and any employees you have for the services and products that you offer. Similarly, make sure that any other professionals who you work in conjunction with or refer clients to are properly covered. If there is a professional liability claim, the client typically sues all members of the planning team. If your other team members are properly covered, your case will get the benefit of their attorneys and insurance company joining in on the defense.

Property insurance and liability insurance are also at the top of the list. Property coverage would replace the contents of your office in the event of a loss. The contents would include the obvious, such as computers, furniture, and phones. But also consider coverage for the cost to reproduce client files, works of art, or the costs to relocate your office. Ask your agent about business interruption insurance. This coverage will pay you money to cover overhead during a time when you cannot possibly operate the business. Fires, earthquakes, and hurricanes are examples of perils that can keep you from accessing your office for a long time.

If you maintain a staff, you are mandated by law to pay unemployment insurance and disability insurance in accordance with state regulations. Don't play games in this area to try and save money. In the event of a claim that should have been covered by this type of coverage, a judge may order the claim to be paid from your personal assets. You should also consider health and medical insurance for your employees. Make sure that you comply with all local laws regarding discrimination and who must be covered. A professional specializing in group or individual health plans can advise you with respect to these regulations, which vary from state to state.

Whether your business owns vehicles or you (or an employee) use personal vehicles for business, make sure that your business policies cover you. If you have outside company directors or officers other than yourself, consider insurance for them. Known as D&O insurance, this policy protects a corporation's officers and directors from personal liability in the event of a claim or lawsuit against the company.

A key-person life insurance policy is also encouraged. Key-person life insurance is a policy taken out on the owner of the business or any key person involved in it. This important insurance will provide the business with the liquidity to weather any storm caused by the loss of a key person and will allow a business to continue operation in the event of the key person's death. If you are the owner and the only key person, you still need this coverage. It will provide your family with the resources to replace your earnings and to keep the business afloat long enough to sell it to another practitioner.

> **In the Know**
>
> Business insurance is a specialty that is separate from personal insurance. Speak to a business insurance specialist—maybe even one who has other clients in the financial planning business—before you just accept what your personal insurance agent recommends.

Professionals whose businesses are located in their homes have to pay special attention to those insurance needs. It's not that you'll need anything different than what I've already discussed, but it's the form of it. Most self-employed people out of their homes don't realize that many of the traditional homeowner's policies do not cover home-based businesses unless they specifically add that coverage to the basic policy. If the FedEx delivery person slips and falls on your icy porch while delivering an important business document, you may not be covered in the event of a lawsuit unless you have in-home business coverage.

Retain an Attorney

You may look at hiring an attorney as just one more expense that you'd rather not make, but it's wise to look into retaining a business lawyer to assist with establishing your entity, writing contracts, negotiating agreements, and to supply you with corporate and employment advice. Chances are good that you have already dealt with an attorney you can trust or know someone who can recommend an experienced business lawyer.

Keep positive thoughts about not ever having to retain that other variety of attorney: a litigator. Be aware, however, that if you or your business is ever named in a lawsuit, you would be best served by a skilled litigation attorney who can represent your business in court. A major reason for errors and omissions coverage is that after you pay the deductible, the insurance company bears your cost of defense. It will often select an experienced litigation defense attorney to represent you.

Accounting and Taxes

Keeping accurate books is one of the hallmarks of a successful business. You can choose from any number of record-keeping systems, but what it comes down to is the ability to demonstrate a summary of your business transactions—in short, gross income, deductions, and assets and liabilities.

The types of records that you should keep for tax purposes are fairly all-encompassing, but here's the list:

- Gross receipt documents, including bank statements and deposit slips, receipt books, invoices, credit card charge slips, and Form 1099-MISC

- Purchase records, including canceled checks, credit card slips, cash register tape receipts, and invoices

- Expense documents for costs you incur to conduct business in addition to purchases, including canceled checks, account statements, and invoices

You must also be able to substantiate travel, entertainment, or gift expense deductions. The best way is to maintain a calendar, electronic or manual, that shows who you went to visit and the round-trip mileage involved. For entertainment expenses, the IRS requires that you document who you saw, what the business purpose was, and the outcome. Beware that outlandish business entertainment expenses such as skyboxes or chartered airplanes can be disallowed or severely limited by the IRS.

In addition to the IRS, state or federal regulators can audit your financial records as a financial planner. Without warning, a regulator can come to your office for a routine compliance audit—which would include a review of your books and records.

A good manual system will suffice, but with accounting software that is so inexpensive, you should consider a computerized accounting service. Software packages such as QuickBooks or Peachtree are very simple to use and are helpful when it comes to organizing your checks and bank records. Most accountants and bookkeepers are proficient at both and can even help you set them up.

If you have employees, consider using a payroll service. These outsourced specialists will make sure that your paychecks are accurate, that withholding taxes are done properly and submitted in a timely manner to the government, and that year-end payroll reports are promptly and accurately filed with employees and the proper taxing authorities.

Although it all sounds so simple, you should hire an accountant. The basic bookkeeping may be something for you or an assistant, but preparing year-end tax forms is something best left to those who do hundreds of them.

Furnishing Your Office

As you already know, perception counts. The penny-pinching part of you may want to skimp on furniture for your office digs—but even if you're operating on the proverbial shoestring budget from a makeshift office space above your garage, take some time when deciding how to spend money on decent furniture.

If the chance of client meetings in your home office is negligible, by all means forego that designer suite of furniture—but don't sacrifice comfort for price. Invest in a good, solid chair and a desk/workstation that has ample space and a number of filing compartments. When choosing your workspace location, keep lighting and proximity to equipment in mind. Lighting increases in importance the larger your working quarters are.

If you're outfitting an office for a small staff, be aware of lighting and equipment factors. You want an office space that provides all employees with decent access to the fax machine, copiers, filing cabinets, and so on.

Consider purchasing or leasing a copier with dual functions, such as print, fax, and scanning capabilities. A paper shredder and a multi-line telephone system should also be on your must-have list. While we're on the subject, think in terms of shelves or short-depth bookcases to store binders or industry literature. That space-saving measure will keep filing cabinets free for client documents and will keep your floor space from becoming too crowded.

Your filing system for clients' confidential data should be fireproof and secure. Locking file cabinets stored in a locked room would be ideal—not only because perception counts, but an auditor may find you in violation of the industry-required privacy policy for leaving client files in visible or open areas. And always maintain a clean, clutter-free, and private area for those regular or occasional in-office meetings with clients.

Hardware and Software Requirements

While some may argue that the incredible array of hardware and software solutions available to today's small business owner can be overwhelming (and sometimes confusing), there's no question that technology has made the life of today's financial planner a lot easier. From data backup systems designed for safekeeping and restoring valuable data to software tools developed specifically for financial planning, technology options are giving financial planners the capability to get to the business of doing business more rapidly.

Types of Hardware to Consider

With regulatory mandates on record retention and client privacy in place, maintaining up-to-date records is vital to the office of a financial planner. A number of backup and restoration options are available—but before deciding on a system, make sure it's the right one for you and your office staff and one that you are comfortable using. It makes no sense to invest in a costly backup system if you're afraid to use it or won't take the time to use it.

An extensive line of removable backup/restore hardware includes any number of formats, such as tapes, CDs, DVDs, flash drives, and external and removable hard drives. Also known as storage devices, they can be used to back up data and then removed to a location outside the office for safety or long-term storage. Most computer systems are equipped with one or more types of removable media. There are many companies that can do this for you using an Internet connection, thereby avoiding the need to buy any hardware. The ability to maintain and restore critical data is at the heart of your career as a financial planner. Establish a backup routine—and use it.

You may also consider implementing a paperless office environment. Several companies have customized solutions for financial services professionals that are compliant with state and federal record retention requirements and are very efficient. Just look through any financial planning trade magazine and you'll see several companies pushing their paperless systems. These paperless solutions are especially easy to implement in the early days of starting your own practice. Consider these before you invest in lots of file cabinets and need space to store them.

Pitfalls

Don't skimp on hardware. Buy the most advanced computer you can afford. While it may be cheaper next year, if you skimp, what you buy cheap today may not work with next year's release of your favorite software package or the next Microsoft Windows upgrade.

How to Choose Financial Planning Software

Many financial planning software tools are available—some basic, others complicated. The number of bells and whistles attached to the program that you select will have a lot to do with your desire or ability to take advantage of them, but keep the basics in mind. There is no such thing as the best package on the market. Each is different, and the trick is finding the one that is best suited to your practice's specific needs. One may provide great detail while another has great graphics. One may offer direct links to your clients' accounts while others require manual updates each time you want to revisit your clients' plans. None of them do a great job creating recommendations. You will have to come up with the solutions based on the analysis provided by the software.

Start by asking yourself what you want the software to do for you. Do you want great graphics? Do you want 50 years of projections? Do you want one general package, or are you willing to buy specialized programs that may provide greater analysis? Do you want it to integrate with your contact management system?

Ask your colleagues what they use. Find out what they like about the software and what they wish it did. Call the vendors and ask for a free demonstration. Look through the trade association magazines and websites for recent reviews. This market is developing so fast that a review from 12 months ago may be totally obsolete today.

When it comes down to purchase time, realize that affinity discounts are available for most of the packages offered today. You may get a discount as a member of a broker dealer, the Financial Planning Association, or one of the many mutual fund or brokerage firms you may encounter.

Contact Management Software

Having client contact information at your fingertips is fundamental to operating a successful financial planning business. A constantly growing number of contact management programs that are easy to install and administer are available, requiring no more special skill than it takes to use a word processor or send e-mail.

The importance of a comprehensive content management system cannot be overemphasized, particularly for the one-person or small-staffed office that does not have an administrative assistant. Content management software can provide a large number of functions, including an address book, an appointment calendar, and a to-do list activities organizer. It can also help systemize tasks, such as automatically sending out annual review letters, inviting clients to events, or sending them articles or other news of special interest to them. There are many specialized contact management programs that even link to financial planning programs so that you can have the clients' financial information right in front of you every time you speak or even think of them.

These systems used to be very time-consuming to learn and expensive to acquire. Today—fortunately—that's not the case. There are systems like Act for financial advisors, Redtail Technology, and www.salesforce.com that work well for financial services professionals.

> **Walking the Walk**
>
> A good CRM [client relationship management] system will be the backbone of your planning business. Access to the information that you want, when you need it, is critical to running an efficient financial planning practice.
>
> — Jeffrey N. Tomaneng, CLU,ChFC,CFP, Financial Planner, U.S. Wealth Management, Braintree, Massachusetts

Your Initial Image

Anyone who has ever been interviewed for a job, visited with a client, or merely been part of the business world knows how important projecting a positive image is to achieving success. Our personal hygiene, wardrobe, and even choice of vehicle are image-building elements—but just as important to creating a winning reflection is your company's logo and the way in which you present yourself to the world through business stationery, business cards, brochures, and your company's website.

Company Logo

Visual identity is critical to anyone who is setting up a business. A good company logo that identifies who you are and what you do can go a long way toward building a brand. Logos get a lot of mileage—appearing on company letterheads, business cards, brochures, and websites. For that reason alone, unless you have true talent in graphic design, you may want to consider hiring a professional to design that all-important business logo.

A designer will probably have his or her own ideas about what type of logo will work well for your business. Before you hand this assignment over, however, have an idea of what image you want that business emblem to portray. A logo should have a memorable impact on its target audience, so keep it simple yet eye-catching with a good balance between symbols and the written word. You could also opt for a symbol-less logo, letting the name of your business and/or slogan take the lead. Don't spend a fortune on your logo. Local designers should be able to give you a fixed fee estimate for a few design concepts. Ideally, your logo will be with you for a long time and will become the hallmark of your brand.

Since color will play an important role in your logo, keep in mind that financial logos should be in universal colors. In other words, stick with the color basics—such as blue, green, black, and silver. Use conventional fonts that are easy to read and are appropriate to the financial planning industry. And always choose a logo that will translate well to both black-and-white and colored paper, a computer monitor, or a television screen.

Letterhead

There's no question about it: first impressions count. And for the startup financial planner, the first impression that you make on a prospective client may come from the letterhead on your stationery. Spend a few bucks on a professional-looking stationery package—letterheads, envelopes, business cards, sticky notes, invoices, receipts, and so on. Choose a heavier-weight stock, and keep graphics limited to your business logo and contact information.

Business Cards

There may be no quicker way to create a business identity than with a business card. Again, go the extra mile by having this highly important element of your marketing campaign designed and printed by a professional. A clean-looking business card with appropriate contact information printed on high-quality stock will help deliver the message that you're in business to do business.

E-Mail

First, let's discuss your e-mail signature—the wording at the bottom of every message you send. Think of your e-mail signature as an electronic business card. Include all standard information, such as your name, title, the name of your financial planning business, mailing address, e-mail address, telephone number, cell phone number, fac-simile number, and Internet address (if applicable). There will also be broker dealer or regulation-required disclosures somewhere.

Once you've set up your e-mail account, check it often—several times a day. You may be on the road drumming up business or attending seminars, particularly during the beginning stages of your financial planning career—but people send e-mails because they want quick responses. If a current or prospective client's e-mail is more than a few days old by the time you've opened it, you may never hear from him or her again.

When composing a professional e-mail message, less is more. A couple pleasant-ries are fine—but the quicker you get to the heart of the business matter, the better impression you'll make on your client. Make sure that you've supplied your client or potential client with answers to all of his or her questions in a clear and concise man-ner. And by all means, turn on that spelling and grammar check. While e-mail tends to be less formal than a traditional business letter, sentence structure and spelling should never be sacrificed. Certainly, even with all checking devices activated, some-times a small mistake can occur—but too many sloppy e-mails can translate into lost business. And please, stay clear of the caps lock key. On the Internet, using capital let-ters means that you're shouting. And nobody wants to hear that.

All e-mail messages to clients about financial matters are considered correspondence that needs to be retained. You will need to invest in a system that retains all client correspondence as well as all inbound and outgoing e-mail to your business e-mail address. Advise your friends to keep the jokes and other nonbusiness e-mails to a minimum—or to send them to another personal address not related to your business. A good rule of thumb is to never put anything in an e-mail that you wouldn't want to see in the headlines of your local newspaper.

 In the Know _____

Get you own domain web address for your e-mail. Using a retail-oriented Internet provider does not have the same impact as your own domain that is the same as the name of your business.

Brochures

You essentially have two choices when it comes to designing a brochure for your financial planning business. It can be all about you—or all about what you can offer. Want a brochure that will make people yawn? Go the conventional route and wax poetic about your credentials, education, and impressive client list. But if you want to catch some positive attention and still provide important information about your practice, then copy has to be benefit-driven.

Instead of going on and on about how smart you are, tell your audience how your expertise can benefit them. A successful brochure—one that will bring business your way—should immediately identify the needs of potential clients and succinctly relate why you should be the one to take care of those needs. Remember, the brochure may have your name and contact information displayed in big, bold letters—but its content should be focused on what you can do for your clients.

Websites

As a startup financial planner, you're probably working with a tight budget. But the truth is, websites have become essential to a business's image. And unless you're lucky enough to know someone who is willing to design a site for you for peanuts, retaining a professional website designer should be on that growing to-do list.

A well-designed website is a valuable commercial mechanism, acting as a source of information for present and prospective clients. Your site should communicate who you are quickly and clearly and should provide the information that users need to determine whether they want to hire you. And it should offer clear and consistent page design with straightforward navigation.

Ask your best clients what features they'd like to see on your website. You may even consider having a group of four or five in one meeting to give you guidance and advice on what you'll need.

Later in the book we'll delve deeper into how and why a well-designed website can help add to your client roster. But for now, just remember that you're competing for business in the twenty-first century. You may be one heck of a financial planner, but if you don't employ a full image package complete with a well-designed website, you could be losing precious business.

The Least You Need to Know

♦ Where you set up shop is a big part of the favorable first impression that you want to create with both existing clients and prospective clients.

♦ Proper insurance coverage is a necessity for your new business and a prudent planning move on your part.

♦ Get good professional advisors to point yourself in the right direction during the critical startup phase. You may never get a second chance to fix some bad decisions.

♦ Take advantage of twenty-first century technology and buy the best technology you can afford.

♦ Your printed, written, and Internet image should have a professional and consistent look with a clear message of quality and desirable client deliverables.

Chapter 13

It's Lonely at the Top

In This Chapter

- ◆ Know what you can do well
- ◆ When and how to hire staff
- ◆ Choosing the right business structure
- ◆ Outsourcing, service providers, and fee structure decisions
- ◆ Establishing your level of independence
- ◆ Why should you consider a coach?

Most senior executives would agree that the air becomes thin at the top of an organization. The buck has to stop somewhere, and it usually stops at the top. This is especially true in a small organization, and it's a certainty in a startup practice.

You will start your business journey by taking a good self-assessment and then lining up people who can bolster your weaknesses. Some of your early decisions may impact your business for years to come. You'll be deciding on your business structure and governance, hiring staff, arranging for outsourcing, choosing a broker dealer, and looking for someone to coach you to your highest and best potential.

It doesn't have to be lonely at the top. There are specialty service providers for financial planners whose only business is providing guidance and service to small financial planning businesses. Choose your service providers carefully. Some partners/service providers are optional, and others are required. In this chapter, you will get guidance to pick the best service providers for you.

Know Your Strengths

You would think that after so many years, you would know your strengths and weaknesses. But this is not always the case. If you've worked for a large organization and lived through the discomfort of a *360-degree review*, you may have some insight into what people think of you and what they see as your strengths and weaknesses.

def•i•ni•tion

A **360-degree review** is a feedback process where everyone in an organization—managers, coworkers, and subordinates—has the chance to give their opinions about you and your performance. This gives you valuable feedback on your strengths and weaknesses, personal and professional, from all levels and perspectives.

Key to the success of your new venture is to understand your signature strengths. More than technical stuff like taxes or investments—instead, it is more about your unique personal characteristics and building tasks that highlight your strengths. Throughout your entire life, teachers and mentors have told you about your weaknesses and how to improve them. While you can't be horrible in any area as a business owner, recent studies have shown that you are better off building around your strengths than to constantly work on bolstering your weaknesses. Hiring staff or outsourcing to people whose strength is where you are weak is more productive in both the short and long term.

Marcus Buckingham and Donald O. Clifton, both former executives of the Gallup organization, have written a terrific book, *Now, Discover Your Strengths* (see Appendix C). It contains a unique identification number that provides access to the Clifton Strengths Finder Profile on the Internet. This Internet-based interview analyzes your instinctive reactions and immediately presents you with your five most powerful signature themes.

When Should You Hire Staff?

Hiring staff is something that most financial planners delay until the last possible moment. Is it because they are undercapitalized, don't know where to find good talent, or think that they can never find someone to do something as good as they can do it themselves? Whatever the reason, it is flawed thinking.

You should hire staff before you actually start on your own. Hire at least one good assistant while you are employed elsewhere as a planner, and you may have your first employee for your new organization. After learning about your strengths and building around them, it will become painfully clear why you need others to support you. In addition to that, you—as the business owner—should not spend your higher earning potential time doing something that can be accomplished by someone who is more skilled and lower-cost than you. If you are still thinking, "I don't cost my business anything, so why should I hire someone to answer phones or send my mail out?"—then you should not have taken the plunge. How would you feel if the CEO of a company that you invested in does his or her own secretarial work?

How to Hire

Make sure that your financial projections for your startup business include hiring a good assistant. It is much harder to get off to a good start if you have to do everything. There are many ways to hire a great assistant and staff. Before you dive into the recommended tactics, be very clear about what you are looking for. Make sure that you have written job descriptions and clear expectations about style, experience, and work ethic. Second, make sure that you consult with a human resources professional about legal issues, such as discrimination and workplace ethics. Even an unintentional error here can cause you more grief than it's worth.

Word of mouth, advertising, and employment agencies are all great ways to start your search. It will be helpful if you hire someone who has prior experience in financial services. The compliance and paperwork issues that you'll want help with are cumbersome and unique to this industry. More than anything, you want someone whose style will complement yours, not mirror it. You may consider having this person also complete the Clifton Strengths Finder Profile assessment that I mentioned earlier. In addition to this service, Kolbe. com has several easy to use and affordable

> **Walking the Walk**
>
> Hiring team-oriented professionals had been a hit-or-miss proposition for our firm until we began to profile our candidates. Once we started using independent evaluation tools, our success in hiring and retention has been far more consistent.
>
> —Jon B. Mendelsohn, president and CEO, Ashar Group LLC, Orlando, Florida

indices that you may want to implement in evaluating a potential hire and accessing his or her fit for the job.

Finding a good assistant may be intricately tied to your ability to conduct a good interview. If you know that you stink at this, hire a consultant to do the interviewing for you. If you think you can do it but just need a little guidance, come up with a consistent list of questions to ask each candidate. This way, it will be easier for you to compare one to the other. Consider first holding a telephone interview, especially if your assistant will spend a lot of time on the telephone with your clients and prospects. A few sample interview questions may be:

- How do you think a friend or professor who knows you well would describe you?

- Describe a situation in which you had to work with a difficult person (another student, co-worker, customer, supervisor, and so on). How did you handle the situation? Is there anything you would have done differently in hindsight?

- What are the most important rewards you expect in your career?

- In what ways do you think you can make a contribution to our organization?

- What two or three things would be most important to you in your job?

- What is the most boring job you ever had? And why was it boring?

Retaining Great Assistants

Part of the key to retaining a great assistant is hiring the right person in the first place. Make sure that you are clear about your expectations and theirs and that their capabilities are compatible with the most important tasks in your job description. Ask your potential employee directly what criteria are important to him or her in rating job satisfaction. This person also needs to know that you genuinely and sincerely appreciate him or her and that his or her work is important to the organization.

Good compensation doesn't hurt, either, but it is typically not the number-one driver for employee satisfaction. But don't be a softie—tie their compensation and bonuses to tasks that you believe will improve your effectiveness and profitability. Incentive bonus compensation—allowing your employees to exceed their earnings expectations—will make certain that they are focused on what you consider to be the most important tasks.

Your Business Structure

The structure of your organization is an important decision that affects the long term, and there are plusses and minuses to each alternative. Most of your choices have some flexibility and can be changed to adapt to your future needs. The comparisons can be broken down into three major areas: taxation, management, and liability.

Sole Proprietorship

The sole proprietor form of ownership is the simplest and most renowned among mom-and-pop businesses. Aside from the states that require you to register the business with the town in which it resides, there isn't much else to do to get it up and running. So the big plus is simplicity and ease of formation.

The downside to a sole proprietorship is that it can only have one owner—and he or she is personally liable for all of the entity's debts. As soon as a sole proprietorship has more than one owner, it is considered a partnership. If you plan to have more than one owner, now or later, move to one of the other two structures discussed.

The personal liability exposure may be much greater than it appears on the surface. Owners of a sole proprietorship are liable for the debts that you can see and those that you cannot. Obviously, trade payables and other expenses of the business become your liability—but so do judgments from lawsuits or any other claims made against you or the business. If you become disabled and miss many months of work and income, the bills will keep coming in—and you are personally responsible for them.

The taxation of a sole proprietorship is really simple. You file a Schedule C along with your normal Form 1040, and the net profit or loss from your business shows up on page one of your personal tax return. The only separate forms that you may need to file would be for payroll of other employees, 1099s for outside contractors, or the tax forms for your retirement plan.

Walking the Walk

Most people who start a new business just get in the driver's seat and go. Without proper legal and tax advice regarding entity structure—and continuing advice regarding short- and long-term strategy—new business owners may encounter problems and additional taxes that they didn't anticipate.

—Scott I. Wolf, Esq., partner, Schlossberg and Associates, P.C., Braintree, Massachusetts

Starting a Corporation

Incorporating your business is a process of filing articles of organization, bylaws, and organizational board of directors resolutions with the state in which you incorporate. This task is followed by the issuance of shares of stock.

Owners of a corporation are protected from the liabilities of the entity as long as the owner-operator did not act with fraud or negligence. The piercing of the corporate veil of liability protection is not easily done and is often challenged by litigators and creditors. To avoid that piercing, officers and directors must act with integrity and not mix business and personal expenses or assets. The entity must stand on its own for all intents and purposes.

A corporation is governed by its board of directors. The shareholders are the ones who elect the board of directors. The directors are responsible for overall management of the company, and they in turn usually elect officers—such as a president, treasurer, and secretary—to run the day-to-day operations. In your small company, you may wear many or all of the hats.

In the Know

Although corporate shareholders are protected from creditors of the company, as a practical matter, this may not be so. As a new company without any track record of revenue and earnings, many vendors will ask for your personal guarantee for the business obligation. Ask for their clarification about when, if ever, your guarantee will no longer be required.

Owners of corporations may be taxed at the corporate level or elect Subchapter S status to have all income and losses flow through to the shareholders according to their ownership interest. Sub S corporations are limited to having 100 or fewer shareholders and only one class of stock. Sub S status is elected by filing Form 2553 with the IRS within 75 days of formation. Sub S status is most common among small business owners, and the detail plusses and minuses are beyond the scope of this book. Call your accountant for help in making the best decision for you.

Limited Liability Company (LLC)

A limited liability company, or LLC, is a legal form of business entity that protects owners with limited liability for entity obligations. In this regard, it is similar to a corporation but is a more flexible form of ownership for small businesses. The flexibility comes in the form of owners being able to distribute profits and proceeds from the sale of the business in a manner that differs from their ownership percentage. The entity is formed by filing the articles of organization or certificate of formation with the state in which the business resides.

An LLC is governed by an operating agreement in which the owners designate one or more managers who may or may not be owners of the LLC. Owners are referred to as members of the LLC and are assigned a percentage ownership.

LLCs are appropriate for businesses that have one owner or many. For tax purposes, an LLC may elect to be taxed as a partnership or sole proprietorship and have its income or losses flow right through to the partners or as a corporation, paying taxes like a large corporation at the entity level. A separate tax form is required for LLCs.

The Outsourcing Decisions

If you were thinking of going out and establishing your own financial planning practice in 1999, it would have cost you a lot more than it will today. Today, you can outsource just about any service and get away with paying as you go instead of having to own everything before you get started.

Most of your financial planning-specific software can be outsourced or paid for as you use it and hosted on someone else's server. Practices could easily spend more than $100,000 in acquisition fees for software to do money management, financial planning, contact management, investment research, and client reporting. Annual renewals and licensing agreements, in addition, could have easily been in the tens of thousands of dollars. Today, all of this is structured with very little up-front investment and monthly fees only. Prices will vary widely from one outsource firm to another. Narrow down exactly what type of service you want, interview several firms, and compare pricing to be sure that you are paying a fair price.

Many services can also be outsourced. Financial planners will commonly send performance reports to clients about their portfolios on a quarterly basis. Each quarter, it is a time-consuming process that can take weeks to complete. Most firms would employ one full-time person just to run the system—let alone the price of the system itself. Today, there are outsourcing companies for this job, such as Orion (orionadvisor.com) or Bridge portfolio (bridgeportfolio.com).

Outsourcing is such a serious business that financial planners can use outsourced services to deliver greater and broader service to their clients without incurring any additional overhead. These additional services can be performed simply by paying your outsourcing partner on a variable basis for exactly what they do. For your client, he or she gets the benefit of a coordinated financial relationship where you will know more about your clients' financial situation and be in a position to deliver better advice. Common examples of outsourced services include tax preparation, trust administration, retirement plan administration, banking, account aggregation services, database management, cash management, bill paying, and document storage.

Service Providers You'll Need

No matter how much capital you have, there are some service providers you will always need. Examples include a firm to do custody and clearing for investment advisors and network or technology services.

Custody and clearing are functions that are outsourced by even the largest investment advisory firms in the industry. Custody refers to the firm that actually holds your clients' investments in a brokerage account. The regulatory and net worth requirements for custodial firms are far greater than any financial planner should encounter. Furthermore, it gives your clients some comfort to know that their accounts are actually being held by Fidelity or TD Ameritrade—instead of your small practice. You will gladly let them know that you cannot access their accounts for any purposes other than executing trades or having your quarterly asset management fee removed from the account. Even the fee removal process comes with a notice and explanation requirement before it actually leaves the client's account.

A clearing firm actually performs the trades directly with the various exchanges. Like custody, this service requires too much capital and compliance for most planners. Furthermore, the large aforementioned firms receive far better execution and pricing that any small planning practice would on its own—and most money managers are required to look for the best execution and pricing that they can find for their clients.

Pitfalls

Be wary of locking in an outside service provider for too long a period. You may find that the service is not up to your expectation or that the prices for the service drop drastically below the price in your contract because of technology improvements and efficiency gains.

Network administration and technology services are things that you will rarely do yourself. It would be a full-time job just to stay current and way too costly even for a firm with 25 employees to have a full-time employee dedicated to this job. Find a good network administration service, and let them maintain your in-house systems.

The same holds true for other technology services, such as client account aggregation, Internet services, or e-mail retention. Hire a network manager who can either provide all of these services or coordinate the work of various technology service providers to be sure that all of your systems work together.

Your Fee Structure

The fee structure for your firm is a combination of several factors: what the market will bear, the competitive landscape, and the style of firm that you have.

If you are a commission-based planner, you may never have charged financial planning fees in the past. This is a new day, however, and you can change that if you feel that your market will bear it and you are doing holistic planning. Planners who charge fees for advice usually adopt a flat-fee concept or bill by the hour. For flat-fee planners, fees are typically determined by complexity of the case. I have seen planning fees range from a low of $250 for simple cases or commission-based planners who are new to charging fees to a high of more than $100,000 for very complicated situations. Hourly fees range from a low of $100 per hour to greater than $350 per hour.

In the Know

Your fee structure will be disclosed in your Form ADV, which is filed with the Securities and Exchange Commission (SEC). Any deviation from what is published will require an ADV amendment to be filed.

For planners billing for assets under advisement or management, fees are often based on the clients' total assets under advisement. Commonly, fees range from 50 basis points to 2 percent. The trend is that advisors are under growing fee pressure, and gross fee billing rates are coming down. If you are at the high end of the scale, be prepared to charge less in the future as competitive pressures and technology allow clients to get a similar service elsewhere for a much lower fee. Advisors who are truly providing holistic planning in addition to asset services will receive less fee pressure than those who just give lip service to the financial planning part.

Broker Dealer Relationships

If you intend to maintain a securities license to generate commissions—or even to capture *trailing commissions* on financial products you've previously sold—you will always need a broker dealer (BD). Very few financial planning firms will ever start their own broker dealer due to the capital and

def•i•ni•tion

Trailing commissions are commissions that are paid to you as the broker of record for as long as your client holds that investment. It is common to receive recurring commission revenue from some mutual funds, variable annuity and variable life insurance, and retirement plans.

compliance requirements. In order for it to make any financial sense at all, you would need to generate millions in securities commissions.

When starting your own financial planning practice, most advisors will either need to change or want to change their broker dealer relationship. There are lots of slick sales pitches and lures of huge commission payout rates, but there is much more to consider.

Does the broker dealer you are interviewing have a mission and vision? Are their goals and values consistent with yours? Ask them directly about their mission and vision. A focused firm will have them in writing and get it to you. Also ask what their ideal representative is like. You don't want to be a fish out of water and find out that their culture is not compatible with your style of practice. Find out about firm ownership. Sometimes large broker dealers are owned by large insurance companies, and the independent name and appearance is a thin veil for what they really want you to sell your clients. Ask whether there are any proprietary sales goals or requirements of their advisors.

Do your homework on the contracts that they want you to sign. It is a National Association of Securities Dealers (NASD) requirement that all representatives have a written agreement with their broker dealer. One of the more important issues for you in this contract is who owns the clients. Ask about noncompete clauses and find out if you can have your own registered investment advisor firm separate from theirs.

Learn about their technology. Most broker dealers today will offer account aggregation services, online commission accounting, electronic deposits of commissions to your bank account, and good websites that will house resources for you and links to your client accounts.

In the Know

Changing broker dealers is not easy. You will need signatures from all of your clients allowing them to approve the transfer of their accounts. Make sure that your new broker dealer will provide extensive support during the transition and feels as confident as possible that you'll not need to do this again.

Ask about their compliance department. Some firms are very lax in the compliance area; others have a reputation for their compliance staff acting like the business prevention department because they are so slow to approve things for you. And then there are some firms that put their money where their mouth is and have a great compliance staff that knows it is their job to keep you out of trouble and to make your job in the field easier.

Take a look at their errors and omissions insurance and feel comfortable that it is adequate for your and their needs. Some firms have a very low aggregate amount of coverage that could leave you in the dark if they are served with a rash of lawsuits that all result in judgments against them. Ask if they have had any prior regulatory complaints or settlements. All large firms have had complaints, settlements, and litigation. If you go deep in this area for your diligence, try to notice if there are any patterns that would make you feel uncomfortable with the culture. The salesperson trying to recruit you may be telling you one thing, but the reps in the field may be doing quite the other.

Does your broker dealer prospect offer any marketing or practice management support? By now it should be clear to you that to be successful, you need a business plan. Does your prospective broker dealer help with that? What about succession in the event you get disabled or die while still active in practice?

And last, but not least, ask for references. You want the references to be planners whose practice is similar to yours. Interview some who just made the switch and others who have been there for a long time. Ask if the firm has delivered on the promises that the recruiter has made to you.

In the Know _____

Ask the same questions to more than one person in each broker dealer firm that you interview. Consistency in the answers from firm employees and other representatives should give you comfort in your findings.

How Independent Do You Want to Be?

Some planners want to be in their own business to be completely independent and others want to be associated with a big firm. To make matters more complicated, some big firms allow you to be completely independent, while others do not. Independence can be defined in terms of whose name you must use on your cards and letterhead, limitations imposed on implementation recommendations for clients, and varying rates of compensation depending on which products you recommend.

Independence in the financial planning world has many interpretations. Let's start with the most literal interpretation of independence as promoted by the National Association of Personal Financial Advisors (NAPFA) crowd of fee-only advisors. The fee-only advisory community feels that the only way that an advisor can possibly be independent is to only work for fees paid by the client. They feel that if an advisor receives commissions for any implementation work, he or she cannot possibly be independent. While in theory this sounds accurate, I feel that it is way too restrictive and self-righteous. It casts doubt and aspersions on anyone who receives commissions and helps to foster distrust in any advisor who is not fee-only. Furthermore, when a client of a fee-only advisor needs to buy insurance, for example, they are likely to buy products with commissions from someone referred by the fee-only advisor. How independent was the referral? Sometimes the referral is completely independent and sometimes it is to an agent who is captive, sells primarily the products from one company and is also a good referral source to the fee only advisor's business.

The next level down the independence chain is someone who does receive commissions, but who is not obligated to work with any particular products and has no limitations on what they advise their clients to buy. These advisors will work with an independent broker dealer and insurance brokerage firm, and work diligently to find the best products available for their clients' needs. The gray area is, how does a client or any third party really know that the advisor has in fact compared all available options and chosen what they truly believe is best for the client? The trust factor has to be extremely high here, and the advisors need to act with prudence and objectivity to earn that continued trust.

Pitfalls

Beware the recruiter who touts the firm's independence if you have reasons to question the statements. Ask for verification of firm revenues to see that their revenues are evenly distributed across several product manufacturers.

The next level is an advisor who does accept commissions, and is affiliated with a broker dealer owned by an insurance company or some other product manufacturer and has proprietary products for their advisors to sell. Most advisors in these firms will tell you that they also have many other companies to recommend, but that their parent company's product is fine and as good as any other. This is not always true, and sometimes the advisor won't do a complete market survey on behalf of the client. Some of these firms even pay their advisors more if they sell a minimum of the parent company's products. Now the independence lines are starting to get hazier.

The lowest level of independence is the firm that restricts what a financial advisor can recommend and sell to their clients. Believe it or not, there are still many firms that operate this way. Ask about their product offerings before you decide to join and make the choice that is in the best interests of your clients, for that will be the best choice for your business in the long run.

Working with a Coach

It may be lonely at the top, but you can join the ranks of other top professionals and hire a coach to guide you to your highest and best use. People like Tiger Woods, Larry Bird, Celine Dion, and Jerry Seinfeld have used coaches and will use them again. So … why wouldn't you hire a peak performance coach?

Coaching is now the rage for all lines of work. In the financial services business, coaching firms are finding great success. Much of this has to do with the self-employed nature of the business and that lonely feeling that owners of small businesses develop. Professional coaching is an ongoing professional relationship that helps people produce extraordinary results in their lives, careers, businesses, or organizations. Through the process of coaching, clients deepen their learning, improve their performance, and enhance their quality of life. This interaction creates clarity and moves you into action. Coaching will accelerate your progress by providing greater focus and awareness of choice. Coaching concentrates on where you are now and what you are willing to do to get where you want to be in the future.

You can hire a coach on an hourly basis or for an annual retainer. Most of the well-known, respected programs for advisors are annual retainers. The fees range from a low of about $5,000 per year to over $20,000 per year. While this figure sounds expensive, look at it this way. Most of the top-earning financial advisors either currently are or have been enrolled in a coaching program.

> ## Walking the Walk
>
> I have been a successful insurance advisor for 20 years. I have enrolled in a coaching program because of encouragement and input from people with a wide range of talent. Since I began the program three years ago, our firm has become more focused on our strengths and grown more than any time in our past.
>
> —Thomas Barnes, managing member, Brighton Consulting, Salt Lake City, Utah

Some coaching programs have regular monthly or quarterly meetings or group sessions. Others are more focused on content and web-related material that you can use for your practice. Carefully do your homework, the same way you would when changing broker dealers, and join the coaching program that fits your level of practice and needs.

Implementing Coaching Tools

Most coaching programs will offer many tools for your business that have been successfully implemented by many advisors before you. Some will be usable in their original form and others will need adapting to your style and practice. To get the most out of any coaching program, you must implement something. Having a full-time assistant who is also involved in your coaching program will speed up the utilization and maximize the benefit from the program.

The best tactic would be to block time out on your calendar each week to work on your coaching. This way you are learning the material and implementing on a regular basis. As the Strategic Coach Program based in Toronto and Chicago states, "progress, not perfection" is the key to benefiting from your coaching program. If each tool and program just gets you a little further ahead, and moves your subconscious thoughts in the right direction, you will improve.

Being a Coach

In addition to being a coaching client, you must also learn to be a coach. In this case, I use the term *coach* in the same light as I would the term *leader*. You need to be a coach to your staff. Part of retaining good associates is working with them on a regular basis to reach their personal and career goals.

You also need to be a coach to your clients. Without your active involvement, encouragement, and direction, their financial plans would be nothing more than a road map that never comes out of the glovebox. The role of a personal financial planner is really that of a personal financial coach who is accountable for results.

The Least You Need to Know

◆ Focus on your strengths, and surround yourself with people who are strong where you are weak.

◆ Learn how to hire great people for your firm—or use someone else who can do it for you.

◆ Choosing the right business structure for your situation is best done right the first time. Know whether a sole proprietor, partnership, LLC, or corporation is right for you.

◆ Line up your broker dealer and outsourcing partners before you start your own business.

◆ Hire a good coach; most of the highest-earning financial planners have a coach.

Chapter 14

Who the Heck Are You?

In This Chapter

- ◆ What is your brand?
- ◆ Creating visibility in the marketplace
- ◆ How your clients can help spread the word
- ◆ Effective marketing tools and techniques

Those hard-earned credentials are yours. That home office—or shared or leased office space—is occupied and broken in with client meetings and revenue. You may already be working with a short list of clients, but your goal is to grow. Things may be going well, but now is not the time to rest on your laurels. In fact, now is the time to evaluate what you bring to the table as a financial planner. As with any industry, it's a competitive world out there—and you must be prepared to gain an edge on your competition, now and in the future.

Certainly, knowledge and the ability to provide the best possible service for your clients are the most important aspects of your career as a financial planner. No amount of glitz and glamour can compensate for unsound fiscal advice. But in order to get the word out that you have arrived, sometimes it's necessary to create your own buzz.

Establishing yourself as a go-to financial planner requires effort beyond what it takes to perform regular daily tasks. It will take some time to build a positive reputation and create the type of professional persona that keeps you in the forefront of your present and future clients' minds.

In this chapter, we take a look at the many ways you can set yourself apart from the competition. From branding strategies to marketing plans to comprehensive public relations campaigns, there's a lot to consider as you determine who the heck you are.

A "Brand" New You

Regardless of the type of industry you're in, the ability to be recognized and stand out from the competition is a key component to success. The growing need for financial planners has placed you in a good career position. But remember, you're not only competing for business with well-established financial planners—you are also vying for clients with other new kids on the block. It's true that education, ability, and a positive reputation are the foundations for business success, but the way in which you "brand" yourself in the early stages could be crucial to your long-term practice.

As the financial planning business matures and major firms spend millions on advertising, the base service of financial planning will become more commoditized. The quickest way to create a successful brand image is to differentiate yourself from the competition. Learn as much as possible about your competitors' strengths and weaknesses—then begin a branding campaign that highlights your strong points.

A brand is more than a catchy slogan, motto, or fancy business card. In fact, branding has as much to do with your competitors as it does with you. Take time to study your competition. Examine what does and doesn't work for them. Then identify what makes you distinctive from your competitors and make those qualities your dominant message and advertising feature. In a perfect world, your brand will conjure up a favorable image about your firm—just like the consistent image we all have when we think of Lexus, *The Wall Street Journal*, or Kleenex. Look at your business brand as your marketing resumé. Know who you are, get that message out, and then go after your target clients!

Keep your target market in mind. If your financial planning practice focuses on retirement-age clients, make sure your image and professional literature drives home the point that planning for retirement needs is at the heart of your practice.

Ask yourself just what you want your practice to be known for. Do you want to be "the" expert on small business financing? Are you trying to build a reputation as the go-to source for families who are financing multiple college educations? The surest approach to getting the word out is to first establish who you want to be for your clients.

Make a list of all the good things that you do for clients. Ask your best clients what they like about you and find unique about your services. From this list, pick out a few items that can be the foundation of your brand. These elements could be specific to the financial planning industry or more generic. Say, for example, that you're a whiz at keeping up to date on changing tax laws. That can be part of your brand. Maybe you're becoming known for an ability to deal with small problems before they become crises. That, too, can be part of your brand.

In the Know

There have been many great books written on branding and market positioning. You may want to read *Purple Cow* by Seth Godin or *Blue Ocean Strategy: How to Create Uncontested Market Space and Make Competition Irrelevant* by W. Chan Kim and Renée Mauborgne (see Appendix C). Both of these books will get you on the right track toward developing a brand as strong as any in the marketplace.

Creating Visibility

You have established who you are and what makes you stand out from the rest. Now it's time to put those features into action and attract enough clients to actually turn your new practice into a successful business. But before you go blindly into a full-out marketing campaign, sit back and think about its desired outcome.

Maybe your goal is to attract two dozen new clients a year. Or perhaps you want to secure a reputation as the premier financial advisor for small business operations in your region. Identify your business goals, and then create a marketing plan that will help you achieve those targets.

No matter how solid your credentials or what a great job you did for your last client, the need to constantly create visibility for your fledgling practice is vital to its future. What we're talking about here is public relations, pure and simple. While retaining the services of a professional public relations firm may not fit your budget right now, there are many media and other marketing opportunities to explore by yourself.

A good public relations (PR) firm can assist with your marketing campaign—especially if you are unfamiliar with what the media considers newsworthy. Aside from any costs you may incur for a professional firm, most of these activities are free and require only a commitment of your time and travel.

Before we take a look at some of the most successful marketing approaches, keep in mind that no single marketing effort works all the time—regardless of the type of business you own. If you only have one song to play, chances are that prospective (and sometimes existing) clients will tire of listening to it. Plus, you'll feel the boredom kicking in. A diverse marketing program can help communicate your value, so remember to mix it up when mapping out your publicity efforts.

Get Yourself in Print

You may be up to your eyeballs just trying to get your practice off the ground. But if you want it to really fly, then you're just going to have to use leverage. There may be no more effective way to get the word out to thousands of prospects about your practice than through the written word. But remember, that written word has to be something that a newspaper or industry publication editor will find newsworthy enough to print.

def•i•ni•tion

A **press release** is a written or recorded communication directed at members of the news media for the purpose of announcing something newsworthy. Typically, it is mailed, e-mailed, posted to a website, or faxed to assignment editors at newspapers, magazines, radio stations, television stations, and/or television networks.

You can begin your print media campaign with a *press release*. Basic, brief, and to the point, a press release should ideally be no more than one page long and include all pertinent announcement and contact information. Make the five W's—who, what, when, where, and why—your press release mantra. When writing a press release without the assistance of a professional PR firm, it's important to do your homework. Make sure your release will be a good fit for intended publications—and always get the correct name and spelling of the editor whose eye you hope to attract.

Don't run the risk of appearing as if you're looking for free advertising by churning out press releases that don't include some legitimate business news. A simple initial news or press release announcing that you have opened for business at a specific location is usually considered business newsworthy. There are a number of other news items that an editor might publish. The addition of staff, a change in location, seminars that you or staff members have recently attended, new certifications or awards—these are all valid reasons for press releases.

Pitch a Local Newspaper Column

If you are fairly comfortable with the written word, try contributing a column to a local newspaper. If, for example, your explanation of the major differences between standard and Roth IRAs hits a chord with readers (or the editor), you may be invited to contribute a regular financial column. While opportunities to write a regular column are not abundant, however, newspaper editors are sometimes on the lookout for new industry expert columnists who can relay meaningful information in an entertaining and concise fashion.

Service columns are also used to dress up a business page. As far as payment goes, well … unless you have already made a name for yourself as an industry leader, chances are you will not receive money in exchange for your knowledge. What you will receive, however, is what is known in the newspaper industry as a tagline. Typically, editors have no problem including the name of your business and your contact information in italics at the end of a one-time or regular column. It may not amount to "free" advertising, given the amount of work that writing a column will require of you—but having a tagline establishes you as an industry expert. And that's the type of promotional tool that money can't buy.

You have to do some homework to break into print, though. Start by compiling a list of publications where your advice and writing style would fit. Then follow the publication's guidelines on submissions and inquiries. Know how to spell and pronounce the name of the contact editor—and if the answer is no for now, ask whether you can be in touch in a few months to see whether the publication's needs have changed. Then move on to the next name on your list.

In the Know

Create about four or five sample articles. It's one thing to pitch an editor on the concept, but it's far better to make that pitch with a stack of samples for him or her to review. Make sure that you have your samples reviewed by a professional writer. This may be the only chance you get to impress the editor.

Print a Company Newsletter

You may be a company of just one, but that doesn't mean you have to take a backseat to larger financial practices with full staffs when it comes to sharing news about your practice. A newsletter can be a cost-effective way to keep in touch with clients—particularly those you haven't worked with for some time. You can also send the newsletter to all of the editors and others you are approaching with your PR effort. The newsletter will keep you in the front of their minds and may even give them ideas for a story. Keep costs low by producing a newsletter—complete with company news and a few financial planning tips or short articles—every other month or quarterly.

There are many sources for article content that you may obtain for little or no cost. Many professional associations produce articles for your use, and professional publishing companies offer articles for a very reasonable cost. In fact, some, such as Forefield (www.forefield.com), will assist you with everything you need to publish a complete financial newsletter for as little as $500 per year. You can even save thousands of dollars by not printing the newsletter and simply e-mailing it to clients and prospects.

Join the Crowd

Networking is an important element to any startup business, and one of the easiest ways to network is by joining your local chamber of commerce or other business-related organizations. But you can't stop there. Make yourself visible—and elevate your status by volunteering for committees and attending as many after-hours and meet-and-greet functions as possible. The idea is to have your face stand out from the crowd. Generally, the more you give to an organization like the chamber or Rotary Club, the more you will be recognized and perhaps receive some ancillary business benefit.

In the Know

Don't join a chamber of commerce or local service group merely for business development purposes. Find an organization in which you have a genuine interest, and become an active member whose efforts will be appreciated.

Hosting a meeting is another powerful way to get some one-on-one time with key business leaders, prospective clients, and any number of others who might want to add your business card to their files. For the fairly small cost of supplying a few platters of cheese and crackers and bottled beverages, you will be seen by other business leaders in your area and may reap big benefits.

Point of Reference Source

If you've been able to parlay your expertise as a financial planner into an occasional or regular column on the business pages of your newspaper, bravo! If not, that doesn't mean you should give up on becoming a source for feature writers or editors doing broad-based theme articles.

Send a letter of introduction along with a couple of your business cards to the business editor of your local and regional newspapers. Often, the need for insight or a quote from an industry expert arises. You could become that industry expert if your name and contact and credential information is at the fingertips of an editor or business reporter. Make sure to include your cell and home phone numbers. It is common for editors to work nights and weekends, and they might need you when you're not at the office.

Radio and TV Opportunities

When orchestrating your marketing campaign, don't stop at the printed word. Industry sources are often needed on talk radio and TV or cable network programs. Abrupt shifts in the stock market, new IRS regulations, a breaking international financial news story—these events are all fodder for special radio or television segments that require words from an industry source. If your contact and credential information is quickly accessible, you may find yourself behind a microphone or in front of a camera.

As with print media, you will need to become known by show hosts, producers, and program directors. They all need outside experts, and often it is the show host who chooses those experts. Realize that these people receive many solicitations and are very difficult to reach. Be professional and persistent, and you may find yourself in the spotlight. Unlike print media, where knowledge and insight is mainly required, radio and TV programs will need your ability to engage and entertain the audience. It is okay to lighten up a bit if you do get the chance to speak with someone about an appearance.

> **In the Know**
>
> The key to success in a media PR campaign is to be available when they need and want you—not when you want them. If your opening happens to come on a day when you have something else planned, figure out a way to make yourself available.

Public Access Television

Getting a "we need your expert opinion" call from the media may be a great ego booster, but sometimes you have to take self-promotion by the horns.

Most communities carry public access channels as part of a franchise agreement with a cable television company. Typically earmarked for municipal, high school sports, or other education-oriented programming, these local origination programs are a great forum for citizens to produce and broadcast their own shows.

The mission of public access channels is to encourage the widest spectrum of local programming and to provide ordinary citizens with access to the tools for producing shows.

Each community has its own rules about what can air and what can't, but most require that the programs be noncommercial. Often, a business can produce an informational show about its industry as long it's not a blatant sales program. Contact your local cable access channel director about programming requirements in your community.

Go "on Tour"

A number of local organizations would be grateful to book you for an appearance. Local councils on aging are always on the lookout for experts in the health, legal, and financial fields who are willing to donate an hour or so of their time and expertise to speak before a receptive and appreciative audience.

Offer yourself as a guest speaker to an investment club in your area. Arrange for a speaking engagement or mini seminar at your local library. Check out the club/organization section of the telephone book to determine which venues might have an interest in your presentation.

Pitfalls

Do not turn any public speaking opportunities into a big sales pitch. The less you promote, the more effective the presentation will be for growing your business. Your job is to educate and entertain. Your content and style will hopefully encourage the audience to seek you out.

Wherever your appearance schedule leads you, always bring enough business cards and brochures to go around. And don't forget to dress the part. That first small-hall appearance may not seem too glamorous, but it could be the first step down the road toward public speaking success.

Also, look into trade groups where you have particular expertise. Many professional organizations meet monthly or quarterly and seek a guest speaker on a topic of interest to their membership.

Clients: Your Best Marketing Partners

Even the most expensive and sophisticated marketing campaign can be essentially worthless if it doesn't help achieve your goal of reaching and retaining clients.

As a fledgling financial planner, you may have just a few great clients. The key to turning that small number into a booming business is to set a system in place that will convert existing clients into advocates for your work—and ultimately, as your referral system. Keep in mind, though, that a referral relationship is not a slam dunk just because you have met a client's expectations. You need to go that extra mile, constantly building the trust and loyalty of your clients. We're talking about customer service—and if you serve your existing customers well, they in turn will assist with your goals to increase your client base. Client referrals are not automatic, however, and good clients need to know that you want to work with similar people.

The primary role of a financial planner may be cut-and-dried: managing assets and providing financial advice. Those essential services may be enough for some in the industry—but to rise above the competition, a savvy financial planner cannot rest on number-crunching and investment counseling alone. Establishing a solid foundation of customer service will set you apart and encourage clients to share your name with prospects.

Show Your Appreciation

A personally written thank-you note sent via snail mail is a small yet often overlooked touch that tells new clients how much you value their business. But don't stop there. You can show your appreciation throughout the year with an occasional gift such as a useful desktop item that you know they'll appreciate.

Consider sending your clients a gift basket randomly during the year, perhaps filled with a mug, a couple pens, and a few pads of stationery (of course, with your name and company logo on all items). Your clients will receive the message that they are important year-round—plus, those practical presents serve double duty as advertising tools.

Some advisors will also send nice gifts that do not bear company logos or promotional material. A sincere, appreciative gift centered on something that you know your client likes will also show him or her that you care and pay attention.

Client events are another way to show your appreciation, and they come in three varieties:

- An *educational* event is geared to a topic that you know is of interest to your clients. For example, you may host an educational event on the benefits of charitable giving for clients who are charitably inclined.

In the Know

Make any day-to-day mailings work double time by enclosing your business card, brochure, or any other appropriate company literature. It won't cost additional postage, and if you ask a client to pass the extras along to someone else who may benefit from your service, who knows the number of prospects that might come your way?

- A *pure appreciation* event is something fun with no promotional purpose other than to show appreciation and get to know your clients a bit better. It will help if your event is centered on something that is a core part of your life. For example, if you are a painter, hold the event at an art museum. If you are a baseball buff, hold it at a local ballpark.

- A *referral* event can be a blend of pure appreciation and education, but there is a hook. For these types of events, you are asking clients to bring someone just like them who may benefit from your service.

Status Reports

Maybe you're researching a potential investment for a client. Or perhaps you've been asked to look into various ways to fund a college education. Typically, a financial planner juggles a number of requests from clients—some with high priorities and others filed under the "when you can get to it" category. If you really want to impress a client, you can deliver the message that all of his or her requests are equally important to you through a brief but regular status report. It doesn't have to be a formal mailing; in fact, a brief e-mail that says, "I'm working on it, and this is what I've found so far" will keep your clients current. It will also show that no small detail gets past you. And if you make a mistake, own up to it. Be honest, apologize, and then fix the problem.

Never underestimate the power of a routine. Some days in your career as a financial planner will be better than others. It's important to keep up with regular maintenance and communication tasks. Stay on top of your clients' accounts by regularly reviewing their statements and activity reports. In this way, you'll know what each client owns, how much, and why. While this sound approach to genuinely knowing your client should be a constant in your practice, it will really come in handy during volatile stock market periods. When the market takes a hit, so do portfolios. You can be sure that a triple-digit loss day on the *Dow Jones Industrial Average (DJIA)* will result in questions from clients. You should know the effects of a bad (or good) market day on individual portfolios and try to contact clients before they make a call to you. You will help relieve their concerns and demonstrate how good you are at the art of the personal touch.

def•i•ni•tion

The **Dow Jones Industrial Average (DJIA)** is an index representing 30 of the largest companies in America. While not that broad, the DJIA is an indicator of how the stocks of many large companies may have performed over a certain time period.

Good communication with clients may not sound like an exciting marketing idea to you. The reverse, however—poor communication—is the number-one reason why clients look for new advisors.

Taking an Interest

When possible, take a step beyond the service relationship you've established with clients. Ask about their interests, their families, and other appropriate aspects of their lives. Not all clients will be receptive to taking a business association to a more friendly level, but others will appreciate your genuine interest. Maybe you'll find that you share a hobby or hometown. By creating business friendships, you will increase client loyalty. And there's another bonus to this marketing tool: it will also boost your referral system.

As you come across articles or anything related to your clients' personal or business interests, drop them a note with a copy or make a call to let them know about it. A few small value-added touches can go a long way toward creating a positive relationship with your clients.

Effective Marketing

You may have the good fortune of a healthy client roster today, but in order to maintain that work (and cash) flow, your marketing maintenance program must have tomorrow in mind. While much of your PR can be done inexpensively, marketing can cost you serious money. The difference is that marketing entails reaching out to get in touch with someone proactively. Some of your marketing efforts will assist you with the PR efforts. Tools that you will want to use for marketing your business include advertising, brochures, websites, sponsorships, exhibitions, seminars, and direct mail.

Even if you have experience in marketing, it makes sense to hire an outside professional who can help you. Sometimes a marketing professional who has experience in your industry can give you new ideas or information about the most effective tools that are currently working for other clients. It can also be a time-saver. Just like a financial planner, a marketing professional cannot possibly be great at all aspects of the job. No one person can do a fantastic job of writing copy, creating the layout, art, and graphics, and knowing where to deliver the message. You may be able to get started with the written message, but a professional writer may have to put it in a form that fits brochures or websites.

Interview several marketing firms before you make a commitment to hire one. You want to see samples of their work, speak with clients who have used them for projects similar to yours, and understand how they price their services. Marketing firms will work on an hourly or project basis or on a monthly retainer. If you choose the hourly method, be careful. Time racks up pretty easily, and the final bill for a project may surprise you.

> **Walking the Walk**
>
> Firms don't need to spend their entire marketing budget just creating the material. Have an idea what you want to say, and tell your marketing firm how much you have to spend. They should be able to design something within the constraints of your budget.
>
> —Ken Groppi, president, Groppi Advertising and Design, Plymouth, Massachusetts

Brochures That Work

You don't need a brochure that will rival the largest firms in the industry. Their brochure budget is more than you make in a year. The purpose of your brochure is to have a printed piece that succinctly says who would want to work with your firm and how it would benefit them. Spend as little time as possible talking about yourself and more about the prospect.

Good graphics printed on high-quality stock will also make a difference. The brochure doesn't have to be very long and feel like a magazine. A business-size envelope piece may be adequate as long as the message, look, and feel are professional.

Websites

In the early stages of your practice, you don't need to spend a lot of money on a website. You do want it to have the same look and feel as your brochures, letterhead, and other printed material, however.

The most important part of your first website is to get clients to use it. How? Have valuable material there, and constantly let your clients know why they should visit your business online. You may have the portal for them to view their investments on your website. You also may want to archive your client newsletters on the website in case they are looking for something that they read a year ago or so. You also want to have some links to other popular financial websites that clients may frequently visit.

You should also personalize your website. Have a section dedicated to current happenings in your firm, such as upcoming client events, press releases you have issued, or news about new hires. It is also a good idea to have profiles of your firm's employees on your website for clients to see pictures and to learn a little more about your staff. The key here is to keep it current. Nothing will turn a client off more from going to your website than finding stale and outdated material on the site.

From a design perspective, keep it professional. Don't use animated graphics unless it is a part of your company's logo. Maintain the same font style throughout the site, do not use popup ads, and limit the number of colors.

Advertising

Don't expect the phone to ring off the hook from advertising unless you have a huge budget. The type of budget that would get you a good lead flow would have to include a three-way campaign: print, radio, and TV.

For the most part, small financial planning firms are talking about local radio, cable TV, or newspaper advertising. Start very small with your advertising budget, and don't waste money on anything except what is geared toward your target audience. The Yellow Pages, for example, are not geared toward any specific target audience—and you can rarely expect to get a quality lead from a substantial Yellow Pages presence.

If you are inclined to advertise, bring a short, consistent message to your medium on a regular basis. Repetition of the same message will be more effective and will cost you less than running one ad now and then. Expect your advertising efforts to help build your brand, rather than provide direct prospects. The only time an ad may begin to drive prospects to you is if you have a very special offer or an event to attract prospects.

Seminar Marketing

Holding workshops can be a timely and cost-effective way to attract new clients. Issue the particulars about your event to all area newspapers. If you're unsure as to whether that press release will be printed, invest in a small advertisement in the business section of one of the larger daily newspapers in your area. There are unknown numbers of prospective clients out there who are either dissatisfied with their current financial advisors or who are taking first steps into the investment realm. By making a name for yourself as "that financial planner who does those good workshops," your developing competitive edge will only become sharper.

There are specialized marketing companies who only help advisors fill the room for a prospect seminar. Between the mailing, the venue, and any food or snacks offered, one good seminar can easily cost $10,000 for about 100 prospects. The better the free offering, such as dinner or a well-known guest speaker, the more you will get to attend. Do the math first, and know exactly what you will need in order to attract or convert enough attendees into clients. That will justify your steep investment.

Your content has to be appropriate for your audience. Don't get too technical or specific unless you are sure that the audience wants that. Your talk should be no longer than 90 minutes, and you should leave time for questions and answers. Make sure that you let people know you are offering a one-hour complimentary consultation to discuss their specific situations. It is also helpful if you have an administrative assistant on-site to book these appointments right at the seminar.

In the Know

Make your seminars entertaining. They don't have to be circus acts, but guests should enjoy themselves and leave with a favorable impression of you. This may relieve some of the natural stress and break down a barrier that builds up over addressing such personal financial information with someone they barely know.

Sponsorships

We wouldn't expect to see a major league ballpark sponsored by your firm, but the local Little League team or the high school dance team may make sense. You can really help out local community organizations and simultaneously get your name in front of your target audience.

Some firms get really creative and sponsor an event that they have created. Perhaps your town is in need of funding for a particular project. Your firm can sponsor the fundraising event.

Exhibitions

An exhibit booth at a gathering of people who fit your target market can make a lot of sense. It's common to see financial advisors exhibit at home shows and other consumer venues. But how about trade shows, where you may be the only financial advisor?

Success may be more attainable if you are the only financial advisor exhibiting in a trade show that comprises your target audience. Perhaps it is a local dental conference or a show for building contractors. While financial advisors commonly populate some of these trade shows, perhaps you can find one where you'll be the only one.

Direct Mail

How much junk mail do you get each day? That begs the question, "Is junk mail effective?" We may think not because of all the paper we throw away, but then why do so many firms use direct mail?

For direct mail to work in your financial planning practice, you need to do two things: target the message, and make it creative. Without a good target and a creative reason for people to read your message, your investment may not return very much. If you can send direct mail to a target that knows who you are or is aware of something you've done, such as your sponsorship of the high school dance team, it may be more effective. If you can be creative in the mailing and tie it into the dance team theme, it will be even more effective. Consider hosting an event to benefit the team, and your mailer may pack the house with good prospects. Your event could involve dance lessons for members of the community, taught by members of the team, with all proceeds to benefit the dance team. As emcee for the event, you'll get a chance to give yourself a little commercial and thank your attendees for their interest and support in the high school team.

The Least You Need to Know

- Branding is not only for large companies; startup and small businesses also benefit.

- Creating a public relations campaign may be the best way to let people know about your firm. Using a professional PR firm is likely to increase your effectiveness.

◆ Although it may be tempting to design and create your own marketing campaigns to save money, in the long run, you may have far greater results, and therefore less cost per new client, if you hire a marketing professional.

◆ A marketing campaign is something that builds awareness and brand for you. Don't expect your sales to increase overnight.

◆ A simple website is considered part of the basic promotional package today. You can start small, but you must begin to build your company's online presence now.

Creating a Business Worth Selling

In This Chapter

- ◆ The difference between owning a business and running a practice
- ◆ Taking the time to work on your business
- ◆ How to build good systems and written procedures
- ◆ What happens to the business if you're not there?

I know that selling your business is the last thing on your mind—you just got started! But if you can think in terms of who may want to buy it from you at some point in the future, it will help you think like a business owner instead of merely an overworked practitioner.

As a business owner, it is your fiduciary duty to your stakeholders to maximize the value of this venture. As the only owner, employee and financial planner, you may view yourself as the only stakeholder. Not true. Your family and any other dependents, employees, and clients are all stakeholders in your business.

Someday you may find yourself eager to retire. But rather than doing what planners did 25 years ago—just walking away and letting the business fade into the sunset—today there are real, live buyers with checks in hand. And what if you don't make it until retirement? Your death or total disability would be easier for your other stakeholders if you had a succession plan with value received for the business.

Whether you start with the end in mind or not, building a business worth selling builds you a better business. It will be more profitable and allow you a better work and personal life balance. In this chapter, you'll learn about the ways to turn this goal into reality. What's the worst thing that could happen? Someone tries to pay you a lot of money for your business, and you say no. That sure beats you or your heirs scrambling to find a buyer who ends up saying no.

Owning a Business vs. Running a Practice

Owning a business should be different than any other job you've had. It should deliver all that you hoped it would. Whether that's more money, more free time, greater value, or something to pass down to the next generation, most owners get nothing more than a higher-paying job. In many cases, that higher-paying job also comes with a lot more responsibility and hours—and in the end, many haven't really gained much.

In the financial planning business, most practitioners fail miserably at running their practice like a business. The owner works frenetically to make sure that all clients are well served, that tasks are completed on time, and commonly works nights and weekends in pursuit of success. A business, as opposed to a practice, is something that works when you are not at work. It is akin to a finely tuned machine that generates consistent results with maintenance and upgrading from its creator. That doesn't mean that you do nothing; on the contrary, you will always be quite busy in your business. But it does mean that your efforts alone are not the only ingredient necessary for the business to generate revenue and satisfy your clients.

All small business owners need to recognize this difference before they embark on fulfilling this lifelong dream. It is strongly recommended that any entrepreneur read *The E-Myth Revisited: Why Most Small Businesses Don't Work and What to Do About It*, by Michael E. Gerber (see Appendix C). In short, *e-myth* refers to the entrepreneur myth. According to Gerber, the entrepreneurial myth is "that most small businesses are started by entrepreneurs; the truth is that most small businesses are started by technicians suffering from an entrepreneurial seizure—the pie maker goes into the pie business and the mechanic opens an automotive repair business. The technician makes the fatal assumption that because he knows how to do the technical work of the business that he knows how to build a business that works. Unfortunately for him and for the business he creates, the opposite is true; and so most businesses fail, or if they don't fail outright, they fail to realize their potential."

This myth is extremely prevalent in all areas of financial planning. For the CPA, attorney, insurance professional, investment advisor, and financial planner, some do fail—and most never realize their potential. If you want to have a job with greater pay, longer hours, and more responsibility, then you will be a financial planner who will not fail. Your clients will probably love you and refer you even more clients—and you'll be even busier next year.

> **Pitfalls**
>
> Be aware that working nights and weekends, a necessary ingredient in the beginning, easily becomes a habit that is tough to break as your business matures. Learn early on to use assistants and outside professionals to strike a good work and personal life balance.

Working *on* vs. *in* Your Business

To break the historical cycle of financial professionals being slaves to their businesses, you need to take time to work on your company. Just like an outside consultant would look at everything you do, you must take the same approach to how you can make your business better, more efficient, and more profitable. It will pay huge dividends for you to figure out a way for your business to become less dependent on you.

Many technicians struggle with this concept and don't even know where to start. Perhaps it's an outside consultant or coach that you need to hire to get you moving in the right direction. The business world suffers no shortage of coaches, consultants, and books that want to teach you to be a better business owner and manager. An outside advisory team made up of other professionals and clients can provide valuable insight and information about the work that you need to do on your business.

While working on your business, you will look at your marketing and client acquisition efforts and process. You will also examine how you do your planning from start to finish. You will consider everything from the software you use and the research you do to how you communicate planning recommendations to clients. You will look at time and effort compared to results and client satisfaction.

You will need to block out time in your calendar to work on your business. Do this every week, and don't worry about what you are going to do—there will be plenty of issues. As you get good at it, you can begin to challenge yourself and focus on industry best practices and how to implement these in your business. You can again bring in outside consultants to help you discover the next level, and you can use this time to implement all of the wonderful coaching tools you'll learn about from your coaching program.

Working in your business means time spent doing the things that actually generate revenue for the company. Meetings with clients, reviewing portfolios, writing financial plans, filling out paperwork for your clients' investment transfers or insurance purchases, and returning phone calls and e-mails are all common tasks associated with working in your business. As you'll soon see, these in-the-business tasks can easily consume 100 percent of your time if you let them.

The Keys to Creating a Valuable Business

If this sounds like a lot of work and you're confused about where to start, don't sweat it. There is a well-worn path to creating a valuable business. It also isn't your first priority as you get started, but it should always be on your mind. Think of everything you do and each new idea that you get as if you were a third party evaluating your business for a possible merger or acquisition.

Systems and Processes

While every business—even the smallest—has systems and processes, how good are they? By good, I mean are they efficient, widely understood by all employees and clients, and consistently applied across the broad spectrum of business transactions? Good systems and processes are crucial ingredients to creating value in your business. It also prevents employees from knocking on your door for every little issue that arises. It helps to set expectations—expectations that you have of your staff, that clients have of your firm, and that your staff has of you. Meeting or exceeding expectations is a huge part of success.

You may devote most of the time spent working on your business in the first few years on the first step of creating systems and processes. You start with a notepad and write down every minute detail of any process. Don't assume anything, and pretend that a complete stranger will open your door tomorrow.

In the Know

You can get great tips and samples of written procedures from your broker dealer or professional associations. Or consider forming a study group of practitioners in a similar situation as you to share the responsibility for creating written procedures that work well.

In fact, that is a good place to start. Write a procedure for opening and closing the office each day. Details are important. If you forget to be sure that the coffee pot is turned off at the end of the day, there may be no office to come back to tomorrow.

You should document the process followed for new clients, referrals from existing clients, client account transfers, annuity transfers, investment changes and trades, mutual fund purchases, compliance issues, client appointments, client events, and the hiring and firing of employees. If you have any complicated technology, such as a computer in your conference room that ties into a projector with a built-in screen, then document it. It will be very helpful when you are running late for an appointment to have your new assistant just pull out the written procedure and have it set up for you when you get there. By no means is this list inclusive of all the written procedures that you'll need, but it should give you an idea just how extensive a job it can be.

What Works and What Doesn't

I've already discussed how focusing on the positive can help with productivity and efficiency. It's the same with your systems, so consistently use and enforce the use of your good systems to the point where they become second nature. Unfortunately, from time to time you will find a kink in a system or a process that simply doesn't work. How can you turn those lemons into lemonade? You need to create a system for fixing what doesn't work.

Simply write down what didn't work. Ask yourself what went right—and what went wrong—with the situation. If you had the chance to run through everything all over again, what would you do differently? Now, begin to reconstruct the situation from the point of view of what you could have done differently for a fantastic result, instead of the lousy one that you already had. From here, you are now ready to document the new system and avoid lousy results a second time.

> **Walking the Walk**
>
> There are always going to be systemic breakdowns and resulting errors or deficiencies. I use these as opportunities to capitalize these deficiencies into better systems and written procedures.
>
> —Peter V. Donohoe, CFP, U.S. Wealth Management, Braintree, Massachusetts

Is It Reproducible?

Have you ever gone to a restaurant with more than one location and had a completely different experience in one than another? Of course—and that's why that restaurant will never be as successful as a chain restaurant such as Outback Steakhouse or McDonalds. Even if you do not envision having more than one location, the McDonalds template for having reproducible systems and experiences for your clients is a good practice.

In your small startup practice, you want your client to have consistent experiences from one month to the next. This will become even more important as you begin to hire people. If you add advisors to your business, you want their clients to have the same consistent experiences that your clients receive. This will also help with client referrals. If a client can tell a referral what to expect, and he or she receives just that, then that client will be satisfied.

Someday, the fact that your business is reproducible may factor into your success. For the past several years, banks and accounting firms have actively acquired advisory practices. This trend does not appear to be slowing down anytime soon.

If a bank wants to acquire an advisory practice, it will be most interested in the firm's ability to offer its core service to all qualified customers. If that bank has more than one key location, you may need to reproduce your operation and client experience in more than one location with more than just you as the sole advisor. You never know when this type of opportunity will present itself or when you may become interested in this avenue, so be prepared. If you operate from day one with good systems and written procedures so that your business is always reproducible, there is no downside.

A Working Business Plan

There are two sides of having a working business plan. First: have a business plan that works. Second: have a business plan that is alive and working all the time. The first part is easy; just find what works for you and perfect it. Where it can become dicey, however, is when you try to expand too fast or get into lines of business that aren't compatible with your core business, abilities, or clientele.

Pitfalls

A business plan locked up inside your head is a great start—but not valuable. You must share it, document it, and allow others to be part of the plan implementation for it to evolve and add value.

Financial advisors rarely have a working business plan that is updated and followed. Just having one puts you at the head of the class. It will get you a premium on sales and set you up as a prime target for others wanting to buy a practice.

In Chapter 11, you learned about the preliminary factors to consider in creating your business plan. Now, let's delve a little deeper. Your business plan should start with an executive summary. This is a high-level, one-page description of your business. In this summary, you should talk about your target market, how you plan to find it, what you plan to do for these prospective clients, and how many you plan to serve. Long before you are thinking of selling, this will be helpful to any new employees—and it can reinforce your mission and vision. This executive summary will also help with your elevator speech (what you would say to someone in 30 seconds or less to get him or her interested in learning more about your business).

The next part of your working business plan should lay out your firm's marketing and communication strategy in detail. Ideally, you would have such detail, including written procedures for achievement, so that you can hire an administrator to implement all of the tactics. On the marketing side, you will want to lay out your schedule for the next 12 months. Always have the next 12 months laid out in front of you, instead of doing it at a fixed point each year. As you get good at this task, you may even have plans in the books for more than one year in advance.

Plan your advertising, direct mail, seminars, client events, and sponsorships now for the next year (see Chapter 14). It will help you with the budgeting process, and you may even get a discount for a long-term commitment. Seeing the whole year laid out in front of you prevents you from taking on more than you can effectively do and helps create a consistent routine for your staff.

On this same 12-month schedule, plan your client communications. You may want to send out monthly newsletters, quarterly performance reports, quarterly status reports, weekly market reports, annual planning update meeting requests, holiday cards, event invitations, and purely random and unplanned notes. One thing is certain: clients want good communication from their advisors. Marketing and communications experts mention that in excess of 50 communications per year, including mail, voice, and face-to-face meetings, is what may be necessary to keep A-list clients satisfied with your communication.

In the Know

Always keep your clients informed about what to expect by having an upcoming events section in your newsletter and on your website.

The next part of your working business plan will be the numbers side. Here, you can track your actual results and compare them to your goals. You should track everything. Track the number of mailings you do to the number of prospects you get to the number of prospects who become clients. You should compare your actual revenues to what was projected and explain any variance, positive or negative. You also want to track your clients' event success. How many clients were invited? How many attended? How many brought a prospective client, and how much new business was generated because of the events?

From your measurements, you will have hard data on what works and what doesn't. From here, you will adapt and change your plan to focus on what works best and eliminate those tactics that haven't worked at all for you. You now have the template for gauging success for any new programs that you want to roll out.

Empowering Managers in Your Business

Your ability to empower others to take responsibility and get things done is a key part of creating value. Don't think of managers in the traditional sense—MBAs who wear expensive suits that you can't afford in your small business. A manager in your startup shop of two will be the other person in the office. You must make that person responsible for and the manager of some things in your office. Even if it starts with the opening and closing of your office, you can end up delegating all of the ministerial and administrative tasks.

Empowerment begins with ownership. When your employee takes ownership in his or her task, he or she is empowered. Getting an employee to take ownership is not something that you can simply give away; the employee has to willingly accept it. The best way to gain their acceptance is to have them involved in the creation. You can start with written procedures. Assign the documentation of procedures for some of the person's tasks as soon as possible. You will still be involved in approving the final written procedure, but if your employee is the creator, it will be much harder to disregard it.

You also empower people who work for your business through their success and achievement. With each new success, their confidence—and their willingness to accept more responsibility—grows. To get to this point, you can't hang them out to dry for everything that goes wrong. You should value their mistakes and errors as opportunities to learn from the experience and transform it into a system that will prevent the mistake from happening again.

Of course, this doesn't mean that you hold on to a subpar performer forever. If you have someone who just can't get things right, you must remove that person from your office. What is helpful to your

In the Know

Employees who are given responsibility and understand how success will be measured are far more satisfied with their jobs than others who wonder how to please the boss.

business is an employee who is willing to take risks for the sake of being efficient and productive. If you have employees who are not willing to take risks, they will come to you for every little thing to seek your approval. Some owners will attach incentive compensation for each mistake that is made when accompanied by a new written procedure to avoid that mistake in the future.

Making Sure the Business Runs When You're Not There

One of the great fire drills for your systems and processes is how well your business runs when you are not there. It would be nice if you could take a vacation now and then and not have to shut down the office. This is tough for a two-person business, but not impossible. You will need great systems and processes and a backup plan for anything that is clearly beyond the scope of your helper.

Here's an example. A client passes away while you are on a camping trip in the wilderness with no access to a cell phone or e-mail. Your assistant should have a written procedure regarding what to do so that the client's survivors can begin processing the insurance death claim or gaining access to the deceased's accounts to pay for final arrangements. But if the survivors want information regarding something requiring more technical or greater knowledge of the family's dynamics, you would need to rely on your systems so that your assistant knows what to do. There should be a process directing your assistant where to find files containing contact information for other advisors on the deceased client's planning team to provide immediate help.

Many advisors want assistants who are also licensed. They might not be as skilled or experienced as you, but at least they are legal to perform those services that require a license when you can't.

This process to help you while on vacation could mean the difference between a good check and a failed business if you can't work. I suggested in Chapter 4 that you set up a good financial plan for yourself with all the proper and necessary insurance coverage in place. But beyond the insurance, how does your business operate for a time frame longer than a two-week vacation without you? And what happens if you can't make it back to work?

If you have followed the direction of this chapter, you or your heirs should get paid handsomely for your business. If you have not followed these suggestions, your heirs will struggle to find a buyer. And if they do find one, it will clearly be for a bargain sale price.

What If You Get Sick or Become Disabled?

Believe it or not, this situation is tougher to deal with than dying (discussed in the next section). You have to worry about getting income for your lifestyle, revenues to support overhead, replacing your services so that your clients don't bail out on you, and maintaining any momentum that you have built up with marketing, referrals, or other planning-team members.

I know that I've strongly encouraged you to be properly insured. And for now, let's assume that you've done that. But if your company had other shareholders and you were charged as chairman of the board to increase value, you'd be forced to come up with a plan to keep the company growing when the chief cook and dishwasher is down. So, for you and your stakeholders' benefit, that's how I will approach your disability.

Momentum from marketing and referrals should be on cruise control because of the systems and written procedures you have built. Those wheels should keep turning in your absence with your assistant and outsourced professionals assuming charge.

The momentum with other team members should also keep going strong. In many cases, your other team members will be small business owners like you. They, too, realize the vulnerabilities of being a small business owner and should empathetically rise to the occasion to help you out. But beyond pure hope and optimism, you could actually have a plan for their extra assistance. In the course of building your dream team, you should hold practice management meetings among all team members no less than quarterly and talk about business planning issues and contingency planning. Make it clear that the team is in place to support each other on client matters as well as your own business continuity.

 Pitfalls

Do not simply have a word-of-mouth agreement with another professional. Hire competent legal counsel to draw up a written agreement that will cover all of the important issues.

Although you have a team in place and are standing by for each other in the event of a disruption in service, you and the other team members may need to plan further. It is likely that your services are not completely replaceable or even well covered by your team members. Part of building a successful team involves members who have unique abilities and specialties that are not easily duplicated. It is imperative that you have a contingency service plan that goes beyond your team.

If you are the only planning professional in your organization, you should have a contingent service agreement with another planning professional. A contingent service agreement arranges for someone else to step in and perform your professional duties if you are unable. Choosing your contingent service partner requires care and diligence. You will need to compare cultures, services, and products offered and the pricing schedule to line up as much similarity as possible. It's ironic that most planning professionals do not have such an agreement in place.

Your contingent service agreement should discuss a few major components, including compensation, duration, and possible buyout provisions. The duration of the agreement should provide for some reasonable notice to the contingent service provider when the service is no longer required. Typically, the recovery period is a gradual process—and the contingent service partner will know when you are recovering and aim to be back to work. But what if the contingent service partner is doing a terrible job and is not living up to the terms of the agreement? Your representative should have the authority to revoke the agreement for causes such as client complaints or deviations from the service expectations.

Make sure that there is someone else who can ask the contingent service provider to start work. Also, make sure that each party to the agreement knows that alternate person. You may be in such shape that you can't make the call yourself.

For compensation, be very generous. This person is being called upon at the drop of a hat to disrupt his or her practice in order to save yours. For that, you should be willing to share a majority of the revenue generated during the contingent service period. Allowing 60 to 80 percent of the revenue generated during the contingent service period would be reasonable. You will need special language in the agreement for one-time earnings when the majority of the work is already complete. A good example is a large investment account where the transfer is in process at the time of your disability or a large life insurance case that is in the final stages of underwriting and issuance.

> **In the Know**
>
> Ask all of your team members to have a contingent service agreement in place with another professional from their areas of specialty. The team is stronger if all members are prepared to practice what they preach.

The last component of the agreement should be some sort of buyout provision. In many cases, a short-term disability can turn into something long term where you never return to work. The agreement should state that after a specified period of time, such as 12 or 24 months, the contingent service partner has the option to buy your practice for a fixed formula price.

Another great reason for this agreement is probably the most important. It is a critical component in satisfying your fiduciary responsibility to provide ongoing service to your clients. You can make this a part of your differentiating factors when obtaining a new client. You practice what you preach and even make arrangements for your clients' continuing service in the event of your disability.

What If You Die?

Of course, it's tougher on your family. But your death is easier to deal with from a business continuity perspective than a disability—as long as you have a plan in place.

def•i•ni•tion

A **buy-sell agreement** is a legal agreement between two parties where one is obligated to buy and the other is obligated to sell a business upon the death of an owner.

Similar to the contingent service agreement, you need to have a *buy-sell agreement* that provides for uninterrupted service in the event of your death. If you have already found a contingent service partner, you probably also have your buy-sell partner.

The buy-sell agreement solves several obvious problems. It provides for uninterrupted service for your clients, and it provides value to the heirs of the business owner. But the buy-sell agreement itself often causes a problem. Careful drafting and regular reviews are necessary to be sure that it is appropriate for the circumstances.

The first problem in many buy-sell agreements is the valuation language. There are many ways to value a financial planning practice, and valuations seem to change with given market conditions and supply and demand. Today, for example, there are far more buyers than sellers of financial planning practices—causing practices to sell for a premium.

Many businesses have a fixed price in their agreements but fail to update that price regularly. The price in the agreement may have no correlation to the real value of a practice upon the date of death. This contract, if negotiated at arm's length and agreed upon by both parties, will stand up under challenge—possibly leaving heirs of the deceased in an unfortunate position. The fixed-price method can work if both parties agree to update that price each year.

Other agreements call for a fair market value definition of the purchase price. While this may sound like the fairest way to reach a valuation that is acceptable to both sides, it is time-consuming and expensive. Both sides will often hire their own valuation specialists, and lawyers for both sides will agree on a third independent valuation specialist who is acceptable to each party. The parties then negotiate the price based upon the findings. This process can take months or longer. In a financial planning business where clients expect regular and timely service, the business could lose its most valuable asset during the negotiations: clients.

In the Know

Put a process in place where you are forced to review, acknowledge, and sign off on the terms of this buy-sell agreement each year with the other party.

The formula method for valuing a practice is most common in buy-sell arrangements. This would articulate value as a multiple of gross revenue or net profits. Even a formula requires some maintenance as the landscape for valuing a practice evolves.

Regardless of the method chosen, it makes the most sense to have life insurance on each party to a buy-sell agreement. This is the most cost-effective way of completing a purchase and is a guaranteed way to get the heirs paid on a timely basis.

The Least You Need to Know

- Working *on* your business is just as important as working *in* your business.

- Good systems and written procedures for everything will make your business inherently more valuable than another company that does not have such documentation.

- Turn lemons into lemonade by using errors to create good written procedures to avoid making the same mistake again.

- A contingency plan for your death or disability must be prepared when you are healthy and least expect to need one.

Part 4

Growing Your Success

Not growing your business is the equivalent of shrinking it. You can build your business by offering additional services to clients, buying a practice, taking on a partner, and using technology to become more efficient. Your living business plan will be the best way to help your practice move to the next level. Your success as a financial planner will be determined by your growth and how much you help others grow.

Chapter 16

Building Your Business

In This Chapter

◆ Expanding your business by offering clients more services

◆ Working with ideal clients

◆ Niche markets and specialization

◆ "Wow" your clients—and attract new ones

◆ Your centers of influence

◆ Going with the trends

In any business, growth of your practice is fundamental not only to build the lifestyle that you want for you and your family but also to enhance the capabilities and quality of services that you offer your clients. Building your business could entail adding new services or raising your fees, but it almost always entails adding additional clients to your client base.

In structuring how you will grow your business, it is imperative to first identify what you actually want to end up building. Obviously, it is very possible that you could double or even triple your number of clients and end up with a business that you hate—and one that doesn't make a profit.

It is understandable that as you grow and increase your capabilities to serve your existing and growing client base, surviving, eating, and paying the bills is important. Yet forgetting or losing track of where your practice growth is headed could create self-imposed roadblocks for sustained growth.

Begin by imagining your business three to five years from now, and you're looking backward over that time frame. What has to have happened in the growth of your practice for you to be able to say, "I did it—I built exactly what I set out to build"? Are you doing what you want? Are your clients ideal for your skill set and business vision?

Is this a perfect science? Will you really know what you want until you have experienced multiple phases of the growth process? The answer is no. In this chapter, I will map out the steps to grow your business and enhance the probability that you end up building a business that you are proud to own.

Expanding What You Do for Clients

Expanding your service platform is certainly a key factor in building your practice. By adding services that complement your existing specialty, you not only strengthen your relationships with your existing clients but also open up new revenue centers and make your business even more attractive to prospective clients.

In Chapter 4, I discussed how becoming a specialist would help you market your services in a more efficient manner. When you add additional services to your practice, it doesn't mean that you have to make a dramatic transformation in the way you personally hone and apply your marketing efforts. It just means that you will work to expand the areas in which you can add value to the lives of those existing and prospective clients who have come to you for what you already do well.

> **Walking the Walk**
>
> When we considered offering financial planning services to our tax and accounting clients, we were pleased to find out how thrilled our clients were to receive that advice from us.
>
> —Michael Alexander, CPA, Kolbrenner and Alexander, Greenwich, Connecticut

Adding additional services needn't be an albatross and certainly shouldn't entail more cost than the derived benefit. If you have an established client base already and additional time to spend with them to help in other areas of their financial lives, you may want to expand your personal capabilities. You can employ additional services yourself or with the help of an assistant.

If you are encompassed with your specialty and have more clients and prospects than you can help already, consider partnering with other professionals in diverse yet financially related areas of expertise to provide clients and prospects with access, through you, to an expanded menu of services. Chapter 17 covers the details surrounding partnering with other professionals. Either way, applied appropriately, your clients will view their newfound confidence and clarity as a direct result of their relationship with you.

The One-Stop Shop

As a financial advisor, your clients expect you to help them make investment decisions. Whether they express it or not, they also expect you to help them identify and articulate their goals and dreams, to protect those dreams from obstacles and deterrents, and to help them meet those goals while they are alive and fulfill their dreams even after they are gone.

Whether you are there to help in other areas or not, people need someone to give them tax advice, prepare their tax returns, insure them against loss of property, health, or life, help them buy and sell property or a business, and help prepare a succession plan. And they are willing to pay you and your team—or others independently— big dollars to help them. Establishing yourself and your firm as their one-stop shopping concierge for assistance in these areas is a sure way to help your clients prosper, strengthen your relationship with them, and substantially increase your business revenues.

In analyzing your service platform expansion, take a look at what your clients already expect from you. If you have established yourself as an investment advisor, for example, a natural extension of this process would be to add computerized financial planning to accompany the investment strategies you design. Adding this particular service will not only separate you from the majority of advisors in your area but will also provide your clients with what they truly look to you for: confidence and clarity about their financial future.

In addition to providing investment advice and composing and documenting financial plans, another natural extension of your service platform is helping your clients make sense of the insurance policies they have accumulated or the ones they should

In the Know

If you are considering additional services for your clients, ask your best clients whether they would utilize those services as a yardstick for how they will be received across the practice.

consider. Clients or prospective clients who have been fortunate enough to accumulate investment assets have also likely established insurance contracts to protect their chances of achieving their goals. If they haven't done this already, they are very likely to do so in the future. To that end, I can assure you that they would certainly welcome your advice and guidance before they would welcome the insurance company calling to talk about adding yet another policy to their collection.

The good news about adding insurance planning to your menu is that there are hundreds of brokerage firms that employ insurance professionals who are more than willing and able to make you look like the expert without taking the credit, spotlight, or your clients.

You probably already have some extensive knowledge about insurance contracts. If you didn't, you wouldn't be a financial advisor. If you are not employing insurance needs analysis for your clients already, you probably just don't feel comfortable with the process or you don't view this type of consulting as a viable revenue source. Either way, your current and future clients need help in this area—and designing a process to add this service could prove to be a very valuable resource for you in maintaining and growing profitable relationships.

In the Know

Take note of the areas where clients often ask for guidance or referrals to other professionals. Chances are, your future growth lies there.

If you are not yet an insurance specialist, your first order of business in providing your clients advice on their insurance needs is to train yourself to recognize their needs and what data to gather to make an informed computation. At this point, you simply need to utilize the insurance brokerage professionals to help you calculate and present the most viable solutions and then learn how to complete the contract applications.

Once you have built processes for the services you have added and tried them on for a while, you will easily identify many other areas in which to serve your clients. You may find these additional services ranging from tax preparation and planning to real estate consulting and will and trust compilation.

Whether you personally acquire the capabilities to provide additional services for your clients—or you establish networking relationships or hire team members to lead these various platforms—the expansion of your value proposition for your clients and prospective clients will help you build stronger and longer lasting relationships. As these relationships grow in value, so, too, will the fee your clients are willing to pay you for the value that you bring to their lives.

Pricing Additional Services

A very important component of adding additional services is your introduction of these services and the pricing structure that you design. Many advisors give away some of these services in light of investment advisory fees that they receive from working with a client. In their mind, they have misconceived that these services are not as valuable to the client as the investment advice they offer. Or, they feel like they have to give away these services to be more competitive in the marketplace. That's a mistake.

In the absence of the investment advice you might offer, clients and prospects are willing to pay very competitive fees for these valuable services alone. As you add additional services to your menu, make sure to segment and individually price these offerings. Carry that same theme forward in how you design the introduction of any additional services to your clients.

What Is an Ideal Client?

For many advisors, when they started out in the business, a client was anyone who could fog a mirror or sign his or her name. You can accumulate just about as many clients as you would like if you only use this or limited criteria in your selection process.

Bringing on just any client in this manner may feel like progress at first. Yet not only do these people provide little or no income to pay the bills—they also expect more of your same free help and guidance from here on. Do this for very long, and you will not only stifle growth but may also be out of business.

Growing a valuable financial advisory practice means developing quality relationships that are profitable. Starting with this mind-set and practice will help you grow with momentum. Restructuring your client base as a result of failing to establish the criteria for an ideal client can be costly and time-consuming.

From this moment on, identify and document your minimum criteria for the type of client you will work with or the minimum fee for which you will work. Slowly integrate these criteria into your marketing and public relations efforts. Once you have established these goals, stick to them. A few years from now, you will be very glad you did.

Defining Your Ideal Client

By definition, in any service business, an ideal client is one who needs your help, wants your help, values your relationship and what you do for him or her, has and applies the resources to pay you well for your services, and refers you to others who are similar. You likely have a few if not several of these clients already. But if you use these criteria to filter your client base, you will clearly identify those clients who you should be looking to duplicate and exactly what you are looking for in any prospective client.

A good idea to help cement the process of clearly defining your ideal client is to document your selected criteria in a questionnaire format and filter each client and prospect. Some advisors ask clients to complete the questionnaire before coming in; others like to complete it as a part of the first meeting. If you can develop a process that works for you and have the discipline to stick to it, you will save yourself a lot of time, headaches, and money as your practice grows.

Quality prospects for you and your firm don't know whether they are ideal clients or not. It is your responsibility to broach the criteria-filtering process. Yet, it is paramount to clearly let your ideal clients know that they are ideal.

In the Know

Document your ideal client profile in a format that is suitable for distribution to prospects and referral sources. This clarity regarding what types of clients you are looking for will yield you more ideal clients.

When you bring on a new client—or when you are in meetings with existing ideal clients—let them know exactly what you value in your relationship and what defines the ideal relationship for you and your firm. Once you are certain they have a clear understanding of your definition, make sure they know that you are available to others like them who may benefit from your help. Once they know who or what to look for, they will certainly begin to identify those qualities in their relationships with their friends and family.

Too often, ideal clients may feel a sense of reluctance to refer others to you if they don't know exactly what you are looking for. You can recognize this situation by the fact that they don't refer—or when they do, they preface the referral with, "I don't know if it will be a fit, but ..." If your ideal clients know that they are ideal because you have expressed that to them, they may be able to introduce you and your firm to many quality prospects for relationships just like they have with you.

Ideal Clients Are a Win/Win Situation

If you surveyed the clients you work with to get a measure of your success in exceeding their expectations, you would likely notice that the majority of those who produce high ratings are those who you would define as your ideal clients. Ideal clients should get the majority of your attention and efforts because you like working with them and the relationship is profitable for both of you. Clients who give you lower ratings are likely those who you really don't enjoy working with or that are not profitable.

Focus your efforts on identifying, working with, and attracting your definition of ideal clients. The better job you do at qualifying and selecting new clients will directly impact the value proposition that those clients receive from you and your team.

The more you enjoy working with your clients, the better job you do for them. The better job you do for them, the stronger the relationships you will build. Build strong relationships with clients, and they, too, will do their part in helping you grow your practice by referring others to you who are just like them. The net result is a better quality of life as a result of the value that you bring to each other.

Do I Need a Niche?

The most successful professionals you know are likely specialists in their chosen fields. They are the first people (or their firm is the first that the public thinks of) when needing a particular service. They likely encompass many other skill sets that they can help their clients with. But, in building their reputation by design or accident, they have become known for being the person or firm to go to for a particular specialty. This niche recognition is what attracts people to them.

When you put yourself out as a specialist—or if a client or prospect thinks of you first when it comes to a specific service need—you have established a niche. This niche may be working with a particular professional group, such as physicians or attorneys; an age group, such as high-net-worth retirees; or a specialty service, such as tax-free real estate exchanges.

Creating a niche in your financial advisory practice can help you enhance profitability and create a working environment that gives you continued energy and personal fulfillment. It will also help you hone your desired professional skill set and create a

 Pitfalls

Don't spend too much money on your niche until you have thoroughly researched the opportunity and feel confident that it is a niche with enough demand for what you offer.

more congruent flow of clients who need and are attracted to the results that you can provide them.

Choosing One That's Right for You

If you haven't identified your niche, this certainly doesn't mean that you don't have one in the making. Everybody has a niche or unique ability. Defining one that is the most appropriate for you and your business entails two very basic but fundamental and identifiable characteristics. You simply need to identify what particular client group or service area you enjoy and in which you excel. Identify areas that you are already working in or would feel comfortable and motivated in as a specialty. You want this to be something that is in high or growing demand from a demographic group and is broad enough to support the sustained growth of your business.

Spending your time and energy on establishing a particular niche that makes a profit for the business—but that you view as lousy work—is not a prudent strategy for long-term growth. You may make profits, but you will eventually build a practice that you really don't like. Make sure that niche you focus on is both profitable and enjoyable.

The Benefits of Specialization

It is impossible to be the best in your market in working with a multitude of services, age groups, or professions. Many advisory firms attempt this broad approach only to end up being pretty good at a lot of things but finding themselves chasing the competition in several areas of specialization.

In the Know

To practice effectively as a specialist, consider obtaining an advanced designation or training to evidence your commitment to this specialized area. Offer educational workshops to centers of influence, prospects, and existing clients to teach them what they need to know and how you can help.

When you find a true niche or the right area of specialty, you are able to truly optimize your time, energy, and resources to move your practice forward. Specializing in working with retirees, for example, allows you and your firm to focus only on those concerns and opportunities that retirees face and to develop unique processes and service platforms to help them specifically. This specialization also allows you to focus your marketing efforts on one specific demographic, which is certainly more efficient than blanketing a larger, more diverse group.

Perhaps the most important attribute to specialization is the mind awareness that this creates with both current and future clients. Done appropriately, establishing yourself as a specialist in a particular area helps you be the first person or firm that a client thinks of when he or she needs your particular service.

In most any endeavor, very few people prefer the services of a generalist over a specialist. Establishing the rapport as a specialist with your clients and your market will produce a much more congruent stream of qualified prospects for what you love to do well.

Creating Enthusiastic Fans

Any client has a certain level of expectation when he or she does business with you. Meet this expectation, and most of the time your clients will say that you have done your job. Yet doing your job will likely not inspire your clients to become clients for life and help further your cause. To do this, you have to create raving fans who feel empowered to work with you and tell others about you.

Most anyone in the financial advisory business can develop a financial plan or talk about an investment product. Inspiring clients to become marketing machines for your business is directly related to how you make them feel in this process. When clients and other professionals speak up about how great your services are, people listen more than when you tell them the same thing.

In all that you do and facilitate, focus your thoughts and efforts on creating a truly unique experience for your clients that goes well beyond what they expected and touches their lives in a way no other service has before. This process involves constantly asking the question, "How or what can we do in our next high-touch service effort to 'wow' the client?" From providing refreshments when a client comes to see you and a customized company binder to organize his or her financial plan and investment statements to inviting the client to workshops, calling your client on his or her anniversary, and sending him or her a baby bib congratulating them on a new grandchild, consistently wowing your clients well beyond their expectations is the key to creating raving fans in any service business.

Adding New Clients

Adding new services for your existing clients is certainly one way to grow your practice, but most any effective growth plan will involve adding new clients. New relationships—the right ones, anyway—mean more revenue for your firm.

As I've mentioned, it's important to first identify who or what type of person you want to bring on as a new client. Then, think about how you and your team will facilitate the addition of new relationships, how many new ideal relationships you need in order to meet your growth goals, and specifically how you will attract and acquire these client relationships.

An important tip here is to make sure that you have systems and processes in place to provide continuous value to those new relationships you create. Client retention is just as or more important than the plan you have for acquiring new clients. New relationships will grow your business only if you retain these relationships and add to them, instead of constantly having to replace them.

Pitfalls

With poor or no planning, many advisors end up having to acquire 30 or 40 new clients a year to replace the 40 they lost as a result of poor value creation. This is not growth. It is survival. Having to acquire new clients to survive is a vicious cycle.

Temper your new client acquisition plan to the growth that your services platform and team can facilitate. Always factor in the addition of resources needed to walk the talk.

Don't spend all of your time and resources acquiring new clients that you and your team can't handle. Start with building your client services system first, which will enable you to painlessly grow through adding new relationships in addition to those you are already servicing.

Centers of Influence

Educating centers of influence about the value proposition you offer through your advisory services could prove to be one of the best marketing efforts you make. A center of influence may be another professional or simply an influential person because of their status, position, or nature. People want to do what others have already done (and succeeded at). It is human nature to think that if someone they respect uses a certain service, product, or program, they will also be inclined to use it.

If you take a close look at your current client list, you can identify those leaders or centers of influence who might, given the right direction, help spearhead the growth of your business. These people have already influenced many others who surround them. Create a list of these influential people and stay in touch with them as you would an ideal client. Let them know that you need their help in growing your business, and show them exactly how they can participate.

A center of influence could be an allied professional who services your ideal client—but for something other than what you do. Attorneys, insurance agents, bankers, and personal trainers are examples of other professionals who deal with people who may be ideal prospects. Some will be thrilled to refer ideal prospects to you simply to see that their clients get top-notch professional services. Others will look for some reciprocity. You have to be willing to help them grow through your existing clients or marketing efforts.

If you don't have a client base yet, identify those immediate centers of influence who are open to test-driving your services. Meet with them, and let them know that you want them to experience the unique processes and quality of services that your other clients experience—and that you need their help as a center of influence. To most people, this is a compliment—and many, if not all, of these same people will be more than happy to help you.

In the Know

Don't compromise your pricing structure or "give away the farm" in this process. Remember, people place little value upon something that is free or that is offered at a significantly reduced price. Simply let the center of influence know that you have identified him or her as such and that you would like help in sharing with others the value that he or she will experience in the relationship with you.

Advanced Referral Strategies

In any business, it is universally held that a referral from an existing client is the most efficient marketing plan. It is also the best testimonial of your effectiveness in providing a product or service. Given that you are doing your job and exceeding your client's expectations, most clients are more than willing to refer others to you. They just need your help.

Too often, as I have previously mentioned, advisors do a great job servicing their clients but a poor job helping their clients help them grow their business. Most of the time, it only takes asking for a referral. Yet, there are several ways to do so more effectively than just asking for a referral in a client review.

If you are not putting on educational workshops for your clients, shame on you. This is the perfect opportunity to add value to your current relationships and to provide your client with an easy, nonintrusive way to introduce others to you and your services. Consider providing these group workshops at least three to four times a year.

Pitfalls

Don't beg for referrals and give the appearance of desperation. Your requests for referrals should be about allowing your client to help his or her family and friends by introducing him or her to you for great advice and guidance.

In your invitation, always list that the price of admission is to bring a guest who would gain value from the information to be covered.

Consider providing your clients with an agenda of their review meeting by mail and in advance notice of the meeting, and include on the agenda the discussion of any new relationships that they think would benefit from working with you. Leave two blank spaces on the agenda form for the client to complete. Have the same agenda on the table when the client comes in for the review, and make this discussion a part of your review process.

Another advanced referral strategy that many advisors have found works well is periodically mailing out response-requested, postage-paid referral cards allowing the client to fill in the name of a person who he or she feels might receive value from your newsletter, e-mail commentary, educational sessions, seminar invite, or a scheduled meeting.

You might also consider starting a referral club and recognizing in your newsletter—and at client events—those clients who are part of the club at different levels. At the end of a specified period, recognize the clients publicly at your annual client banquet—and enter their names in a drawing for a door prize.

Going with the Trends

As a nation, over the past 40 years, we have evolved from a product economy to a service economy. Similar trends can also be identified in the financial advisory industry, as it has evolved from buying and selling products to providing investment and financial planning services.

With 78 million baby boomers beginning to enter the 30-plus years they will spend in the new definition of retirement—with more net worth than any generation before them—they will define the next trend. What these people truly want today and in the immediate future is a financial partner who can provide them with guidance and advice from a holistic point of view regarding multiple needs and overcoming obstacles they will face in managing their accumulated wealth. The industry now calls this new paradigm "wealth management."

As a result of the massive wealth creation around the world in the past two decades, combined with the tremendous scientific and technological advancements we have seen through this same period, mass quantities of people have created an entirely different set of wants, needs, and concerns than the previous generation. Whether it is the new focus on making their incomes last the full length of their retirement years or staying healthy and being able to pay for health care in the future, today's retiree is different—and so must be their retirement planning and investment strategies.

In the Know _____

You don't need to be a futurist to know what the trends of the industry are. Read trade magazines, attend conferences, and talk to your peers about their best practices. Then you must implement them. To know the trend and not act is like business suicide.

Following this trend, the most successful financial advisors will meet these new and changing needs by developing one-stop, concierge centers that create the utmost in unique experiences for their clients.

Today's leading advisors will be the first to truly define wealth management by combining networks or teams of professionals who create these experiences for their clients by employing a series of unique processes to give them confidence and clarity about their ever-changing futures. Advisors who fail to accommodate this trend by concentrating their efforts on finding and selling just the right product will quickly be commoditized and eventually become extinct. Evolving their service and experience offerings through creative destruction of outdated thinking to accommodate these ever-changing trends will define the most successful financial advisors in the years to come.

The Least You Need to Know

- Expanding what you do for existing clients is the best way to grow your practice.
- As much as possible, work with ideal clients to maximize your enjoyment, satisfaction, and profits.
- Developing a niche or specialization will help build your reputation.
- Referrals are the best way to reproduce your best clients.
- The trend in the financial planning business is to provide guidance to clients regarding their entire financial picture, giving them confidence and clarity.

Chapter 17

Partnering with Other Professionals

In This Chapter

- ◆ Formal or informal, partnerships work
- ◆ The benefits of a formal partnership
- ◆ Partnership agreements
- ◆ Joint ventures with CPAs and other financial professionals
- ◆ Diligence and courtship before partnership

Buzzwords come and go in the business community. One of those words gaining prominence since the late 1990s is "partnering." Everyone who wants to sell you something is trying to partner up with you. Office supply companies consider themselves a valuable business partner, and mutual fund wholesalers insist that their firm can be your partner and help you grow your business.

It is possible that some outside parties have been so helpful they deserve to be your partner. Some give more than their fair share to gain your business loyalty and to genuinely assist you—even before you start doing business with them.

Beyond vendors and suppliers, some practitioners really do want to develop close relationships with other professionals. Some of these may end up in formal legal partnerships, where you share expenses and profits from a certain line of business (or the entire business). Others will stay informal, simply expecting that you will always do your best to help them or their clients.

In this chapter, I will talk about why you may want a co-owner for your financial planning business and what you need to do for protection. You will also learn about other professionals who are actively seeking partnering opportunities with financial planners, and how to make the most of these opportunities.

Formal vs. Informal Partnerships

A formal partnership is a business entity owned by two or more people. Law and accounting firms have been operating as partnerships forever; yet, in the financial planning business, partnerships are uncommon. The spirit of a partnership is that two or more people will combine their talents to make something better or stronger than it would be without the other. It could be that each brings a different talent to the table, or two or more people may simply want to share expenses.

Whatever the reason for your formal partnership, make sure that you have ironed out in a written agreement all of the details regarding responsibilities and revenue and expense sharing before you start. A partnership gone bad can sour you against future partnerships in a hurry.

Informal partnerships may result from office sharing to occasional client sharing. Many financial planners have informal partnerships with other planners that are developed on a case-by-case basis. Depending on the experience or specialty required in a given case, you as the planner may decide to ask another planner to work with you and share revenues. Just like a formal partnership, have a written agreement with that informal partner to state the revenue split, the share of the work for each of you, and the terms for ending the relationship. There are many reasons why you may want to end this informal partnership in the future. The person you need today may lose his or her license, relocate to another part of the country, or join another firm that will not allow the two of you to split revenue. In the latter case, your agreement could protect you from the former informal partner soliciting your client to transfer accounts to his or her new firm.

Pitfalls

Do some background and credit checking of an informal partner. It would be horrible to find out that you are the only one whose guarantees are worth anything.

In the case of office sharing, where no formal partnership exists, you still need to have some written agreement. The office lease is probably signed by both of you in addition to leases for copiers, computers, and phones. Both sides would want protection in case the other planner's business fails or the other professional is unable to earn revenue because of illness or death. Your agreement could even provide for contingent service or buyout of the other's business in the event of death.

Your informal partnership may be with someone who is not even a financial planner. Maybe he or she is a lawyer, accountant, or insurance professional looking for overhead sharing. In this instance, you are less concerned with contingent service or buyout provisions and more worried about the details of tracking expenses, such as long-distance phone service, postage, and copiers. You will need to be especially clear about any employees you share. Many an informal partnership has ended up problematic because of bickering over one getting more resources than the other.

The non-financial planner you share the space with should be strategically chosen for more than his or her ability to share overhead. You should choose this person because you think that beyond expense sharing, you will each benefit from the other's existence. You can benefit from referrals, professional mentoring of each other, or expertise on demand for client situations or questions.

Why Have a Partner?

The best reason to have a partner is when you believe that 1 plus 1 equals 3. (Sorry, math majors—I know that it will take you a while to figure out this equation.) I am talking about the "X" factor … synergy … symbiosis; something that happens because of your combination that is greater than it could have been if you had not become partners.

In an accounting firm, it is common to have partners who offer specialties in different areas, such as taxation, auditing, or industry specifics. In a financial planning firm, it could be for the same reason. You may be able to offer services that your partner cannot—thereby enabling the firm to deliver greater services to its entire client base or attract a type of client that neither partner would be able to attract without the other.

> **Pitfalls**
>
> The downside of a bad partnership is not pretty or fun. Perform an analysis of the strengths, weaknesses, opportunities, and threats of your combination before it becomes formal.

It could make sense to build a partnership because of your combination of unique abilities. Perhaps you're a sales maven. You can attract more business than any other financial planner known to mankind. Therefore, you would benefit from a partner who is a technical and operations maven. A partner who delivers quality work on a consistent basis and makes the clients as happy as you promised they would be could make the harvest of your sales ability that much greater.

Shared Risk

In business, you inherently assume risks. With a partner, you are inherently sharing those risks. Hopefully, by sharing, you are not assuming new risks that you wouldn't have had but are instead cutting the risks that you could have had. You can cut your risks by asking your partner to review client work products, thereby reducing errors and poor judgment. You will reduce risk by sharing responsibilities and assigning each partner to those tasks within their realm of abilities and desire.

You are also sharing financial risk. Of course, in tandem, you are sharing the financial reward also. The financial risk you share is another guarantor on the business lease or other expenses. You also get the benefit of having two people think like owners and think about ways to improve the business and make it more valuable.

In the Know

It is fair to directly ask about and evaluate the personal financial situation of your partner before you get into business. You want to know early on whether your partner will be able to contribute capital if and when needed. You should also put the prospective partner through all of the same background checks that you would a new employee. These may include a credit report, driving record survey, and criminal investigation.

On the financial risk and reward side, there is no requirement for everything to be shared equally. You may agree to have disproportionate shares of both based on facts and circumstances. For example, if you are the sales partner and the other person is the technical partner, you may both agree to a guaranteed base salary or commission level for sales. It is not uncommon for the sales professional to be the highest-paid person in an organization—and perhaps that should be the case in your partnership. Don't be too liberal with these guarantees, however; your entity still needs to be profitable.

There are two levels of compensation for you as the business owner. The first is the compensation for your labor. You should be generating enough revenue in the business to pay what you would have to pay to a third party to do the same work. The second level of compensation should be your compensation because of your equitable interest in the firm. This would be your share of profits.

Each year, Moss Adams, LLP, the twelfth-largest accounting and consulting firm in the United States, conducts a survey of compensation and profits for financial planning firms. The latest survey revealed that profits in financial planning practices should be around 20 percent of gross revenues.

> **Pitfalls**
>
> Carefully evaluate the compensation method for each partner before going into business together. Compare yourselves to the industry at large and to conditions in your local market.

Enhanced Capabilities

Even if you and your partner have identical backgrounds and levels of technical expertise, the two of you combined are likely to bring enhanced capabilities. To reveal these possibilities, you each need to discover your strengths and try to support each other to work only on what brings greatest value to the partnership.

Once you discover each other's strengths, you can begin to take advantage of each in a way that will help your business development, client service, staff, revenue, and profits. Beyond unique abilities, each partner brings his or her own business development possibilities to the partnership. They may lie in their circles of influence or from past jobs, and may be solicited. A client service enhancement can add great value to the practice if each partner brings services to the business that the other would not be able to do without the partner. The combination of these factors will deliver greater revenues and profits to the business.

Greater Bargaining Power

Even your small financial planning business may receive greater negotiating strength from a good partnership. The two (or more) of you combined may be able to extract higher payouts from broker dealers or insurance companies and purchase some of your outsourced services at a discount.

Two independent practitioners may receive a payout rate from an insurance company or broker dealer of x percent of gross revenues. If those two were a part of the same financial planning firm, the payout rate could easily be x plus 10 percent. Most firms do pay a higher percentage for the additional volume, and it is more cost-effective for a firm to manage two professionals in one location than two independent representatives as part of two separate financial planning practices.

The same holds true for outsourced services. Generally, the more you outsource, the less you pay on a per-unit basis. So if your partnership brings twice as much activity to a service provider, chances are high that you will pay less per unit for that service.

Speak to other professionals about their financial arrangements. Vendors will never tell you how low their pricing can go. You need to discover that from other buyers of the same services.

Built-in Succession

Succession planning is one of the largest areas of vulnerability for a small financial planning business. Ironically, most small practitioners do not have a succession plan in place despite preaching this concept to their clients. Having a partner gives you a natural platform from which to have built-in succession.

Similar to a succession plan with an independent third party, your partnership's succession plan should provide provisions for the death or disability of a partner. It should also provide for what happens if the parties decide to split up or one simply wants to quit.

In the Know

Just because you have a partner and a succession plan doesn't mean that the financial side of your plan will work out easily. You must still have insurance to cover both the death and disability contingencies.

The simple fact that you have a partner and a succession plan may be the reason why some clients hire you. Some clients who have sophisticated needs are drawn to larger firms because of the impression that any one person is not too critical to the planning team. Use your built-in succession to your advantage, and make it known to prospects and clients alike that you have a plan for them in the event that their primary advisor cannot do the work.

Legal Agreements

Way too many business partnerships are formed and operated without the benefit of a formal partnership or shareholder agreement. This is simply a bad choice. Handshake agreements may work fine when you are both healthy and contributing daily, but when that is no longer possible, you will stress the relationship to a point of breaking.

Don't be cheap when it comes to your business agreement with your partner. Keep the agreement current, and make sure that the language regarding valuation is accurate and appropriate. Hire an attorney who is experienced and competent at business law and agreements. It may cost you a little more today, but maybe a lot less in the long run.

A good example is if a partner becomes disabled. Let's say that both partners agree they will keep each other's salaries going and profits equally divided under any circumstances. This arrangement sounds good and may work for a while—but what if you are permanently disabled and never able to return to work? How long will the working partner be willing or able to afford this same cash outflow? How long will there be profits? Furthermore, where does the moral obligation end in favor of what is the right thing to do for the long-term health of the business?

Your partnership agreement would, of course, cover issues such as death and disability, but it will also cover issues that may govern certain day-to-day circumstances, such as the loss of a partner's license because of a regulatory issue or how to break a stalemate regarding business policy. The agreement will also have important nonsolicitation or noncompetition language that would apply in the event of a breakup. You would also have salary and profit-sharing guidance from your business agreement.

In the Know

Have your legal agreements prepared by an attorney with experience in this area and signed by both parties before you start the business. It is worth delaying the opening day rather than going forward without any formal agreement.

Working with CPAs

For CPAs, being active in the financial planning needs of their clients has always been an afterthought. But in the 1980s, personal financial planning was touted as a major growth area for CPA firms. Laws had recently changed, enabling CPAs to accept contingent fees and commissions. Prior to that law change, it was considered unethical for a CPA to work for a contingent fee or for a commission.

Because of a drastic reduction in the number of candidates in school for accounting and the CPA exam, this profession has been suffering through one of its most severe staff shortages. Starting with the dot-com era, not many college students were willing to go through the pain and long hours suffered by young CPA candidates when working for an Internet startup company was so fun and lucrative. Now, follow that up with the Sarbanes Oxley Act—requiring much greater scrutiny of a company's records by outside firms—and CPA firms are busier than ever. The end result is that financial planning has been very slow to become a major force in the CPA industry.

In the Know

Find a CPA who has started a financial planning division and has not met with much success. He or she will be more motivated to create success than someone who is just getting into financial planning.

Despite the slow start, some firms have embraced personal financial planning as a firm offering and seen tremendous success. There are just as many, however, who have not found success because they have not devoted the proper time and resources to launch this department. Many client surveys have revealed the CPA rank as the most trusted among all professional advisors. Further surveys have even pointed out that a majority of small business owners would prefer to receive their investment advice and purchase their insurance through their CPAs.

The CPA has a reputation for not being the most polished of business development professionals and rather slow to move. These statements are both true and are exacerbated today by the huge demand for CPA services and the undersupply of CPAs. They don't need to be good salespeople, and they don't need to do anything different to make a good living. CPA partners are making more money today than they ever imagined they would 10 years ago. But for the CPA who is not merely content with doing historical analysis and tracking billable hours, the financial planning world has great appeal—leaving the door open for financial planners to build relationships with CPA firms whose attitude is similar to a business owner looking to do what is right for clients and shareholders. Working with CPA firms today can have several potential outcomes.

The framework for how you may develop a relationship with a CPA firm is not exclusive only to CPA firms. The possibilities that follow can be applied in any professional joint venture.

Referrals

Successful financial planners have been getting quality client referrals from CPAs for years. Even firms that have taken the plunge to start a financial planning division will still occasionally refer a client who does not want to use the CPA for financial planning. If you expect a steady referral relationship from a CPA firm or two, you will need to be clear about the type of clients you want to service and also be in a position to refer good CPA clients to the firm.

Revenue Sharing

Many CPA firms that are not willing to commit fully to a financial planning division have set up revenue-sharing arrangements with financial planners. Depending on the type of revenue, the CPA firm may need to have licensed professionals to receive the revenue share. For securities or insurance commissions, only a licensed professional can receive a revenue-sharing payment. For investment advisory or financial planning fees, no licenses are required. A firm member must merely sign a solicitation agreement with the provider and disclose that relationship and revenue-sharing agreement to clients.

Pitfalls

Make sure that CPAs only share securities and insurance revenue with licensed professionals. Any deviation would cause a regulatory problem for them as well as for you.

Fully Licensed Affiliates

A CPA firm committed to the financial planning business will become fully licensed and is a potential affiliate for your firm. This is the ideal situation because of the firm's alleged commitment. You may need to champion the plan and take charge of the marketing and communication efforts so that the firm's clients are aware of their desire to perform planning services for their clients.

In these situations, there is likely an across-the-board revenue-sharing agreement in exchange for services. You provide the actual planning, investment, or insurance services; the CPA firm provides the client and client relationship services. Revenue splits are commonly anywhere in the 40 to 60 percent range for you, with the balance to the firm.

Walking the Walk

I have been a financial planner since 1996, always working directly with CPA firms. In 2002, I joined a firm that showed me how to work specifically inside a CPA firm. Now, five years later, I am a partner in a fast-growing financial services division of a prominent Connecticut accounting firm.

—Kevin P. Major, Kolbrenner and Alexander, CPAs and financial advisors, Greenwich, Connecticut

A Financial Planning Partnership

This method may be the best situation of all if the CPA firm is substantial enough. You would want to gain comfort that the firm's clients fit your ideal profile and that the partners are committed to promoting the financial planning division and encouraging clients to use your services. In this case, a new advisory firm is started where you and the members of the CPA firm share ownership. You will often be asked to roll your book of business into the new venture in exchange for your ownership interest in the new entity.

Just like any other partnership, make sure that you can see how less is more and that your reduced ownership in this new deal is going to be a better financial deal for you. You will also need to be sure that a strong business agreement exists between you and the firm, spelling out all of the same details that you would expect to find in any partnership or shareholders' agreement.

Winning with Attorneys

Attorneys have been much slower than CPAs to start a financial planning practice as a part of their law practice. Part of this is because there are so many legal specialties out there, many of which are not related to the financial planning business in a congruent way. However, attorneys who do practice estate planning or business law are well suited to add the financial planning discipline to their firms.

Many of the very large law firms have established trust departments with billions in assets under management, but the smaller firms have yet to follow suit. It's only a matter of time until law firms follow the CPA firms and start personal financial planning divisions. In the meantime, the most common relationship between lawyers and financial planners are mutual referral relationships. A referral relationship with a qualified estate or business lawyer can yield great results, but don't expect it to evolve into much more in the near future. It would be acceptable and wise for you to inquire about the firm's interest to enter the financial planning business and to let them know why you think they should do it and how you can help—but don't expect immediate results.

In the Know

If you do partner with a lawyer, ask that partner to introduce you to other attorneys who may refer ideal clients to your new venture.

Leveraging with Mortgage Brokers

The mortgage brokerage business has really grown since its mainstream acceptance in the real estate market in the 1980s. It is, however, a boom-and-bust business. When the real estate market is hot, it prints money. When the real estate market is soft and sales are off, it suffers.

To level out their revenue flow, it makes sense for mortgage brokerage firms to consider a financial planning division. With the current slowdown in real estate transactions, some firms are beginning to diversify their service offerings for past customers. The problem for many has been that they have customers, not clients. What's the difference? A customer is someone who may have conducted a transaction with you but has no loyalty or intention of using you again unless you have the best deal. A client, on the other hand, is someone who looks to you for your guidance, has a relationship with your firm, and the expectation of doing business again.

In the Know

When partnering with a mortgage broker, find out how many customers have come back for second or subsequent transactions. That is an indicator of a good relationship that can be built upon.

When the real estate market is off, a mortgage broker is looking for alternate sources of revenue. The easiest services for these professionals to offer would be ones that impact the real estate transaction—namely, homeowner's insurance, life and disability insurance, and estate planning. It would be appropriate for any lending professional to ask questions and offer services to help with these issues. This is where you enter. While the firm can ask the questions, its employees are probably not knowledgeable enough to deliver the answers.

You and the Insurance Professional

A good insurance professional is very well suited to add a financial planning division to his or her practice. Most insurance sellers are good at relationship building and have clients who know them well. There are, however, two distinct divisions in the insurance industry: property and casualty lines and life and health insurance lines.

Property and Casualty Agents

Property and casualty agents who have a good number of business clients would be well suited to add financial planning services. The small agent who has primarily homeowners and auto insurance clients is not a good prospect for you.

Pitfalls

Beware the insurance agency that is unwilling to prepare a business plan or commit resources to the new partnership. Its commitment has to be deeper than a few good clients that it already knows need your services.

Business insurance is so expensive and complex that many agents build a good relationship with their clients and interact fairly often. The agent is often consulted about many business issues and risk management in general. The relationships are commonly with the owners of the firm and their key management personnel. Issues such as succession planning and key person insurance are a natural for owners and their business agents. These business-focused property and casualty agencies are often involved in the group benefits of their clients, as well. A clientele in group benefits provides an ideal entry into the retirement plan and 401(k) business.

Life Insurance Agents

Many life insurance agents already do financial planning, but there are many who do not. Even for those who already call themselves planners, many do not have a formal planning offering for clients and do not have a division to offer fee-based asset management.

Like the business property and casualty agent, the life insurance agent often builds a good relationship with his or her clients. The relationship naturally traverses topics regarding family, money, and estate plans. Top agents are usually great salespeople, too, and find it easy to launch another division or service as long as they have the professional talent to provide that service.

Can You Help a Bank?

As I discussed in Chapter 6, many banks are in the mainstream of financial planning providers already. Many smaller banks, however, still need your help. Many of the very small community banks—with a couple of branches or fewer—don't even have a representative on the floor of the bank to sell annuities or mutual funds. And then there are some of the smaller banks that have a branch sales program for financial products but no financial planning offering for clients needing greater guidance and service. These small institutions are ideal prospects for your financial planning services.

Walk Before You Run

The possibilities to partner with any of these financial services professionals provide you with enormous potential. But potential alone does not bring success and profits. It takes a burning desire to succeed and a dedication of resources to realize the potential.

Evaluate the Fit

Before you snap at an opportunity to partner with another financial professional, do your homework to see whether there is a long-term fit. Start by examining the types of services that the firm offers. Just because it's a CPA firm doesn't mean that it has ever ventured beyond audits and taxes. You want to make sure that the addition of financial planning services to your partner's business is not culture shock for his or her clients.

In the Know

Prepare a diligence checklist, and ask your potential partner to prepare as much of the information for you as possible. The diligence checklist will ask detailed questions about the partner and his or her clients and practice. You may ask for the number of clients served, the average longevity of existing client relationships, the gross revenue per client, the source of existing clients, and details of all revenues and expenses for the practice. This will help indicate your potential partner's level of interest and give him or her an opportunity to see what is important to you.

Evaluate the quantity and quality of the partner's client base. A good partner will already have enough clients to support the financial planning division. It is not only important for them to have enough clients to build a successful planning practice, but they have to be the right clients. Ask the partner to rate his or her clients by criteria such as fees paid, premiums paid, or other benchmarks that will tell you about their potential as planning clients. Then you rate their clients by criteria that are important to you as a financial planner.

On the quantitative side, you want to make sure that their income levels, net worth, and investable assets meet your criteria as ideal. Qualitatively, you should stick to clients who are fun to work with, who are willing to refer you to other ideal clients, and who view you as the head coach of their financial team. In a new venture like this, you should be picky enough to only work with ideal clients. The reality of working only with ideal clients may be tough to do when you're just starting out, but do not stray too far. Many advisors devise a scoring system using grades from A through F. An ideal client is an A. B clients have the potential to become A's. C clients have the potential to become B's or even A's someday. Stay away from D and F clients at any stage of practice.

Get Engaged Before You Marry

Every now and then, you'll find a potential partner who is ideal and as excited as you are for the joint venture. But don't go right to the attorney to draw up a partnership agreement. You need to "date" a while first. Share a few clients, spend time together in the conference room, and meet a few of each other's clients and centers of influence. After you hear each other tell your stories to others a few times, you'll begin to develop a deeper understanding and comfort.

You can begin your relationship with a simple revenue-sharing agreement and a plan to move forward upon attainment of a few key milestones. Your milestones may be related to net revenues, numbers of clients, or compatibility on a stage when doing marketing seminars together. After you have witnessed the business potential firsthand and you know that getting along is not a problem, then you may move forward to a more formal arrangement.

The Least You Need to Know

- ◆ Whether your partnership is formal or informal, have a written agreement to document the key business terms, purpose, and goals of the relationship.

- ◆ Partnerships work best when the combination of two or more individuals brings more value to a business than you could have had alone.

- ◆ Other financial professionals who are looking to offer financial planning services are ideal candidates for growing your business.

- ◆ Take your time when making formal partnership arrangements. Make sure that you have thorough quantitative and qualitative comfort with your partner.

Chapter 18

Keeping Ahead of Technology

In This Chapter

- The effectiveness of a good business website
- Protecting yourself, your clients, and their data
- Content management for profits
- Necessary electronic client services
- Using the Internet as a marketing tool
- Operating efficiency gains never go away

Keeping ahead of technology may be a bit of an oxymoron. The only people who are truly able to stay ahead may be Bill Gates or Steve Jobs. But to run a successful financial planning business today, you need much more than good client relationships and a personal computer.

Websites have become central to the success of businesses. A well-designed website is a valuable commercial mechanism, acting as a proven source of information for present and prospective clients. It's a rare business today that does not maintain a website. But a good one doesn't start and end with you ponying up the money to retain a website creator. There are a number of elements to consider when designing your site. Download time, navigation structure, overall usability, and general appearance are a few.

In this chapter, I'll explore the key elements of a professional-looking website and then look at proven ways to attract leads to your site. This brief tutorial in technology will provide an examination of sound efficiency methods, such as content management software, in addition to a few words on electronic client solutions.

What would a chapter on technology be without a segment on information protection? I'll examine a few measures necessary to secure the confidential data entrusted to you by clients—from the very hands-on to the more technical. Advancements in technology have made it easier and more efficient for financial planners to conduct business. This chapter will give you a snapshot of the variety of technology-based marketing and client solutions available as you begin your business in financial planning.

Websites: More Than Electronic Brochures

Much more than an electronic brochure, a well-designed and well-maintained website can draw volumes of business to a financial planning practice. Unlike a handout brochure that provides the most basic information about your practice, a website can become an infinite source of new clients. Considered a virtual window display for business, a well-designed and properly maintained website can be a go-to source for existing clients and a built-in referral service for new prospects. If a website is built right, it will at least attract curious Internet surfers—but there are a few essentials to follow to attract visitors and ultimately generate new business. Updated content, appropriate graphics, and easy navigation are the ultimate goals of every business website.

Go with a Pro

You may be tempted to set up your company website by yourself as a cost-saving measure. Unless you have the technological savvy and an eye for online design, however, the fairly small investment that you'll outlay for a professionally designed site will be well worth it. Hiring a professional to design and maintain your site will ensure that styles and formatting remain consistent, and you'll have the benefit of someone who has designed sites for usability.

A website is a visual mechanism that, when designed correctly, will educate and advertise to your advantage. Perception counts for a lot, and if your site evolves into a couple of sloppy windows and assorted fonts, frames, and columns, the perception that you will convey is one that may actually drive clients away.

Chances are that you know a few business-people who are pleased with the way their website is performing. Likely, they'd be happy to share the name of their website designer with you. Also, check with other planners at professional meetings and trade shows for a designer you can afford. Don't be bashful when conducting interviews with potential designers to be certain that they have a good grasp on the type of website your financial planning practice requires.

In the Know

There are many web designers who cater to the financial services business and work from templates that already have a fair amount of financial planning content and infrastructure. You may need to further customize these sites to meet other goals you have.

Looks Count

The look of your website should immediately convey your line of work. As a financial planner, your accreditations, specialties, and contact information should be up front and easily readable. Neatness counts, as does organization and content. To achieve a well-organized site, remember that all information should never be more than a mouse click or two away. Also, try to keep the content of each page to one page—limiting the users' need to scroll down. Easy navigation is vital to a business website.

Choose carefully when deciding on background and text colors. Steer clear of bold, bright colors that may not be appealing to the eye. Dark background colors can also be a visual turnoff. A white background with a few well-placed graphics that say something about your work as a financial planner is the best way to go.

Want to draw prospects away from your site quicker than you can say "fiduciary"? A business site that contains even one sloppy error will work bad magic. Incorrect spelling and grammar conveys carelessness and laziness, while a properly edited website will communicate the image that you want to suggest. Let's face it … if your website is a mess, why would a prospective—or a loyal, existing client for that matter—trust you with his or her finances?

Outdated information on any website is another kiss of communication death. Product line changes, staff additions, and contact names and numbers must all be kept up-to-date. You need to have a process in place to regularly allow you to eliminate stale press releases, industry articles, upcoming events, and so on. That doesn't mean that you want to clear them from the site entirely; you just want them archived somewhere other than in what should be a time-sensitive location.

In the Know

To even out the ratio of copy to graphics on your website and to drive the marketing point home in an illustrative way, mix things up a bit with well-placed and industry-appropriate graphics. A professional photographer or high-end stock photography source can help you achieve that winning look.

Instilling confidence in clients is vital to your success as a financial planner. Your website should convey this message, and the best way to deliver it is through a separate page that clearly details your privacy policies—including whether or not you share e-mail addresses, how you will use information gathered, and its intended use. A privacy statement should also cover restrictions on your website's use and appropriate industry disclaimers. Regulators also require that you furnish this privacy policy to clients at least annually. Your broker dealer or compliance consultant can give you a sample privacy policy.

Attracting Visitors

It's the small business person's dream—achieving a high ranking in major search engines. You can attain that goal by keeping your target market in mind. Keyword phrases are what drive search engines; therefore, your site should contain phrases that prospects will likely type into a search box. Confer with your website designer about keyword phrases, or use research tools available through the major search engines. Because major search engine companies such as Google change their formulas so often, you may need to retain someone who is always on top of this for you.

Search engine optimization will increase the number of visitors and potential clients to your site, but there are other measures you can take to increase the number of hits you receive. Consider having industry-related websites link to your site. This will draw attention to your site and at the same time optimize your ranking on the major search engines.

You can also sharpen your competitive edge by offering a website that "speaks" another language. A second language version will not only bring additional clients your way, but it will also increase your visibility in the major search engines. But if you are doing this, be prepared to start getting prospects that expect you to speak the language also. It may be worth brushing up on that high school Spanish or French.

One of the best ways to keep traffic coming to your website is by making sure that it loads quickly and efficiently. Keep the information on your home page to a minimum. The idea is to get visitors to explore your site and discover who you are and what you have to offer. You may be tempted to blow your own horn, but don't overwhelm visitors with 500-word testimonials and other self-congratulating copy on your home page.

Having a website that you believe is valuable to your clients is one thing; getting them to go there and use it is another. You need to develop a regular marketing campaign reminding clients why they should visit you online. Take every opportunity to direct attention to your website by including its address on all of your marketing efforts, including business cards, brochures, newsletters, and other promotional items. That also goes for the contact information included in your e-mail signature.

The reverse is also true. Too many virtual companies don't want prospects to call them. You, on the other hand, need the personal contact. Your website should invite the personal contact and have your firm's contact information prominently displayed on every page with an encouragement to call for more information.

Staying Protected

Providing sound advice in a timely manner may be the foundation of a successful financial planning practice, but instilling trust is at the heart of good client relationships.

That time-built confidence can come crashing down in an instant if client information has been compromised. Unfortunately, financial advisors are high on the target list for identity thieves. Think about it. You maintain sensitive, confidential information in your office files and on your computer. Social Security numbers, tax returns, driver's license information, estate planning documents … in the wrong hands, this information could create a nightmare for your clients—and you.

Before you scream, "Stop this train … I want to get off," take a deep breath and read on. A number of technologies exist to safeguard your electronic network from these scoundrels. And you can use a few tried-and-true measures to ensure that your office passes the security test.

> **Pitfalls**
>
> A small business can often be more attractive to an identity thief or hacker than a large corporation for one simple reason: the big firms have deeper pockets and can afford every security measure that comes down the pike. In fact, most large companies maintain information technology (IT) departments that keep on top of advances in network security.

Shielding Your Practice

A number of technologies are available to protect your computer and network system from being invaded by information thugs. First and foremost, no business—regardless of size—should be connected to the Internet without firewall protection. In basic terms, a firewall is a combination of software and hardware that acts as a security inspector between the Internet and the information on your business network. A firewall protects your computer network from intentional intrusion that could result in compromised confidentiality or data corruption. That's the good news. What a firewall cannot do, however, is prevent someone with a modem from dialing into your network—thereby bypassing the firewall. Make sure that your technology consultants have a written security plan that you are comfortable with and can publish for clients who inquire about it.

Antivirus software is another must-have for a business network. Installation of this software will detect, isolate, and eliminate code that is meant to compromise your networking system. Fairly simple to install, antivirus software can be set to automatically scan hard drives and e-mail for viruses, often referred to as worms or Trojan horses.

An intrusion detection system, referred to in the computer biz as an IDS, can scan for suspicious activity on your network. An IDS works in partnership with firewalls to help block unwelcome traffic and examine remaining visitors to ensure that they are valid.

Just because you're a small-scale company doesn't mean that you should throw security caution to the wind and hope that a hacker doesn't worm his or her way into your systems. You can't afford not to spend a few extra dollars on protection systems. Your clients have entrusted you with extremely sensitive information. Maintaining it is not only your responsibility—it is the key element to your continued career as a financial planner.

A Few "It Goes Without Saying" Measures

I'm going to mention them anyway. If you're taking on a partner, an assistant, or even part-time help, conduct a thorough background check. It may seem like you're getting into their business, but if you don't check a prospective employee's criminal record (and their credit rating while you're at it), then you may find that you have been compromised by someone who wanted to work you over, not work for you. Securities regulations will even require fingerprinting of any employee who handles client checks.

Speak to your attorney about drafting offer letters and consent to investigation letters in such a way that you make potential employees aware of the checking, and obtain their written consent. The letters may also state that you will, from time to time, conduct random checks without the need for additional consent and require that they disclose to you any changes that would be discovered in a subsequent check.

Secure all filing cabinets with high-quality locks, and by all means be aware of what's sitting on your desk. All client information should be kept safe from eyes that have no business looking at it. And if you're going to leave your desk for any length of time— including a lunch break and definitely at the end of the day—clean off your desk and put all confidential data away in a secure area.

A paper shredder can be one of your best friends. You need to destroy all copies of confidential data that you do not need to save. Also, make sure that your shredder does cross-shredding. A good crook can take the trash from a cheap shredder and piece together enough of the shredded material to obtain meaningful information.

Speaking of security, did you know that identity thieves "case" parked vehicles for laptop computers? Don't tempt a scam artist by leaving this fountain of confidential information in sight. If you must travel with a laptop, keep it with you at all times. The same is true for hard copies of client files. Do not, under any circumstances, leave any client files in your car. Get a bigger briefcase if needed.

Pitfalls

Never use an obvious computer password, such as the names of your children or the year you were born. Use an obscure password and mix it up by using symbols, numbers, and upper- and lowercase letters. It's also a good idea to change passwords regularly—as often as once a month.

Backing up your data is critical and needs to be a regular part of your routine. Daily backups are best. You can outsource this task to a firm that backs up and stores your information off-site in its vaults, or you can do it yourself (but someone has to physically be there to assist). While you can program the system to perform a daily backup, someone needs to be present to at least change the tape or CD used for the backup. Backup disks should be stored in a safe place away from the office and retained at least until the next backup.

Practice Management Is a "Contact" Sport

The busier your practice becomes and the more networking you do, the more contact information you'll encounter. You may be tempted to keep that growing pile

def•i•ni•tion

Content management systems are database systems that maintain all of your clients' contact information. They are easily customizable, enabling you to track projects and schedule tasks for future dates.

of business cards on a rolling device or in a file cabinet, but the important information that they contain could do your practice a lot more good if they were immediately accessible.

That's where handheld personal information managers and *content management systems* can come into play. In the competitive financial planning profession, having quick access to all contact information can increase your prospects, sales, and customer service—and give you yet another edge over the competition.

PDAs

No longer considered highfalutin' address books, handheld personal digital assistants (PDAs) typically focus on the individual user. Most have a few central functions, including a daily calendar, phone book, to-do list, memo pad, calculator, and e-mail system. Most also have Windows-portable computing features, such as Excel, in addition to your cell phone.

These little computers have become bare minimum requirements for the professional who spends a lot of time away from the office. If you have an assistant or another employee who needs to communicate with you at the drop of a hat, you will also need to have your device synchronize remotely with your computer network. You can have the synchronization performed with Microsoft Outlook or with many other content management systems.

If your handheld isn't set up for remote synchronization, make sure that you back it up at least once per day. This little guy will keep track of all of your appointments, to-do lists, and address book—and that loss would be painful. Also, be sure to password protect the device. If you happen to leave it in an airport or inside a rental car, you may never see it again. The loss of data may be something you need to disclose to regulators or clients.

More Than a Database

The most essential function of a good content management system is to keep you updated on your clients' current and future financial needs. It may take a little time and effort to get a handle on how to get the most from it—but once it's mastered, a good content management program will help run your financial planning practice with increased efficiency.

Still, don't get more than you need in a content management system. Some programs are just a little too complicated to get a firm grasp on if you're not technologically savvy. If operating a contact manager requires more technical ability than you have, either find a technology guru who can guide you through the learning curve or consider a program without as many bells and whistles.

You should design your content management system to be the core system for executing many of your marketing and communications initiatives. You can use it to send out newsletters, performance reports, or news tidbits. If you put good data into the system, you will get better results from it. For example, if the tax laws change with respect to retirement plan distributions, it would be very cool to send a notice to all clients with retirement plan assets about the change on the very day that it's announced. Being the first one to provide your clients with information specific to them is wonderful for your professional relationships.

If you plan on hiring employees, make sure that the content management system you utilize will accommodate a growing practice. Most systems are flexible enough to add and delete users with very little effort. Also, make sure that the system you use will easily export data to another program. With all of the rapid developments in technology, you may find the system you are using today outdated and dysfunctional a year from now.

Electronic Client Services

Most clients hire a personal financial planner because of the high touch and ensuing relationship. They also expect, however, not to have the services you offer be so technologically outdated that everything is ink and paper. In addition to your website, clients might like to receive other valuable communication from you electronically.

Your newsletters and quarterly performance reports are great starts for electronic communication. This will also save you a bundle in printing and postage.

You should have links on your website to client account information. Some content management systems will even allow client access to those portions of the system that you grant them permission to access. Some clients will want to fiddle around and look at their accounts on a regular basis, and

In the Know _____

Before you go crazy with building electronic capabilities that your clients may want, invite them to help. Asking your best clients what electronic services they would like to see can get you closer to their needs and save you time and money.

others will not. You can easily set up your client investment performance system for client access. The client will then have the ability to look at his or her performance over any particular time period, whenever it's most convenient.

Some of the most recent versions of financial planning software allow for data integration from banks and investments not serviced by your firm. These same systems will incorporate that updated information into the financial planning calculations, and conclusions can change daily. It's not that financial planning conclusions need to change that often; it's just that this "information now" world we live in is creating expectations that the small financial planner needs to be aware of.

At a bare minimum, you should have financial calculators and simulation capabilities on your website. Why send clients to other websites for them to calculate how much it will cost to educate their children or how much they will need to retire comfortably in 15 years? You should also have educational information available electronically for your clients. Whether you push that information to them or they pull it down from your website, you need to be an educator to your clients about financial information that's of interest to them.

You should provide some shopping services to your clients electronically. I'm not talking about books or handbags; I mean insurance or other readily available financial services. Why let your clients go to another website to shop and buy term life insurance or long-term care insurance when you can set that up for them? The same goes for clients who want an investment account where they play trader for fun. Why let them do it at some discount broker who will keep soliciting them for all of their investment assets when you can provide that service for them?

Many advisors have added storage vaults to their electronic client services. Most clients have a bear of a time locating important documents, especially when they need them. Copies of insurance policies, wills, trusts, prior tax returns, and important business documents can easily be stored in your systems and set up to allow client access and downloading 24 hours a day, 7 days a week.

The Internet as an Advertising Tool

Mostly large companies use the Internet as an advertising tool, but there are also opportunities for the small business. Start by asking your more technologically savvy clients what websites they find interesting and often use. See whether there are any sites of particular local interest that are common among a few or more clients where you may reach other good prospects within your geographic area. You can purchase banner ads from other popular sites visited by your ideal clients and publish articles on websites looking for good financial content. (A banner ad is an advertisement that you place on a company's website. This ad will prominently display when any user of that site opens it as a link to your message.) Most site publishers will allow a tagline telling readers who you are along with a link to your firm's site.

You can use your firm's newsletter as an e-mail solicitation to prospects. You may even use your banner ads simply to get subscribers to the firm's newsletter. Spam laws do prevent mass marketing via e-mail, but you wouldn't want to do something as offensive as spam anyway. Start building a newsletter distribution list of ideal client prospects, and always have an opt out button clearly labeled. This will get some new readers and eventually some new clients.

Consider joint venture Internet marketing with other firms that are looking for a similar client but are offering different products and services. You could do a marketing joint venture with restaurants, wine stores, travel companies, attorneys, mortgage brokers, realtors, contractors, clothing stores … the list goes on.

Operating Efficiency Gains

Operating efficiency gains is a fancy term for doing things better and more quickly. The single largest benefit of technology in all sectors of the financial services business has been operating efficiency gains. The CPA can prepare financial statements and tax returns in far less time; the attorney can get your new wills and trusts drafted much more quickly; and the financial planner can examine what-if scenarios for clients while the client is seated in front of them.

There may be a point where operating efficiency gains stop or at least slow down. But that is not the case for the financial planning industry. Expect information about new tools and technologies to flood your inbox for the foreseeable future. You'll always need a good budget of time and money for new technology. Just because the cost of hardware continues to come down doesn't mean that you'll spend less next year. You'll just have better equipment with greater output.

If there is a downside, it will come from a few various perspectives. First is that the big will get bigger. The large firms—some with a decided technological advantage already—will continue to invest in and develop new technology, distancing themselves even further from the small practitioner who refuses to invest in new technology. In today's world, there is no reason that you, as a small practitioner, cannot have similar technology as the big firms. It will just cost you more on a per-client basis.

A second downside is that client expectations will begin to grow regarding what they perceive is available in the marketplace. People talk to other people about their financial issues; ads during the Super Bowl sometimes work; and newspapers and magazines will write about what a client should expect. As a result, you need to be prepared to meet those expectations to keep your clients believing that their advisor has the best technology for their needs. Your technology tools for clients are worth talking about in your firm's newsletter and during client events. If clients perceive that another firm has something they wish you had, your client is at risk to leave your firm.

The Least You Need to Know

◆ Your business needs an effective, well-maintained website to be competitive.

◆ Small financial advisory practices are particularly vulnerable to client privacy issues and scoundrels looking for information.

◆ A good content management system can be the backbone of your organization.

◆ View the Internet as a tool that enables you to compete with larger firms by offering a robust menu of electronic client services.

Chapter

Spread the Wealth

In This Chapter

- Giving back to the community
- Doing pro bono work
- Teaching others about financial planning
- Becoming a mentor
- Creating the time to give

There are many ways to spread the wealth of your knowledge. From special guest appearances at local senior organizations to sharing your expertise with nonprofits, we'll take a look at a variety of venues where you can give back. For whatever reasons—be they utterly selfless or to boost your business—now is the time to give back by sharing your hard-earned wisdom.

Performing your services for free, to people who really need them and probably cannot afford them, is another valuable way to give back to your community and to assist with national causes. Offering free professional services is a fine approach to gaining recognition for your professional services and being a good citizen. But there are guidelines to consider when offering your expertise for free. We'll examine these boundaries and offer a few suggestions on where to provide good public services.

This chapter will also discuss the commitment and preparation involved when volunteering your services. I'll also say a few words about ways to share what you've learned by becoming a mentor to a novice financial planner. For many of you, those first steps into the challenging, interesting, and rewarding profession of financial planner were not that long ago. If you were fortunate enough to have benefited from the encouragement, advice, and support of a more seasoned advisor, perhaps now is the time to consider paying back that favor.

Giving Back

People volunteer for a wide variety of reasons: from an altruistic desire to assist to more self-interested reasons, such as networking for business prospects. Volunteerism has career-enhancing power, demonstrates your abilities, and offers a way to share your financial planning knowledge. Your volunteer efforts will help this new industry by spreading goodwill about financial planners.

Among the many motivations to volunteer are a desire to …

- Share a skill
- Get to know a community
- Have an impact
- Keep skills alive
- Gain recognition
- Build a resumé
- Help someone

Chances are, this short version of a very long list of reasons to volunteer includes a couple that have your name on them.

Maybe, though, you're one of those people who just can't wrap your head around the concept of volunteering. You know it's the "right" thing to do, but something about volunteering puts you in a position of thinking you don't have the time and you're simply not motivated by a desire to give something for nothing. Don't worry—those feelings don't make you a bad person. In fact, if many people were to be honest, the first question they'd have when asked to volunteer their time and skills would probably be "what's in it for me?"

So to all you budding or fully bloomed financial planners out there who have yet to share their knowledge without benefit of a fee, think of volunteering as an exchange for help you have received in the past or may require in the future.

Pay It Forward

Until the 2000 book by Catherine Ryan Hyde, *Pay It Forward*, and the blockbuster movie of the same name that followed, only a small number of people actually practiced giving in advance of getting. While the spirit of this chapter is really about giving back, let's face it—many of you are still in the early stages, or even the consideration stage, of a career in financial planning.

You may consider this pay-it-forward approach to your career in financial planning by donating services and time before you are financially successful. This can help you be certain that a career in financial planning is the perfect fit for you while helping others who are in need of some financial guidance or knowledge.

Nonprofit Organizations

Becoming involved with community organizations can serve several purposes. You will receive satisfaction from your selfless endeavors, your visibility in the local public and business communities will be heightened, and you may also be on the receiving end of a few new clients. Sitting on the board of a local nonprofit organization, such as a chamber of commerce, hospital, nursing facility, or cultural association, is the most direct way to offer your professional volunteer services. These organizations are often looking for potential board members who can offer financial expertise or make and solicit very large financial contributions.

In the Know

A genuine interest in helping is all that you need in order to give back. Start by attending meetings or volunteering for specific events or fundraising events being held by your favorite organization.

If you decide to seek an appointment to a nonprofit board, make sure that you team up with a board that holds some personal interest. Look to your hobbies and other interests, and get active in organizations that help others get involved with the activity. Maybe you'd like to help promote artistic visibility in your area. That's a good impetus for an appointment to a local art club or regional museum board.

Can't decide which nonprofit best suits you? Check out GuideStar (www.guidestar. org), an online database of nonprofits. The Volunteer Consulting Group (www.vcg. org) is another excellent resource. These websites can help link you to a nonprofit that that will work for you and enable you to do some basic research about the organization's history, financial condition, and current needs for volunteers or directors.

Before you jump on board, nail down what will be expected of you—particularly if you assume the role of board fiscal whiz. Will you be responsible for preparing annual budgets? Are you in charge of cash management? Will you be called upon to make investment recommendations? Know as many of the details of your board position as possible before you say "aye."

Make sure that any board position is not in conflict with your broker dealer or errors and omissions insurer. Make sure you have your appointment preapproved by your compliance officer and insurer before you commit. You should also be aware that accepting a seat on a nonprofit board of directors is typically a multiyear commitment. And you may be called upon to make and solicit monetary donations for fundraising efforts. Nonprofit boards usually meet once a month or every other month for a couple hours. As a board's financial guru, you will likely be asked to sit on board subcommittees—and chances are you'll be asked to chair a subcommittee or be elected board treasurer at least once during your reign. (Not a bad thing to have listed on your resumé or curriculum vitae.)

And in case this point hasn't already occurred to you—you must avoid potential conflicts of interest as a member of a nonprofit board. You cannot do business directly with an organization with which you volunteer. However, that doesn't mean you can't increase your visibility and enhance your reputation through this give-back effort via the many contacts you are likely to make.

 Pitfalls

Ask the charity whether it has director's and officer's liability insurance in place. This coverage protects you from any personal liability that may arise while carrying out your duties as an officer or director. It's an expensive policy for the charity but one that you cannot afford to be without as a member of the board or as an officer of a charitable organization.

Professional Industry Associations

In Chapter 9, I made a strong recommendation for you to join a professional organization in your area of interest. Well, here's the rest of the story.

Joining is great and is something that you'll never regret. But being active is where it's at. Sometimes getting active is a bit elusive, though, and you don't know where to start. You need to start by speaking with the executive administrator, the board of directors, and the committee heads. All of these folks know where the organization needs help and will gladly direct you to the right people.

Don't expect to jump right to the director level, however; frankly, there is no rush for that, anyway. The real help is needed at the grassroots level regarding issues such as membership, programming, government relations, finance committees, sponsorships, career development, and financial literacy.

Speak Up

Don't yet have the time to devote to active membership or a board of directors position? Not to worry. There are other ways you can give back without giving as much time.

One good way to give back to the community is by offering yourself as a speaker. Organizations of all varieties are constantly searching for speakers who have specific knowledge that's of interest to a broad audience. And let's face it—what has more broad a base of interest than free advice on financial planning and investments? Every opportunity you have to speak before a group is a good one. It provides you with the practice necessary to enhance your performance ability for future speaking engagements.

Before you're booked for a speaking engagement, put some thought into the subject matter. It's wise to match your topic to the organization or event. If you're talking before a council on aging, for example, consider estate planning as your focus. If the median age of your audience is 40s or 50s, plan on a talk about retirement funds or saving for college.

Always provide some autobiographical information for the person who will introduce you. This should be honest and without puffery, but there's nothing wrong with it highlighting a few of your major accomplishments. Keep things moving throughout your talk with well-placed graphics and real-life stories. Depending on the size of your audience and the scope of the topic,

> **In the Know**
>
> There are many groups, organizations, and agencies that could benefit from you speaking. The Society for Financial Awareness is a not-for-profit organization whose mission is to wipe out financial illiteracy and to teach advisors to obtain speaking engagements. Visit sofausa.org for more details.

keep presentations to fewer than 60 minutes and leave time for questions and answers. Also, offer them a way to contact you for more personal questions or issues requiring deeper consultation.

Pro Bono Work

Providing *pro bono* or free service work is not for everybody, but many financial planners find this method of volunteerism to be precisely what they need to enjoy a sense of making a difference.

If you choose to go down this volunteer path, borrow from earlier passages in this chapter and offer your expertise to an organization that is familiar to you or that provides services that you support. The Financial Planning Association (FPA), for example, has an active pro bono movement and a committee dedicated to such.

Often this call to action is precipitated by a particular situation. For instance, charitable consultations from financial planners were in demand following the September 11, 2001, tragedy. Many individuals affected by Hurricane Katrina in 2005 were also in need of pro bono advisors. In times of need, your expertise could have a significant impact on local, national, and global communities.

def•i•ni•tion

Pro bono is from the Latin phrase meaning "for the good." If a professional performs work pro bono, it usually means that he or she is acting free of charge or at a significantly reduced rate.

Offering your services to military families is one way that you can help serve those who are serving their country. Making financial decisions can be a difficult task for any family, but for those whose loved ones are away from home for months on end, it can become overwhelming. You can help lighten the load by providing financial counsel for free or at a reduced cost.

If you're going to do pro bono work, it should be a genuine effort. Do it because you want to help, not because of the glory attached to performing a good deed or any potential business opportunities that may arise. And while you're looking for organizations or relief efforts to lend your considerable knowledge to free of charge, keep your eyes close to home. Chances are you have clients whose parents or grown children need a little financial advice but can't afford your rates. They may be the perfect candidates for your gift.

Share What You've Learned

Most financial planners are essentially teachers at heart. Think about it. Much of your workday is spent imparting the knowledge you have learned, and the remainder is devoted to keeping up with industry changes. You educate your clients on ways to improve their financial well-being. Some graduate early, some drop out, and others need extra sessions and ongoing tutorials to get desired results.

It's natural to include teaching a course or signing on as a mentor to your roster of give-back opportunities. Sharing what you have learned not only provides a great outlet for your altruistic tendencies, but it can also recharge interest in your chosen profession. It's difficult not to get fired up about the work you do when you're talking about it with others.

Go to the Head of the Class

There are opportunities to teach financial planning at all levels. If you don't mind being the center of attention and have a genuine desire to share your knowledge, offer yourself to a local high school, college, or university as a guest lecturer. If you enjoy getting up in front of a classroom, you may be an ideal candidate to participate in continuing education curriculums that offer consumer education or certificate programs in financial planning. Often, local high schools, colleges, and universities will maintain a list of industry professionals that they can rely on to lead either credited or non-credited courses. Now may be the time to get on that list.

Another less time-consuming way to spread your message about the joys of being a financial planner is by volunteering to speak at a high school or college career day. There, you will have the opportunity to "talk up" the advantages of a career as a financial advisor and at the same time position yourself as someone who can be relied upon as a guest speaker. And who knows, maybe Junior will go home that evening and wax poetic about your presentation. Could be that Mom and Dad are in the market for a little financial planning assistance.

In the Know

Many high schools teach independent-living classes where the basics of "life as a grownup" are taught. Offer yourself as a guest speaker and choose a general topic for your talk, such as how to avoid accumulating debt or the general principles of saving.

Junior Achievement

Known for its mission to educate and inspire youngsters to succeed in the business world, Junior Achievement runs programs that globally focus on entrepreneurship, work preparedness, and financial literacy. And the organization has been achieving its lofty purpose since 1916 with the assistance of volunteers.

As a volunteer with Junior Achievement, you can share your enthusiasm for the work you do as a financial planner and also impart your personal story about the roads you have traveled to achieve your professional goals. Commitment to the program varies from a weekly visit to a local school where Junior Achievement classes are being held to appearances just a few times a year. Volunteers are trained by the organization and supplied classroom materials. For more information about the Junior Achievement program, check out www.ja.org.

Be a Mentor

Maybe a more seasoned financial planner took you under his or her wing when you were starting out in the business and you want to return the favor. Or perhaps you have caught the teaching bug and want to share the knowledge you have learned. Becoming a mentor is a volunteer effort that can have lasting impact on your protégé for many years.

Not everyone is cut out to be a mentor, though. Yes, your heart may be in the right place, but you must also be motivated to help and have a great deal of patience to successfully wear a mentor's hat. Sometimes, there are business development opportunities that arise from mentoring. Your less-experienced professionals may run into cases that are way above their capabilities from time to time, creating a joint work opportunity for the both of you. If, on the other hand, your desire to generate more business outweighs a wish to help coach a rookie, then mentoring is not the way for you to give back.

Projecting a positive attitude is another element involved in being a good mentor, as is the ability to communicate with clarity. Being a mentor requires time and effort and a willingness to share the dos and don'ts of a successful practice. Let's look at those words "successful practice" again. To be a mentor worth your salt, your practice must be strong and your clients must be satisfied.

In a Giving Mood

Offering your considerable knowledge to your community, local educators, and startup advisors are all admirable ways to share your expertise and experience. But for many financial planners, there isn't enough time in the day to accomplish their workload—never mind the hours required to fulfill a volunteer commitment. Don't despair. There are numerous other ways to satisfy your desire to contribute to society.

Start a Scholarship Fund

Want to help someone achieve his or her goals in the financial planning industry? Is there a charity that hits home for you? Consider setting up a scholarship fund through a local school, a private foundation, a community foundation, or another public charity. You could also sponsor a scholarship through a club or trade association. Granted, establishing an endowed scholarship fund will require an initial outlay of several thousand dollars—but from there on, an additional contribution of a few hundred dollars a year will keep this mechanism of giving going for a long time. An added advantage to setting up a scholarship with your name is, well, simply put: it has your name on it. That's good public relations.

Of course, you can take the purely altruistic avenue and simply contribute to an already established scholarship that you deem worthy. Remember, in the end it's all about the giving, not the getting.

> **Pitfalls**
>
> IRS rules dictate that scholarship programs benefit a broad charitable class and that the process is not discriminatory. In other words, you can't set up a scholarship that restricts eligibility requirements to the point where only one or two people or a specific family can qualify. The penalty for noncompliance can be quite hefty.

Be a Sponsor

Want a way to give something to the community and at the same time do a little business promoting? By offering to be a sponsor for a local golf tournament, a church supper, or a nonprofit organization event, you can achieve both goals.

As an event sponsor, your name will be included in all advertising and press. Naturally, you'll want to attend the event, where you'll have the opportunity to hand out some business cards or take a few photos for addition to your company literature and website.

You can also offer to be the talent for a church or other nonprofit fundraiser. You can provide a presentation on ways to save or on investing wisely, and the organization could charge a small fee for admission. The audience learns something; the nonprofit earns something; and you get to pass out a few more of those business cards.

Give on a Client's Behalf

During the holiday season, on clients' birthdays, or at any time of the year, make charitable donations on your clients' behalf. Send out cards at the holidays or on birthdays, letting clients know that you have contributed to a local or national charity in their name. During your initial consultations with clients, you may want to ask them to name a couple of their favorite charities. That way, you'll be sure to contribute to a cause that means something to them.

Charity Begins at Home

There's a lot to be said for spreading the wealth of your knowledge and pockets to worthy organizations and causes, but there may be some fellow financial planners in your community whose practices need a little boost. If you find yourself in the enviable position of being too busy to take on every client who graces your door—or you have focused on only accepting clients who meet your ideal profile—then make a referral to an advisor whose credentials and reputation you know to be sound.

Make the Time

I have never met any successful professional, let alone a startup financial planner, who had so much extra time that he or she was looking for things to do. This situation never changes unless you force it to change.

Taking the time to pay it forward or give back often amounts to making the time to do so. In the end, the success you make will be greatly enhanced by the success you gave.

The Least You Need to Know

◆ Giving back or paying it forward will help the financial planning industry gain acceptance and grow.

◆ Speaking and teaching are great ways to give back that only require your time and desire.

- Professional financial organizations need member volunteers for just about every committee. Get active today.

- Pro bono work will assist those who may never be able to afford the life-changing experience that a financial planner has to offer.

- Make time to give. The more you give, the more you get.

Appendix A

Glossary

12b-1 fees   Fees that a mutual fund may charge to cover marketing and advertising expenses.

360-degree review   This is a feedback process where everyone in an organization—managers, co-workers, and subordinates—have the chance to give their opinions about you and your performance. This gives you valuable feedback on your strengths and weaknesses, personal and professional, from all levels and perspectives.

accrued interest   Interest that has been earned but not received.

acquisition debt   Debt incurred to acquire, construct, or substantially improve a personal residence. The debt must be secured by the residence and is limited to $1 million ($500,000 for married couples filing separately).

adjustable-rate mortgage (ARM)   A mortgage loan in which the interest rate is periodically adjusted to reflect current interest rates.

adjusted gross estate   The adjusted gross estate is equal to the gross estate less any deductions for funeral expenses, last medical expenses, administrative expenses, debts, and losses during the administration of the estate.

Adjusted Gross Income (AGI)   Total income less adjustments as computed on page one of Form 1040. AGI is an intermediate step in the calculation of individual taxable income.

annuity   A series of equal annual payments.

balloon payment   The large final payment necessary to retire a debt issue.

Barron's confidence index   An index designed to identify investors' confidence in the level and direction of security prices.

basis point   One basis point is equal to $\frac{1}{100}$ of 1 percent. Conversely, 50 basis points are equal to one half of 1 percent. 150 basis points are the same as 1.5 percent.

beneficiary   The person(s) entitled to receive the death benefit of a life insurance policy upon the insured's death. Also, a beneficiary is the person(s) who hold(s) the beneficial title to a trust's assets.

bond   A long-term liability with a specified amount of interest and specified maturity date.

broker   An agent who handles buy and sell orders for an investor.

broker dealer (BD)   A company registered with the Securities and Exchange Commission (SEC) to sell stocks, bonds, mutual funds, and other securities products for a commission.

business risk   The risk associated with the nature of a business.

buy-sell agreement   A legal agreement between two parties where one is obligated to buy and the other is obligated to sell a business upon the death of an owner.

bylaws   A document specifying the relationship between a corporation and its stockholders.

capital asset   Any asset that does not fall into one of five statutory categories: business inventory, business accounts receivable, real or depreciable business property, creative assets, and U.S. government publications.

capital gain   The increase in the value of an asset, such as a stock or a bond.

capital gain distribution   A distribution of long-term capital gain recognized by a mutual fund to investors in the fund.

capital loss   A decrease in the value of an asset, such as a stock or a bond.

cash budget   A financial statement enumerating cash receipts and cash disbursements.

cash value   The amount that would be received if a life insurance policy were canceled.

Certificate of Deposit (CD)   A time deposit with a specified maturity date.

certificate of incorporation   A document creating a corporation.

charter   A document specifying the relationship between a firm and the state in which it is incorporated.

Chicago Board Options Exchange (CBOE)   The first organized secondary market in put and call options.

closely held corporations   Corporations privately owned by a relatively small number of shareholders.

codicil   A document that amends a will. A codicil is prepared subsequently to and separately from the will to modify or explain the will.

commissions   Fees charged by brokers for executing orders.

confirmation statement   A statement received from a brokerage firm detailing the sale or purchase of a security and specifying a settlement date.

content management systems   Database systems that will maintain your clients' contact information. They are easily customizable, enabling you to track projects and schedule tasks for future dates.

contrarians   Investors who go against the consensus concerning investment strategy.

cost basis   The purchase price of an asset, including any sales tax paid by the purchaser and any incidental costs related to getting the asset in place and into production.

credential   What you want from any credential is knowledge, esteem, and respect— something that clients, prospects, and other professionals will look favorably upon. Other terms used to denote such achievements are certificate holder, certificant, specialist, designee, licensee, and certified.

cyclical industry   An industry whose sales and profits are sensitive to changes in the level of economic activity.

date of record   The day on which an investor must own shares in order to receive the dividend payment.

dealers   Market makers who buy and sell securities for their own accounts.

debt ratio   The ratio of debt to total assets; a measure of the use of debt financing.

default   The failure of a debtor to meet any term of a debt's indenture.

deferred compensation   A nonqualified plan under which an employer promises to pay a portion of an employee's current compensation in a future year.

defined-benefit plan   A qualified plan under which participants are promised a targeted benefit, usually in the form of a pension, when they retire.

defined-contribution plan   A qualified plan under which an annual contribution is made to each participant's retirement account.

dependent   A member of a taxpayer's family or household who receives more than half of his or her financial support from the taxpayer.

designation   *See* credential.

diligence   The process undertaken to verify the viability or integrity of a claim or anticipated result. This would include checking calculations, discussing assumptions, and corroborating claims with independent third parties.

director   A person who is elected by stockholders to determine the goals and policies of the firm.

discount broker   A broker who charges lower commissions on security purchases and sales.

diversification   The process of accumulating different securities to reduce the risk of loss.

dividend   A payment to stockholders that is usually in cash (but may be in stock or property).

Dividend Reinvestment Plan (DRIP)   A plan that permits stockholders to have cash dividends reinvested in stock instead of received in cash.

dollar cost averaging   The purchase of securities at different intervals to reduce the impact of price fluctuations.

donee   An individual or organization that receives a gift.

donor   An individual who makes a gift.

Dow Jones Industrial Average (DJIA)   A stock index representing 30 of the largest companies in America. While not that broad, the DJIA is an indicator of how the stocks of many large companies may have performed over a certain time period.

duration   The average time it takes to collect a bond's interest and principal repayment.

effective interest rate   The interest rate paid, adjusted for any tax savings.

efficient portfolio   The portfolio that offers the highest expected return for a given amount of risk.

emerging markets investments   Investments typically made in companies located in countries that are not major economic centers. These could be third-world countries or countries that have undergone major political change, such as South Africa, Vietnam, or the former Soviet Union.

employee payroll tax   The FICA tax (Social Security and Medicare tax) levied on employees who receive compensation during the year.

Employee Stock Ownership Plan (ESOP)   A qualified, defined contribution plan in which contributions are invested primarily in the corporate employer's common stock.

employer-provided plan   A retirement plan sponsored and maintained by an employer for the benefit of the employees.

enrolled agent   A tax practitioner certified by the Internal Revenue Service (IRS) to represent clients in IRS proceedings.

estate planning   The process of accumulation, management, conservation, and transfer of wealth considering legal, tax, and personal objectives.

estate tax   A tax on the value of a deceased individual's assets.

executor   The estate representative designated in the will by the deceased person. An executor may serve without bond if the bond is waived by the decedent.

expected return   The sum of the anticipated dividend yield and capital gains.

face value   An insurance policy's death benefit.

Family Limited Partnership (FLP)   A limited partnership created under state law with the primary purpose of transferring assets to younger generations, utilizing discounts to create reduced gift tax valuations.

family office   The term used to define a type of practice that serves very high-net-worth individuals and families. These family offices typically offer concierge-level planning and administrative services, from holistic financial planning and tax preparation through bill paying, arranging for domestic services such as home sitting, maintenance and cleaning, and booking travel. Essentially, it is the business office for the family.

Federal Reserve   The central bank of the United States.

fiduciary   Someone who is hired to act or advise on behalf of another. The duties of a fiduciary are to always keep the best interests of the client first and foremost in all decision making and advising.

filing status   A classification for individual taxpayers reflecting marital and family situation and determining the rate schedule for the computation of tax liability.

financial intermediary   A financial institution, such as a commercial bank, that borrows from one group and lends to another.

financial leverage   The use of borrowed funds to acquire an asset.

financial life cycle   The stages of life during which individuals accumulate and subsequently use financial assets.

financial risk   The risk associated with a firm's sources of financing.

fiscal policy   Taxation, expenditures, and debt management of the federal government.

full disclosure laws   The federal and state laws requiring publicly held firms to disclose financial and other information that may affect the value of their securities.

General Agent (GA)   A person who is hired by an insurance company to manage an office often owned by and paid for by the insurance company. The GA's job is to recruit, manage, and train a sales force of agents and an administrative support staff for that sales force.

gift   A voluntary transfer, without full consideration, of property from one person (a donor) to another person (a donee) or entity.

global funds   Mutual funds whose portfolios include securities of firms with international operations that are located throughout the world.

grantor   The person who creates and initially funds a trust. The grantor is also known as the settler or creator.

Gross Domestic Product (GDP)   The total value of all final goods and services newly produced within a country by domestic factors of production.

gross estate   Consists of the fair market value of all of a decedent's interests owned at his or her date of death plus the fair market value of certain property interest that the decedent transferred during his or her life, in which he or she retained some rights, powers, use, or possession.

gross profit margin   Percentage earned on sales after deducting the cost of goods sold.

hedging   Taking opposite positions to reduce risk.

high-yield securities   Non-investment-grade securities offering a high return.

holistic financial planning   Where any financial decisions are made after evaluating the impact on the person or family's entire financial situation.

independent contractor   A self-employed individual who performs services for compensation and who retains control over the manner in which the services are performed.

index fund   A mutual fund whose portfolio seeks to duplicate an index of stock prices.

Individual Retirement Account (IRA)   A retirement plan that is available to workers. Examples include standard and Roth IRAs.

inefficient portfolio   A portfolio whose return is not maximized, given the level of risk.

inflation-indexed securities   Securities whose principal and interest payments are adjusted for changes in the Consumer Price Index (CPI).

inheritance tax   A tax on what an individual receives from an estate.

Initial Public Offering (IPO)   The first sale of a company's common stock to the general public.

innocent spouse rule   The rule of law under which a person who filed a joint return with a spouse is not held liable for any deficiency of tax with respect to the return.

inside information   Privileged information concerning a firm.

installment sale   A sale of property that includes a note from the buyer to the seller. The buyer pays the seller the full valuable consideration of the property over a specified set of terms.

interest   Payment for the use of money.

interest rate risk   The uncertainty associated with changes in interest rates; the possibility of loss resulting from increases in interest rates.

internal rate of return   Percentage return that equates the present value of an investment's cash inflows with its cost.

international funds   American mutual funds whose portfolios are limited to non-American firms.

intestacy   The laws of a state for deceased persons who did not create a will. These laws will govern the distribution of the deceased's property to heirs or closest living relatives.

investment banker   An underwriter; a firm that sells new issues of securities to the general public.

key-person life insurance policies   Insurance purchased by a firm on the life of a high-level employee. The firm is the beneficiary of the policy.

legal ownership   Possessing legal title to the property.

life planning   The process of using a client's life dreams and vision as the centerpiece for the financial plan. All financial decisions are made based upon their contribution to the life goals of the client(s).

liquidation   The process of converting assets into cash; dissolving a corporation.

liquidity   Also known as "moneyness," the ease with which assets can be converted into cash with little risk of loss of principal.

limited liability company (LLC)   A form of entity that combines attributes from traditional corporate structures with those of partnerships. This is the most common ownership form for new entities today.

load fund   A mutual fund that charges a commission to purchase or sell its shares.

margin (stocks or bonds)   The amount that an investor must put down to buy securities on credit.

margin call   A request by a broker for an investor to place additional funds or securities in an account as collateral against borrowed funds or as a good faith deposit.

margin requirement   The minimum percentage, established by the Federal Reserve, that the investor must put up in cash to buy securities.

marginal tax rate   The tax rate paid on an additional last dollar of taxable income; an individual's tax bracket.

market order   An order to buy or sell at the current market price.

market risk   Systematic risk; the risk associated with the tendency of a stock's price to fluctuate with the market.

marketability   The ease with which an asset may be bought or sold.

maturity date   The time at which a debt issue becomes due and the principal must be repaid.

money market instruments   Short-term securities, such as Treasury bills, negotiable certificates of deposit (CDs), or commercial paper.

money market mutual funds   Mutual funds that specialize in short-term securities.

mutual fund   A diversified portfolio of securities owned and managed by a regulated investment company.

National Association of Securities Dealers Automatic Quotation (NASDAQ) System   The quotation system for over-the-counter securities.

natural market   Refers to a group of prospects, often referred to as a market, with which you have a close and personal relationship. This relationship can be from training, experience, or exposure to that group over an extended period in a highly visible way.

net asset value   The asset value of a share in an investment company; total assets minus total liabilities divided by the number of shares outstanding.

no-load mutual fund   A mutual fund that does not charge a commission for buying or selling its shares.

New York Stock Exchange (NYSE) composite index   New York Stock Exchange index; an index of prices of all the stocks listed on the New York Stock Exchange.

option contract   This is a security in which an investor buys the right, but not the obligation to buy or sell a security at a specified price.

organized exchange   A formal market for buying and selling securities or commodities.

orphan accounts   Accounts that were developed by advisors who have left the firm. Managers will assign orphan accounts to new advisors in the hopes of retaining their business, getting you experience and hoping that you uncover more opportunities with these clients.

over-the-counter (OTC) market   The informal secondary market for unlisted securities.

partnership   An unincorporated business owned by two or more individuals.

phantom stock program   This is an incentive compensation scheme in which key associates of your firm receive an amount of money equal to what they would have received if they owned a percentage of the business. These employees would receive that phantom share of profits in addition to any proceeds from the sale of the company.

portfolio   An accumulation of assets owned by the investor and designed to transfer purchasing power to the future.

portfolio rebalancing   The process of selling some holdings and buying others to bring the portfolio back to its desired allocation of holdings. As certain positions grow and others decline in value, the portfolio strays from the original allocation and needs to be brought back into line with the manager's objectives.

portfolio risk   The total risk associated with owning a portfolio; the sum of systematic and unsystematic risk.

power of attorney   A legal document that authorizes an agent to act on a principal's behalf.

present value   The current worth of an amount to be received in the future.

press release   A written or recorded communication directed at members of the news media for the purpose of announcing something claimed as having news value. Typically, it is mailed or faxed to assignment editors at newspapers, magazines, radio stations, television stations, and/or television networks.

principal   The amount owed; the face value of a debt.

pro bono   This word comes from the Latin phrase meaning "for the good." If a professional performs work pro bono, it usually means that he or she is acting free of charge or at a significantly reduced rate.

property tax   A tax levied against the value of real or financial assets.

purchasing power risk   The uncertainty that future inflation will erode the purchasing power of assets and income.

qualified residence interest   Interest paid on acquisition debt or home equity debt allowed as an itemized deduction.

qualified retirement plans   Retirement plans that meet certain statutory requirements. Individuals who recognize gain on the sale of qualified small business stock may be eligible to exclude 50 percent of the gain from income.

rate of return   The annual percentage return realized on an investment.

realized return   The sum of income and capital gains earned on an investment.

recession   A period of rising unemployment and declining national output.

registered representative   A person who buys and sells securities for customers; a broker.

Real Estate Investment Trust (REIT)   REITs come in many varieties, both publicly traded and non-publicly traded. REITs are intended to offer clients a way to diversify their portfolios into professionally managed real estate without needing to be landlords.

return   The sum of income plus capital gains earned on an investment in an asset.

rollover contribution   A distribution from one qualified plan contributed to another qualified plan within 60 days.

Roth IRA   An investment account through which individuals who have compensation or earned income can save for retirement on a tax-exempt basis.

Section 401(k) plan   A defined contribution plan under which employees elect to contribute a portion of current year compensation to an employer-provided retirement plan.

Securities and Exchange Commission (SEC)   The government agency that enforces federal securities laws.

Securities Investor Protection Corporation (SIPC)   The agency that insures investors against failures by brokerage firms.

share averaging   A system for the accumulation of shares in which the investor periodically buys the same number of shares.

sole proprietorship   An unincorporated business owned by one individual.

speculation   An investment that offers a potentially large return but is also very risky; there's a reasonable probability that the investment will produce a loss.

Standard & Poor's 500 stock index   A value-weighted index of 500 stocks.

stock   A security representing ownership in a corporation.

stock dividend   A dividend paid in stock.

stock option   The right to purchase corporate stock for a stated price (the strike price) for a given period of time.

stock split   Recapitalization that affects the number of shares outstanding, their par value, the earnings per share, and the price of the stock.

S corporation   A corporation with a subchapter S election in effect. The corporation is a pass-through entity for federal tax purposes and does not pay federal income tax.

tax-deferred annuity   A contract sold by an insurance company in which the company guarantees a series of payments and whose earnings are not taxed until they are distributed.

tax-exempt bond   A bond whose interest is excluded from federal income taxation.

taxable estate   The aggregate fair market value of property owned by a decedent or transferred because of the person's death, reduced by allowable deductions.

technical analysis   An analysis of past volume and/or price behavior to identify which assets to purchase or sell and the best time to purchase or sell them.

term insurance   Life insurance with coverage for a specified time and excluding a savings plan.

time value of money   A dollar available today is worth more than a dollar available tomorrow because the current dollar can be invested to start earning interest immediately.

total return   The sum of dividend yield and capital gains.

trader   An investor who frequently buys and sells.

trailing commissions   Commissions paid to the broker of record for as long as the client holds that investment. It is common to receive recurring commission revenue from some mutual funds, variable annuity and variable life insurance, and retirement plans.

Treasury bills (T-bills)   Short-term federal government securities. T-bills mature in 1 year or less.

Treasury bonds (T-bonds)   The long-term debt of the federal government. T-bonds have the longest maturity of any treasury debt and mature in 10 to 30 years.

Treasury notes (T-notes)   The intermediate-term debt of the federal government. T-notes mature between 2 and 10 years.

trust   A structure that vests legal title (the legal interest) to assets in one party, the trustee, who manages those assets for the benefit of the beneficiaries (who hold the equitable title) of the trust.

trustee   The individual or entity responsible for managing trust assets and carrying out the directions of the grantor that are formally expressed in the trust instrument.

universal life insurance   A term insurance policy with a cash accumulation account attached to it.

value   What something is worth; the present value of future benefits.

variable universal life insurance   A universal life insurance policy with investment options available for the cash accumulation account.

whole life insurance   A permanent insurance policy guaranteeing that the policy will remain in force as long as the premium is paid. The policy has a cash account attached to it, which grows tax-deferred.

will   A legal document that provides the will maker the opportunity to control the distribution of property, appoint an executor, and avoid the state's intestacy law distribution scheme. *See also* intestacy.

Professional Organizations and Certificate Programs

Professional Organizations

The following professional organizations are mentioned in this book and are worthy of your membership consideration.

The Financial Planning Association (FPA)

Phone: 1-800-322-4237
Fax: 303-759-0749
Website: www.fpanet.org

Denver Office
Suite 400
4100 E. Mississippi Avenue
Denver, CO 80246-3053

District of Columbia Office
Suite 201
1600 K Street, NW
Washington, DC 20006

The National Association of Personal Financial Advisors (NAPFA)

3250 North Arlington Heights Road, Suite 109
Arlington Heights, IL 60004
Phone: 1-800-366-2732 or 847-483-5400
Fax: 847-483-5415
Website: www.napfa.org
E-mail: info@napfa.org

The National Association for Insurance and Financial Advisors (NAIFA)

2901 Telestar Court
Falls Church, VA 22042-1205
Phone: 703-770-8100
Website: www.naifa.org

The Society of Financial Service Professionals

17 Campus Boulevard, Suite 201
Newtown Square, PA 19073-3230
Phone: 610-526-2500
Fax: 610-527-1499
Website: www.financialpro.org

Estate Planning Councils

1120 Chester Avenue, Suite 470
Cleveland, OH 44114
Phone: 866-226-2224
Fax: 216-696-2582
Website: www.naepc.org
E-mail: admin@naepc.org

The American Institute of CPAs (AICPA)

AICPA Member Service Center
220 Leigh Farm Road
Durham, NC 27707
Phone: 888-777-7077
Website: www.aicpa.org

Million Dollar Round Table (MDRT)

325 West Touhy Avenue
Park Ridge, IL 60068-4265
Website: www.mdrt.com
E-mail: info@mdrt.org

CFA Institute

560 Ray C. Hunt Drive
Charlottesville, VA 22903-2981
Phone: 1-800-247-8132
Website: www.cfainstitute.org
E-mail: info@cfainstitute.org

The American Society of Pension Professionals and Actuaries (ASPA)

4245 North Fairfax Drive, Suite 750
Arlington, VA 22203
Phone: 703-516-9300
Fax: 703-516-9308
Website: www.aspa.org
E-mail: asppa@asppa.org

The International Association of Registered Financial Consultants (IARFC)

The Financial Planning Bldg.
P.O. Box 42506
Middletown, OH 45042-0506
Phone: 1-800-532-9060
Fax: 513-424-5752
Website: www.iarfc.org

American Bankers Association (ABA)

1120 Connecticut Avenue, N.W.
Washington, DC 20036
Phone: 1-800-BANKERS
Website: www.aba.com

American Bar Association

Website: www.abanet.org

Chicago Office
321 North Clark Street
Chicago, IL 60610
312-988-5000

District of Columbia Office
740 15th Street, N.W.
Washington, DC 20005-1019
202-662-1000

American Risk and Insurance Association (ARIA)

Tony Biacchi, ARIA Executive Director
716 Providence Road
Malvern, PA 19355-3402
Phone: 610-640-1997
Fax: 610-725-1007
Website: www.aria.org
E-mail: aria@cpcuiia.org

The American Institute of Financial Gerontology (AIFG)

1525 NW Third Street, Suite 8
Deerfield Beach, FL 33442
Phone: 888-367-8470 or 954-421-1403
Fax: 954-698-6825
Website: www.aifg.org
E-mail: info@aifg.org

Association for Advanced Life Underwriting (AALU)

2901 Telestar Court
Falls Church, VA 22042
Phone: 888-265-0092 or 703-641-9400
Fax: 703-641-9885
Website: www.aalu.org

Investment Management Consultants Association (IMCA)

5619 DTC Parkway, Suite 500
Greenwood Village, CO 80111
Phone: 303-770-3377
Fax: 303-770-1812
Website: www.imca.org

Institute for Divorce Financial Analysts

24901 Northwestern Highway, Suite 710
Southfield, MI 48075
Phone: 1-800-875-1760 or 989-631-3605
Fax: 248-223-0199
Website: www.institutedfa.com

National Association of Independent Life Brokerage Agencies (NAILBA)

12150 Monument Drive, Suite 125
Fairfax, VA 22033
Phone: 703-383-3081
Fax: 703-383-6942
Website: www.nailba.org

Professional Certificate Programs

Certified Financial Planner (CFP)

Certified Financial Planner Board of Standards
1670 Broadway, Suite 600
Denver, CO 80202-4809
Phone: 303-830-7500
Fax: 303-860-7388
Website: www.cfp.net

Chartered Financial Consultant (ChFC)

The American College
270 S. Bryn Mawr Avenue
Bryn Mawr, PA 19010
Phone: 888-263-7265
Fax: 610-526-1465
Website: www.theamericancollege.edu

The following designations are also offered by The American College:

- Life Underwriter Training Council Fellow (LUTCF)
- Financial Services Specialist (FSS)
- Chartered Life Underwriter (CLU)
- Chartered Advisor for Senior Living (CASL)
- Registered Health Underwriter (RHU)

- Chartered Leadership Fellow (CLF)

- Chartered Advisor in Philanthropy (CAP)

- Master of Science in Management (MSM)

- Master of Science in Financial Services (MSFS)

Chartered Financial Analyst (CFA)

560 Ray C. Hunt Drive
Charlottesville, VA 22903-2981
Phone: 1-800-247-8132
Fax: 434-951-5262
Website: www.cfainstitute.org
E-mail: info@cfainstitute.org

The College for Financial Planning

8000 E. Maplewood Avenue, Suite 200
Greenwood Village, CO 80111
Phone: 1-800-237-9990 or 303-220-1200
Fax: 303-220-1810
Website: www.cffp.edu

The College for Financial Planning was the first organization to offer training for the CFP certification. In addition to its CFP training, the college has launched a few other designations worthy of consideration with a good training program to support each of these designations:

- Certified Senior Advisor (CSA)

- Chartered Retirement Plans Specialist (CRPS)

- Accredited Wealth Management Advisor (AWMA)

- Accredited Asset Management Specialist (AAMS)

- Chartered Retirement Planning Counselor (CRPC)

- Chartered Mutual Fund Counselor (CMFC)

Certified Divorce Financial Analyst (CDFA)

24901 Northwestern Highway, Suite 710
Southfield, MI 48075
Phone: 1-800-875-1760 or 989-631-3605
Fax: 248-223-0199
Website: www.institutedfa.com

Certified Employee Benefit Specialist (CEBS)

18700 W. Bluemound Road
Brookfield, WI 53045
Phone: 1888-334-3327
Website: www.ifebp.org

Certified Public Accountant/Personal Financial Specialist (CPA/PFS)

You must be a CPA to obtain this designation.

220 Leigh Farm Road
Durham, NC 27707
Phone: 888-777-7077
Website: pfp.aicpa.org
E-mail: pfs@aicpa.org

Certified Pension Consultant (CPC)

4245 North Fairfax Drive, Suite 750
Arlington, VA 22203
Phone: 703-516-9300
Fax: 703-516-9308
Website: www.aspa.org/credentials/cred_cpc.htm
E-mail: asppa@asppa.org

Appendix C

Resources

Books

Anthony, Mitch. *Selling with Emotional Intelligence*. Kaplan Business, 2003.

———. *Your Clients for Life: The Definitive Guide to Becoming a Successful Financial Life Planner*. Kaplan Business, 2005.

Anthony, Mitch, and Gary Demoss. *Making the Client Connection: Maximizing the Power of Your Personality, Presentations, and Presence*. Kaplan Business, 2004.

Bachrach, Bill. *High Trust Leadership: A Proven System for Developing an Organization of High-Performance Financial Professionals*. Aim High Publishing, 1999.

———. *Values-Based Financial Planning: The Art of Creating and Inspiring Financial Strategy*. Aim High Publishing, 2000.

Bachrach, Bill, and Karen Risch. *Values-Based Selling: The Art of Building High-Trust Client Relationships*. Bachrach & Assoc., 1996.

Blanchard, Ken, and Ken Muchnick. *The Leadership Pill: The Missing Ingredient in Motivating People Today*. Free Press, 2003.

Buckingham, Marcus, and Donald O. Clifton. *Now, Discover Your Strengths*. Free Press, 2001.

Calloway, Joe. *Indispensable: How to Become the Company That Your Customers Can't Live Without.* Wiley, 2005.

Carson, Ron, and Steve Sanduski. *Tested in the Trenches: A 9-Step Plan for Building and Sustaining a Million-Dollar Financial Services Practice.* Kaplan Business, 2005.

Collins, Jim, and Jerry I. Porras. *Built to Last: Successful Habits of Visionary Companies.* HarperCollins Publishers, 2004.

————. *Good to Great: Why Some Companies Make the Leap … and Others Don't.* HarperCollins Publishers, 2001.

Corrento, Richard J. *Run It Like a Business: Top Financial Planners Weigh in on Practice Management.* Kaplan Business, 2004.

Covey, Stephen R. *The 7 Habits of Highly Effective People.* Free Press, 2004.

Diliberto, Roy T. *Financial Planning: The Next Step: A Practical Approach to Merging Your Clients' Money with Their Lives.* FPA Press, 2006.

Eisenberg, Lee. *The Number: A Completely Different Way to Think About the Rest of Your Life.* Free Press, 2006.

Ferrazzi, Keith. *Never Eat Alone: And Other Secrets to Success, One Relationship at a Time.* Currency, 2005.

Financial Planning Association. *Investment Adviser Compliance Policy Manual Template.* FPA Press, 2006.

Financial Planning Association and Lisa Holton. *The Encyclopedia of Financial Planning: What You Need to Know About Money from the Nation's Leading Financial Planners.* FPA Press, 2006.

Fox, Jeffrey J. *How to Become a Rainmaker (The Rules for Getting and Keeping Customers and Clients).* Hyperion, 2000.

Garlow, James L. *The 21 Irrefutable Laws of Leadership Tested by Time: Those Who Followed Them … and Those Who Didn't!* Thomas Nelson, 2002.

Gerber, Michael E. *The E-Myth Revisited: Why Most Small Businesses Don't Work and What to Do About It.* HarperCollins Publishers, 1995.

Gladwell, Malcolm. *Blink: The Power of Thinking Without Thinking.* Back Bay Books, 2007.

————. *The Tipping Point: How Little Things Can Make a Big Difference.* Back Bay Books, 2002.

Goad, David K., and The Financial Planning Association. *Succession Planning Strategies for the Financial Planner: A Complete Resource Guide, 2nd Edition.* FPA Press, 2005.

Godin, Seth. *Purple Cow.* Penguin Books Ltd, 2005.

Hicks, Grant, and Jay C. Levinson. *Guerrilla Marketing for Financial Advisors.* Trafford, 2006.

Johnson, Spencer. *Who Moved My Cheese?* Vermilion, 2007.

Katz, Deena B. *Deena Katz on Practice Management: For Financial Advisers, Planners, and Wealth Managers.* Bloomberg Press, 1999.

Kess, Sidney, and Alan Campbell. *Financial and Estate Planning Guide. 16th ed.* CCH, Inc., 2006.

Kim, W. Chan, and Renée Mauborgne. *Blue Ocean Strategy: How to Create Uncontested Market Space and Make Competition Irrelevant.* Harvard Business School Publishing Corporation, 2005.

Kinder, George. *The Seven Stages of Money Maturity: Understanding the Spirit and Value of Money in Your Life.* Dell, 2000.

Kinder, George, and Susan Galvin. *Lighting the Torch: The Kinder Method of Life Planning.* FPA Press, 2006.

Lannom, John. *People First: Achieving Balance in an Unbalanced World.* Lannom, Inc., 2005.

Mittra, Sid, Tom Potts, and Leon Labrecque. *Practicing Financial Planning for Professionals.* Random House, 2006.

Nomura, Catherine, Julia Waller, and Shannon Waller. *Unique Ability: Creating the Life You Want.* The Strategic Coach Inc., 2003.

Oglesby, D. W. *Concise Encyclopedia of Investing.* Best Business Books, 2006.

Parisse, Alan. *This Is Your Time: Empowering Today's Financial Advisor.* Flagstaff Publishing, 2003.

Pink, Daniel H. *A Whole New Mind, Moving from the Information Age to the Conceptual Age.* Riverhead Hardcover, 2005.

Rath, Tom, and Donald O. Clifton. *How Full Is Your Bucket? Positive Strategies for Work and Life.* Gallup Press, 2004.

Rattiner, Jeffrey H. *Financial Planning Answer Book*. CCH, 2005.

———. *Getting Started as a Financial Planner: Revised and Updated Edition*. Bloomberg Press, 2005.

Smart, Brandon. *Topgrading: How Leading Companies Win by Hiring, Coaching, and Keeping the Best People*. Penguin Group, 2005.

Stovall, Jim. *The Ultimate Gift*. RiverOak Publishing, 2001.

Sullivan, Dan, and Catherine Nomura. *The Laws of Lifetime Growth: Always Make Your Future Bigger Than Your Past*. Berrett-Koehler, 2006.

Templeton, Tim, and Kenneth Blanchard. *The Referral of a Lifetime: The Networking System That Produces Bottom-Line Results … Every Day!* Berrett-Koehler, 2005.

Tibergien, Mark C. *Practice Made Perfect: The Discipline of Business Management for Financial Advisors*. Bloomberg Press, 2005.

West, Scott, and Mitch Anthony. *Storyselling for Financial Advisors: How Top Producers Sell*. Kaplan Business, 2000.

Winston, William J. *Marketing for Financial Services*. Haworth Press, 1986.

Zwick, Gary A., and James J. Jurinski. *Tax and Financial Planning for the Closely Held Family Business*. American Law Institute-American Bar Association, 1999.

Websites

www.401khelpcenter.com   This site provides unbiased information for plan sponsors, retirement professionals, small businesses, and plan participants.

www.advisorproducts.com   Advisor Products, Inc. is a client communications and marketing company serving more than 1,600 of the nation's leading independent financial advisors. API creates websites, client newsletters, brochures, and stationery and assists advisors with branding, writing their marketing copy, and designing a logo.

www.bc.edu/crr   Center for Retirement Research at Boston College.

www.bankrate.com   News, tips, and advice for comparing mortgage rates, home equity loans, CDs, car loans, credit cards, and money market accounts.

www.bigcharts.marketwatch.com   A good site for historical information, including specific historical closing prices of investments.

www.bloomberg.com   Good, current information about investments and the financial markets; a good source for breaking financial news.

www.bobveres.com Each month, this site offers a separate issue of the *Inside Information* report plus one or more e-columns exploring topics that help you serve your clients better and create a more efficient, effective, and profitable practice.

www.cboe.com The home page of the Chicago Board of Options; good information and education about all kinds of options investments.

www.emeraldpublications.com Emerald provides innovative products to help financial professionals build and grow profitable businesses.

www.forefield.com Forefield is a provider of real-time sales, education, and presentation solutions for financial institutions and advisors. Forefield's Internet-based solutions facilitate the communication of client-centric financial planning knowledge and advice that is current, concise, and compliant.

www.fpanet.org The home page for the Financial Planning Association (FPA).

www.fundalarm.com A website that gives opinions on when it is time to sell a specific mutual fund.

www.guidestar.org An online database of nonprofit entities. Various levels of usage give you greater detail about specific nonprofit organizations for a fee.

www.horsesmouth.com Horsesmouth improves the performance of financial advisors in a continuous process that provides them with access to innovative resources and key people who can help them succeed.

www.irahelp.com A good resource for everything you need to know about Individual Retirement Accounts (IRAs).

www.irs.gov Yes, they are from the government and they are there to help; a great website from the Internal Revenue Service (IRS).

www.joinpeak.com PEAK, based in Omaha, Nebraska, provides training, coaching, and software services to financial advisors across the country. Their goal is to empower financial advisors to achieve the business and quality of life that they desire by offering proven tools and innovative programs that ignite their burning desire to succeed.

www.marketinglibrary.net Thousands of marketing messages—letters, invitations, and notes—for clients. This site has a compilation of the best of these messages with a system for you to add your own, including a supermarket of content from other providers such as Liberty Publishing, Response Mail Express, and Bill Cates. You can download and use these messages, and your compliance department can review the content and track the entire process.

www.medicare.gov   Another great site from the federal government; the official U.S. Government site for people with Medicare.

www.morningstar.com   The home page for the investment analysis publisher Morningstar; good free information and premium subscription services.

www.mystockoptions.com   Independent and unbiased expertise on equity compensation for the people who participate in stock plans.

www.producersweb.com   Online home of Senior Market Advisor, Benefits Selling, Boomer Market Advisor, and Bank Advisor.

www.raintoday.com   An online source for free articles, case studies, and other tools for growing a service business.

www.savingforcollege.com   Contains objective information about Section 529 college savings plans and other ways to save and pay for college.

www.sec.gov   The Securities and Exchange Commission (SEC) site, loaded with good information about brokers, advisors, and compliance material.

www.ssa.gov   The official U.S. government site about Social Security.

www.strategiccoach.com   A coaching program whose purpose is to outfit successful entrepreneurs with the direction, confidence, capability, and focus to get to the next level in their business and create the freedom and income to enjoy a unique quality of life.

www.uswealthcompanies.com   The home page for John P. Napolitano's company, U.S. Wealth Management, LLC.

www.vards.com   An online resource for data and information about annuity products and services.

www.vcg.org   An online resource for information about nonprofit boards of directors and board service.

Magazines

Financial Advisor magazine
www.financialadvisormagazine.com
A magazine created for independent financial planners and RIAs.

Financial Planning magazine
www.financial-planning.com
A magazine that examines news and issues about financial planning.

Institutional Investor magazine
www.iimagazine.com
A monthly magazine covering issues in investing.

Investment Advisor magazine
www.investmentadvisor.com
A magazine that places information and analysis into context, allowing advisors to meet clients' needs.

Investment News newspaper
InvestmentNews.com
A weekly newspaper that combines comprehensive news with accurate, independent reporting on the entire financial services industry.

Journal of Accountancy
www.aicpa.org/Magazines+and+Newsletters
The AICPA publishes a variety of magazines and newsletters containing news, information, and other developments affecting the profession.

Journal of Financial Planning
www.journalfp.net
The official publication of the Financial Planning Association.

Life Insurance Selling magazine
www.lifeinsuranceselling.com
A magazine for life, health, and financial services producers.

Mergers & Acquisitions magazine
www.majournal.com
A monthly magazine that covers the latest methods and influences impacting the buying and selling of businesses.

On Wall Street magazine
www.onwallstreet.com
A monthly magazine that provides insight and analysis into the risks and opportunities of being a financial advisor at national or regional brokerages.

Pensions & Investments newspaper
www.pionline.com
A magazine that delivers news, research, and analysis to executives who manage the
flow of funds in the institutional investment market.

Private Wealth magazine
www.pw-mag.com
A magazine for professionals focused exclusively on meeting the financial, legal, and
lifestyle demands of ultra-high-net-worth clients.

Registered Rep. magazine
www.registeredrep.com
A magazine for the retail investment professional.

Wealth Manager magazine
www.wealthmanagermag.com
A resource to aid investment advisors, brokers, and financial planners who manage
assets for clients with high net worth.

Index